DEATH AND THE MAIDEN

DEATH AND THE MAIDEN

THE CURIOUS RELATIONSHIP BETWEEN THE FEAR OF THE FEMININE AND THE FEAR OF DEATH

BRIGID BURKE

Algora Publishing
New York

Library of Congress Cataloging-in-Publication Data —

Names: Burke, Brigid, 1972- author.
Title: Death and the maiden : the curious relationship between the fear of
    the feminine and the fear of death / Brigid Burke.
Description: New York : Algora Publishing, 2019. | Includes bibliographical
    references and index. | Summary: "Belief in an immortal soul and in
    salvation has a paradoxically negative impact on perceptions of the
    archetypal feminine in myth, religious scripture, and philosophy; this
    can be demonstrated using the lens of depth psychology. This book
    explores the idea from Ancient Egyptian times through the early
    Christian era"— Provided by publisher.
Identifiers: LCCN 2019030592 (print) | LCCN 2019030593 (ebook) | ISBN
    9781628943986 (trade paperback) | ISBN 9781628943993 (hardcover) | ISBN
    9781628944006 (pdf)
Subjects: LCSH: Women—Religious aspects. | Death—Religious aspects. |
    Women—Religious aspects—Christianity. | Women—Religious
    aspects—Judaism. | Greece—Religion.
Classification: LCC BL458 .B87 2019 (print) | LCC BL458 (ebook) | DDC
    200.82—dc23
LC record available at https://lccn.loc.gov/2019030592
LC ebook record available at https://lccn.loc.gov/2019030593

Table of Contents

INTRODUCTION

The ancient philosophers championed humanism, seeing humans with their sense of reason as capable of knowing "truth." We see the true beginnings of morality and ethical thinking in ancient Greece. While this seems like noble progress—and in some ways it is—there are unintended consequences of continually seeking the "good," the "true," and the "pure." We attempt to identify ourselves with these positive attributes while disavowing their opposites, and the consequences can be seen today in a culture where everyone has to be right and everyone has to be perfect. In the broadest sense this is the "good vs. evil" debate. Good and evil are subjective terms, but the "good" has somehow become wrapped up in the "perfect." The word *perfect* comes from *perficere*, which means "to finish." According to the strict Latin definition, we are not perfect until we are dead. This idea comes from the Christian backdrop of Western culture; monotheistic religion demands unerring obedience to dogmatic laws, with dire consequences for those who stray in many traditional dogmas. St. Paul says in Philippians 3:12, "Not that I have already obtained this or am already perfect; but I press on to make it my own, because Christ Jesus has made me his own" ("Philippians"). This idea of striving for something beyond humanity is not unique to St. Paul or even to Christianity. Striving for the "good" means one or two possible things; it can mean continually comparing ourselves to an ideal and falling short, or it can mean believing we have attained the ideal, and judging others who have not.

From this wide view, we see the problem that leads to tribalism and conflict. Erik Erikson referred to this problem as "pseudo-speciation"—the idea that one group of humans is superior to another on some kind of economic, cultural, or moral grounds (10). In short, we have been looking at the problem of division the wrong way. Modern secular society focuses on reason and assumes this as the default behavior for humankind. Modern monotheistic religions focus on obedience, and they blame crises on disobedience, as their ancestors did. The influence of rationality and science combined with monotheistic religious ideas leaves us in a lopsided state, and in these recent years of crisis fear has left us more rigidly polarized. Unless we examine these modes of thinking and make some attempt to consider a new way, we will never get beyond the problem.

What other way is there to look at life, history, and current events? Carl Jung speaks about the Shadow, the weaker side of our psyches that we identify with failure, weakness, shame, and ultimately with evil. The Shadow becomes an amorphous "Other," and our tendency to strive for good over evil makes us think we can banish or eradicate the Other, and everything will be wonderful. But we can never banish the Other; we need to embrace it. Embracing the Other does not mean committing evil acts; on the contrary, we commit evil acts because we are in denial of the Other. The Other is something within ourselves, but it is often projected onto those who are different, hence the tendency to demonize minority groups and immigrants. This allows us to justify keeping "lesser" individuals in their place or getting rid of them altogether. We also live in a culture of "safe spaces" that encourages us to avoid what is uncomfortable, which only adds to the problem. Anything that causes discomfort becomes "bad," or in broader terms, "evil."

It is with this idea of good vs. evil that I begin this work. Belief in an immortal soul and salvation has a paradoxically negative impact on perceptions of the archetypal feminine in myth, religious scripture, and philosophy; this can be demonstrated using the lens of depth psychology. Myth is an expression of fundamental human behaviors, as it provides a narrative of things that cannot be spoken about directly. I am focusing on the mythologies and beliefs about death and the afterlife, as death is the ultimate unknown.

Discussions of death beliefs and associated rituals have not been popular in the Classics or studies of ancient religion; there are only a handful of scholars who previously or currently specialized in this area. Mainstream psychology has avoided the topic as well, until recently. Robert Kastenbaum has provided the only comprehensive survey of the subject, and he takes note of how little was published on death before 1992 (1). Cognitive and behavioral scientists tended to view death as a distortion, and patterns of behavior were studied with regard to anxiety responses. (17) The developmental school of psychology viewed death as a life "task," something that people prepared for as they got older, and it is this latter view that has influenced bereavement and hospice counseling. The "psychoanalytic approach" (including folks like

Freud and Jung) was largely discredited in favor of "evidence based" models dependent on studies. The argument is that there is no evidence for psycho-analytic assertions, because they have not been tested. The volumes of case studies and dream studies collected by Jung in particular were not seen as sound methodology in a field moving toward a neurology-based view of psychology. Jung may have enacted his own researches based on patterns he saw in his own case studies, but these do not carry the "rigor" required of modern psychological studies. On the one hand, this is a sound criticism; it is one thing to say, for example, that our behavior is influenced by unconscious archetypes, but where's the proof? Studies about attitudes can run into trouble, because they are largely seen as the vehicle of writer bias. Ian Morris criticizes Christiane Sourvino-Inwood's theories on Greek death attitudes because "we can't say for sure that this was the attitude of ancient Greeks" (297). This is true—how can we say that we speak for everyone? I may be afraid of death, but I can't simply assume that all people around me have the same fear or the same narrative.

On the other hand, modern psychological approaches to death tend to be limited in their scope. The focus is on attitudes toward physical death; the concept of "death" is much broader. In ritual and myth, it is also connected with major life changes, as we will see: the movement from childhood to adolescence, marriage, and having children all count as a type of "death" in the transformational sense. But they involve "dying" to an old life in order to start a new one. Humans may have many of these cataclysmic changes in their lives. While Kastenbaum cites studies focusing on anxiety about death and its possible relationship to other things like test anxiety (154), there doesn't seem to be much of a focus on these other kinds of "death". For our purposes, both are important. When you look at death in the context of religion, myth, and the complexities of consciousness, there still isn't a better way to look at common stories and symbols than Jung's way, for all of its imperfections. The quantitative side of the question is interesting but does not allow us to go very far with our inquiry into the meta-narrative of death in Western culture.

There is much discourse about "going back to the way things were," which demonstrates a fear of death. Death does not have to be physical; major life changes are also "deaths," and at least one function of religious ritual is to deal with these transitions. There is a loss of the familiar as society changes and time marches on. People's worldview depends at least partially on their attitude toward change—do they welcome it, or fear it? Fear of the unknown or the "other" drives a lot of resistance to social change.

In my research I discovered something curious: there was a time in Greek and Roman culture when death was not about reward or punishment or about how you behaved in life. Death was simply death, and it affected the lowest slave and the greatest warrior the same way. When religion came to be about morals and striving for "spirit" over the "body," our views on death changed, and so did our attitudes about many other things. It also matters if a society focuses on the collective or on the individual; the greater the focus on the individual, the deeper the split, as judgment of the soul after death becomes an issue. In this work I am focusing on how this change in view affected ideas of the archetypal Feminine.

It's important to define our terms at this point. Jung defines archetypes as "primordial types, that is, with universal images that have existed since the remotest times" ("Archetypes" 5). Archetypes belong to the collective unconscious, a layer of consciousness beyond Freud's personal unconscious. Rather than focusing on the thoughts, feelings, and memories of the individual, the collective unconscious is universal to humanity: "It is, in other words, identical in all men and thus constitutes a common psychic substrate of a suprapersonal nature which is present in every one of us" (4). Jung's idea of the collective came from his cases as a psychoanalyst; he routinely found that patients' dreams contained symbolic and mythical narratives relating to stories they never learned in their conscious lives. Understanding these patterns of unconscious narrative helped Jung's patients break through their neuroses and psychoses.[1]

Critics of this approach have trouble with the notion of the "universal." Walter Burkert summarizes the major difficulty with this approach:

> It has the advantage of admitting neither verification or refutation, since those nonempirical entities may be constructed to fit exactly the presuppositions of some set of myths. Still it has been notoriously difficult to maintain any kind of consistency in such constructs, keeping in touch at the same time with the myths as attested and not losing all contact with empirical reality. Granted that there are unconscious dynamics of the psyche, there is no reason to assume that they are isomorphic with any tale, which belongs after all not to the realm of the unconscious, but to language. (*Structure* 4)

As Jung points out, what is universal is not the object, but the story behind it:

> I have frequently been accused of a superstitious belief in 'inherited ideas'—quite unjustly, because I have expressly emphasized that these

---

[1] For more information on Jungian psychoanalytic case studies, see, Fierz, Heinrich Karl. *Jungian Psychiatry*. Daimon Verlag, 1991.

concordances are not produced by 'ideas' but rather by the inherited disposition to react in the same way as people have always reacted. Again, the concordance has been denied on the ground that the redeemer figure is in one case a hare, in another a bird, and in another a human being. But this is to forget something which so much impressed a pious Hindu visiting an English church that, when he got home, he told the story that the Christians worshipped animals, because he had seen so many lambs about. The names matter little; everything depends on the connection between them. Thus it does not matter if the 'treasure' is a golden ring, in another a crown, in a third a pearl, in a fourth a hidden hoard. The essential thing is the idea of an exceedingly precious treasure hard to attain, no matter what it is called locally. ("Structure" 111-112)

I will address Burkert's notion that "tales" belong to the realm of language below. Returning to our definition: archetypes are beyond our conscious understanding; we only see their effects in a crisis situation, when the archetypal material is "constellated" or projected into some kind of form such as a synchronicity (meaningful coincidence) or appears in dream material. For the individual to become completely immersed in an archetype is psychotic; it is through these psychoses that Jung also gained his understanding of archetypal material. Myths and fairy tales also arise out of archetypes. ("Archetypes" 5) "The archetype is essentially an unconscious content that is altered by becoming conscious and by being perceived, and it takes its colour from the individual consciousness in which it happens to appear." (5)

The terms "Feminine" and "Masculine" are archetypal, as they do not necessarily refer to women and men respectively. These terms refer to certain qualities that are often projected onto the social or cultural roles of women and men. Jung does not concretely define these terms; his writings suggest that the reader intuitively knows what they mean. In his essay on the Kore, Jung notes how the Kore is both the Anima and the Mother ("Psychological" 183). The *anima* is the term Jung uses for the soul of a man, and *animus* as the soul of a woman; whatever they are biologically, their "soul" is psychologically the opposite, as the merging of opposites in the process of individuation is the goal of humans, in Jung's opinion. This means that someone becomes a "complete" human being by developing his or her dominant traits and integrating their opposite (and therefore weaker) ones. These so-called "weaker" traits are part of the individual's Shadow.[2] It is metaphorically like the right-handed person learning to write left-handed, or vice versa. Current psychoanalytic thought is critical of these strict categories in men and wom-

[2] See Chapter 2 for a fuller discussion of Jung's ideas on anima and animus.

en, suggesting that the anima and perhaps the animus are present in both sexes. (Relke)

Jung's view of the anima and animus in therapy suggested his own biases about what is Masculine and Feminine, but he never gives a formal definition of either term; one can only infer Jung's definitions from his writings. Cynthia Eller's excellent work on the myth of matriarchal prehistory questions these categories and our uses of these categories. She rightly notes that what is often categorized as masculine and feminine does not necessarily apply to either men or women, and yet those categories are still continually used to define men and women.[3] Are ideas of masculine and feminine somehow predetermined in our unconscious? It becomes hard to separate these archetypal ideas from social constructs of gender, and the reality is that they are still applied to men and women even when they don't apply. Social and biological gender constructs are more in question than ever these days, which makes it more necessary for us to understand what we mean by these terms "masculine" and "feminine," even if they are inaccurate as descriptions of human beings.

One obvious symbol of Masculine and Feminine is the Chinese Yin/Yang symbol, consisting of a circle divided by an s-shaped curve, half black, half white, and with a circle of white in the black half and vice versa. Jung comments on this symbol: "The word *hun* is translated by [Richard] Wilhelm as 'animus.' Indeed, the concept seems appropriate for *hun*, the character for which is made up of the character for 'clouds' and that for 'demon.' Thus *hun* means 'cloud-demon,' a higher 'breath-soul' belonging to the yang principle and therefore masculine. After death, *hun* rises upward and becomes *shen*, the 'expanding and self-revealing' spirit or god. 'Anima,' called *p'o*, and written with the characters for 'white' and for 'demon,' that is, 'white ghost', belong to the lower, earth-bound, bodily soul, the yin principle, and is therefore feminine. After death, it sinks downward and becomes *kuei* (demon) often explained as the 'one who returns' (i.e., to earth), a revenant, a ghost." (Wilhelm 115) This association of women with earthly death may explain why Jung's collective unconscious is associated with the Feminine by Erich Neumann, while the rational conscious mind is associated with the Masculine (172). The collective unconscious is the realm of the irrational and the unknown. Psychological interpretations of the "Hero's journey" involve a descent into the underworld, interpreted as a psychological metaphor for getting in touch not only with what is unconscious, but with that "treasure" that has relevance for humanity as a whole, not just the individual.

---

[3] For a full discussion of archetypal use of these terms vs. gender roles, see Eller, Cynthia. "The Eternal Feminine." *The Myth of Matriarchal Prehistory: Why an Invented past Won't Give Women a Future.* Beacon, 2000. 56-80.

Jung identifies the *hun* as *logos* (Wilhelm 116), and in his essay on the "Syzygy" he describes the masculine as corresponding to *logos* and the feminine as corresponding to *eros*.[4] So, we see an identification of the Masculine with sky, spirit, and rationality, while the Feminine is associated with the earth, the demonic, and desire. But is this accurate, or does it simply represent Jung's own gender prejudices? Burkert noted earlier than myths and "tales" belonged to the realm of language rather than the unconscious, and I believe this supports Jung's assertions rather than disproving them. The Roman grammarian Varro once claimed that words associated with the sky were masculine, and those associated with the earth were feminine.[5] While this is etymologically inaccurate, it shows that the ancient Romans may have had similar prejudices about Masculine and Feminine. Linguistics provides a noteworthy approach to the question. Lera Boroditsky's studies, referred to by Anthony Corbeill in Chapters 1 and 3 of this work, examine associations with masculine and feminine words. Her first study involved taking the German words for "key" and "bridge" and telling one group that the word was masculine, the other feminine, and then asking the participants to provide adjectives describing the words. "Key" is masculine in German and feminine in Spanish, and the participants spoke Spanish or German as their native language. German speakers described the English word "key" as hard, heavy, jagged, metal, serrated, and useful; Spanish speakers described them as golden, intricate, little, lovely, shiny, and tiny (Boroditsky 70). In an attempt to remove cultural bias, she then did a study with a fictional language and pictures. Items were "soupative" or "oosative," and these corresponded to grammatical gender categories (71-72). The results were similar, and the example of a picture of a violin is given in Chapter 4. It would be interesting to see this kind of a study repeated in other parts of the world, perhaps in an African or Asian country, to see if there are also similar categorizations.

Linguistic theories of gender in language have suggested another set of categories for masculine and feminine—that of individual vs. collective, and this will prove to be an important categorization in this study. While there is disagreement about these categories among linguists, Karl Brugmann put forward the argument that Indo-European feminine suffixes (*a, ic, i*) expressed abstracts and collectives (Ibrahim 34). A similar theory was expressed with regard to Semitic language (42). While these ideas are contentious, they do suggest a pattern within language that equates the feminine with the collective in a notable number of examples. With regard to social uses of language, Robin Lakoff offers a syntactic axis with the elements Clar-

---

[4] See Chapter 2.
[5] See Chapter 4.

ity, Distance, Deference, and Camaraderie. She uses Clark Gable and Marilyn Monroe as examples of social ideals of masculine and feminine, and suggests that Gable falls closer to the Clarity/Distance axis of speech (with his infamous line "Frankly my dear, I don't give a damn" as an example), while Monroe is closer to the Deference/Camaraderie part of the axis:

> In contrast to Gable's characteristic poker face, we have Monroe either smiling or looking sensuous, but certainly wearing an identifiable facial expression. She uses interjections and hedges freely and her dialog is sprinkled with 'I guess' and 'kinda' in distinction to Gable's unembellished 'yup's.' Her sentences seem not to end, but rather to be elliptical, as if in invitation to the addressee to finish them for her—classic feminine deference. (66-67)

Lakoff suggests that social perception of the Deference/Camaraderie mode of speech falls into the "nonmasculine" and therefore "nonnormal," and this is viewed as "worse, weaker, or degenerate." (68) This is similar to Carol Gilligan's *In a Different Voice*, discussed in Chapter 1, which suggests that boys tend toward rationalistic and legalistic approaches to questions in psychological tests, while girls tend toward a less definite but more community-oriented response. Gilligan argues that psychologists saw this "feminine" view in a negative light: "When considered in the light of Kohlberg's definition of the stage and sequence of moral development, her [Amy, the girl in the study] moral judgments appear to be a full stage lower in maturity than those of the boy" (30).

We may not "prove" definitively that all people think of masculine and feminine categories in this way, but there is strong evidence that there is some agreed-upon cultural bias that has an ambiguous origin. We could point to the biology of women and the traditional role as child-bearers as possible reasons for the association of women with the earth and fertility. But biology is not destiny, and as we will see, ancient mythologies and histories portray female goddesses in a variety of roles, which may or may not accord with attitudes toward actual women living in those time periods. Eller mentions the comment of a male pilgrim: "the difference between the Goddess and women is like the difference between the stone you worship and the rock on which you defecate" (104). For our purposes, we are interested in the association of male deities with the sky, and female deities with the earth, and how ideas about sky and earth—and by association about masculine and feminine—are altered by attitudes about the soul and death.

This is not about patriarchy vs. matriarchy; there was never a time when women ruled the earth peacefully, as matriarchal feminists would suggest. Cults of the Great Mother engaged in bloody rituals, often meaning castration for men. If anything, the matriarchal myth is metaphorical of our Western male psychological development. Object relations theory tells us that children identify with their mothers as infants and gradually develop a sense of self, and also a sense of others. This sense of self is usually developed by the age of seven, and as a child grows into adolescence there is a tendency to reject the mother and the family in favor of independence. Later, when the child becomes an adult and has gone out on their own, they may revisit those familial things they rejected and reintegrate them into their lives. The idea of "starting from the mother" and the collective and becoming independent is another way of saying that we break away from the comfort of the nurturing mother to face conflict in the world. In the later part of the "heroic journey" of life, the feminine is re-encountered as an anima-figure, and later perhaps as a wife or significant feminine influence that allows the independent adult to share talents and gifts with the community at large. This is not a regression to childhood; it is the mature individual coming into an adult relationship with the "Feminine." While the terminology is masculine, women also tend to follow this pattern of development. Esther Harding notes the discomfort of both men and women with the "feminine" in the modern world (16-17). Independence, rationality, and unemotional decision making are valued as strengths. These are all positive traits in human character, but the emotional and the vulnerable should not be discarded as weaknesses. As Martha Nussbaum states in Rachel Aviv's *New Yorker* article: " 'What I am calling for,' she writes, is 'a society of citizens who admit that they are needy and vulnerable'" (36). Our world today consists of constant tribalism and conflict; there is no middle ground, and yielding to another point of view is often treated as a "cop-out" or an act of treason. There is too much of "standing one's ground" with guns loaded and not enough effort to understand the other and build bridges. Validation goes a long way toward understanding, and it does not necessarily involve adopting opposite views.

This work is dedicated to examining ideas about death and what happens after death and their relationship to the Feminine. Now that we have clarified some definitions and assumptions, Chapter 1 goes back to Ancient Egypt; while Egyptian civilization developed differently and at an earlier time than the Greek, it is impossible to talk about Western afterlife beliefs without examining Egyptian influence. Chapter 2 examines ancient Greek ideas about the Feminine as expressed in goddesses, and Homeric ideas of the afterlife. Chapter 3 looks at changes in Greek society around the 6th to 4th centuries B.C.E., when Greeks were known to be influenced by their Persian neighbors in the Achamenid Empire, and with a change in thought about the relationship of humans to gods with philosophy and the rise of mystery cults, particularly Orphism. The fourth chapter looks at ancient Roman belief, and how these beliefs changed through contact with the East during the Punic Wars, up to the beginning of the Roman Empire. Finally, Chapter 5 looks at the influence of apocalyptic Judaism on the developments of religious belief and philosophy, and how the rise of Christianity solidified split thinking about Heaven and Earth in terms of divine reward and punishment, and the view of lust as the ultimate corrupter of humanity. The ancient Greeks could accept the worship of gods with opposite purposes; the more one strives for the "good" and the "true," the less acceptable this state of affairs becomes. Concurrently, the valuing of the individual over the state played a role in this split between earth and sky and reward and punishment, resulting in a negative association of women in religion.

Works Cited: Introduction

Aviv, Rachel. "Captain of Her Soul: The Philosopher Martha Nussbaum's Emotions." *New Yorker* (July 25, 2016): 34-43.

Boroditsky, Lera et al. "Sex, Syntax, and Semantics." *Language in Mind: Advances in the Study of Language and Thought,* Edited by Dedre Gentner and Susan Goldin-Meadow, MIT Press, 2003, pp. 61–79.

Burkert, Walter. *Structure and History in Greek Mythology and Ritual.* University of California, 1979.

Eliade, Mircea. *Rites and Symbols of Initiation: the Mysteries of Birth and Rebirth.* Harper Torchbooks, 1958.

Eller, Cynthia. *The Myth of Matriarchal Prehistory: Why an Invented Past Won't Give Women a Future.* Beacon, 2000.

Erikson, Erik H. *Childhood and Society.* W.W. Norton, 1993.

Gilligan, Carol. *In a Different Voice: Women's Conception of the Self and of Morality.* Harvard University Press, 1977.

Harding, M. Esther. *Woman's Mysteries: Ancient and Modern.* G.P. Putnam, 1971.

Ibrahim, Muhammad Hasan. *Grammatical Gender: Its Origin and Development..* The Hague, 1973.

Jung, Carl G. "The Archetypes and the Collective Unconscious." *Collected Works.* Translated by R. F. C. Hull. Vol. 9.1. Pantheon, 1959.

Jung, C. G. "The Psychological Aspects of the Kore." *Collected Works.* Translated by R.F.C. Hull. Vol. 9.1. Pantheon, 1959. 182-203.

Jung, Carl G. "The Structure and Dynamics of the Psyche." *Collected Works.* Translated by R. F. C. Hull. Vol. 8. Princeton University Press, 1969.

Kastenbaum, Robert. *The Psychology of Death.* 3rd edition. Springer, 2000.

Lakoff, Robin Tolmach. "Stylistic Strategies within a Grammar of Style." *Language, Sex, and Gender: Does La Différence Make a Difference?*, Edited by Judith Orasanu et al., vol. 327, New York Academy of Sciences, 1979, pp. 53–78, *Annals of the New York Academy of Sciences.*

Neumann, Erich. *The Fear of the Feminine and Other Essays on Feminine Psychology.* Princeton University Press, 1994.

"Philippians." *Interpreter's Bible: The Holy Scriptures in the King James and Revised Standard Versions.* Vol. 11. Abingdon, 1955. 3-129.

Relke, Joan. "The Archetypal Female in Mythology and Religion: The Anima and the Mother." *Europe's Journal of Psychology* 3.1 (2007) ‹http://ejop.psychopen.eu/article/view/389/html›.

Wilhelm, Richard, and C. G. Jung. *The Secret of the Golden Flower: A Chinese Book of Life.* Harcourt, Brace, Jovanovich, 1962.

Chapter 1: Ancient Egypt: Foundations

Introductory Comments

Western civilization has its roots in the Near East, and any discussion of religious beliefs about death in the West must begin with Ancient Egypt. Many Western ideas about the afterlife were adapted from Egyptian belief by the Greeks, Romans, and Jews among possible others. The ancient Egyptians spent most of their wealth on preparations for the afterlife; there is no other culture recorded in human history that invested as much in death. (Müller) The first question that comes to mind is "why"? There is an expression found in Egyptian tombs addressing visitors with, "As you hate death and love life." (Assmann 17). Was it a remarkable fear of death that led to such elaborate rituals and preparations? Jan Zandee suggested that Egyptians were both "monistic and dualistic"—on the one hand, everything proceeded from the same source, and death was part of that natural progression of regeneration and renewal. On the other hand, death was viewed as an enemy (Zandee 2).

We have a wealth of information about these beliefs from the tomb walls of pharaohs and ancient papyri. However, even with these sources, many narratives are incomplete, leaving us to rely on syncretistic Greek and Roman accounts to piece together a view of ancient Egyptian belief and culture. The ancient Egyptians were in an era unto themselves, and they developed sophisticated ideas about life after death long before any mixing with Greek or Roman ideas. Maya Müller succinctly explains the changes in belief from the Pre-Dynastic period of Egypt through the second century C.E. In the early periods, death and immortality was strictly the domain of the pharaoh. By the Middle Kingdom, high ranking government officials also had tombs and were eligible for an afterlife with the gods. Common people had tombs in the later part of this period, though they did not become gods; they lived a life much like the one on earth, only in the other world and with their own families. The New Kingdom showed further changes in belief, with the journey of the sun god Re emerging as the main motif in afterlife conceptions; this was also the first time the afterlife itself was portrayed on tomb walls. By the time Egypt enters the periods of Persian and Roman rule, attempts to hang on to afterlife traditions seem more historical, and there is much mixing of Greek, Roman, and Egyptian ideas as evidenced by Plutarch.[6]

Death beliefs and funerary practices were shaped by political and social forces, with marked changes from the Old Kingdom to the New Kingdom. At first glance, the mythology of the ancient Egyptians seems quite different from that of ancient Greece and Rome, which we will treat in subsequent chapters. However, the psychological changes in Egyptian views of death are concurrent with social forces that democratize the population. The Greeks of the Archaic period believed everyone had the same fate, regardless of social standing or role. Ancient Egyptians initially believed this with respect to everyone but the pharaoh, who was considered a god. As the joyous afterlife of the "beautiful West" (Müller 32) became open to everyone over time, scenes of earthly life gradually disappear from tomb walls in favor of grand depictions of the afterlife. A disconnect occurs between earth and heaven. It should be noted that the earth god in Egyptian myth is Geb, a masculine deity, which is different from its neighbors, and the sky is feminine, the goddess Nut. The ancient Egyptians also did not place the "underworld" under the earth. Nonetheless, changes in attitude toward earthly life and afterlife are noteworthy for our thesis.

This chapter will give a brief overview of the historical forces at play throughout Egyptian history, and examine core mythologies, deities and practices relevant to our discussion of the afterlife. As Egypt is not the main focus of our study, but rather provides background to Classical civilization and Biblical ideas, this will not be more than a concise overview of this rich culture. We will specifically look at conceptions of the Feminine with respect to death beliefs, and conclude with an analysis of foundational concepts that will be important in subsequent chapters, particularly with respect to the rise of mystery cults and philosophy.

---

[6] See: Plutarch. "Of Isis and Osiris, or of the Ancient Religion and Philosophy of Egypt." *Plutarch's Essays and Miscellanies, Comprising All His Works Collected under the Title of "Morals,"* edited by William Goodwin, translated by William Baxter, Little Brown and Company, 1911.

Background

First, we should consider the time period in question. Before Alexander the Great conquered Egypt there were 31 dynasties of pharaohs, with the first dynasty dating from approximately 3050 B.C.E.[7]). Ancient Egyptian history prior to Graeco-Roman occupation is divided into the Old, Middle, New, and Late Kingdom periods, with three intermediate periods. There are three main "texts" offering information about Egyptian afterlife beliefs. The first are the Pyramid Texts from the Old Kingdom period (ca. 2700-2190 B.C.E.); the second are the Coffin Texts from the Middle Kingdom period (ca. 2060-1665 B.C.E.); the third are the Books of the Dead from New Kingdom period (ca. 1569-1080 B.C.E.). We can see the rise and fall of the importance of death rituals if the burials from these periods are considered; there are two distinct trends. There was the traditional Egyptian narrative of Seth and Horus, and the trial vindicating Horus and punishing Seth. During the New Kingdom period, Amenhopte IV (Akhenaten, ca. 1372-1355 B.C.E.) challenged existing beliefs during the Amarna Period, creating a kind of monotheistic religion that worshipped only the sun god, and abolished the idea of the afterlife. The dead dwelt in their tombs, not in another realm. (Assmann 15) However, this belief system did not last, and the Egyptians returned to their previous beliefs about the afterlife, with the Books of the Dead now gaining central importance. (15-16) The resurrection of Osiris by Isis was the central myth in this system, as well as the rise of Horus and the defeat of Seth. After the 18th Dynasty, Amen-Ra became the overlord of Osiris. (Budge Gods 175) The sun was reborn every day, while Osiris remained as a judge in the underworld.

The *Pyramid Texts* deal with the pharaohs and their families exclusively; no one else was eligible for an afterlife with the gods. The *Coffin Texts* of the Middle Kingdom demonstrated a social shift in ideas about life after death; now it was open to everyone. The final text comes from the New Kingdom period, after the Amarna period, and is referred to as the *Amduat*, translated as the *Book of Coming Forth by Day* (Budge Gods 174), or the *Book of the Dead*. The latter book likens the life of humans to the journey of the sun god, who died every night, fought off the monsters of the underworld, and rose every morning in triumph. The *Amduat* was the "chief religious text" from the time of Tuthmosis I to the Amarna Period (Hornung 155). The blazing sun on the horizon was believed to be Amen-Ra burning up his enemies. (Budge *Egyptian* 178) Like Amen-Ra, righteous humans who received the correct rites and knew the correct spells to pass through the twelve gates of the underworld

[7] Dates from: Redford, Donald, editor. *Oxford Encyclopedia of Ancient Egypt*. Oxford University Press, 2001.

could live happily in the other world. The un-righteous (and originally any-one who wasn't royalty) lived in an underworld that was an upside-down and reversed version of earth, where everything was dark and the inhabi-tants ate excrement. The "doors of Geb" (the Earth) must be opened to the dead person, lest he or she be seized by the gods of the earth (Zandee 8). The reverse side of a flat earth was seen as the place of punishment and a gloomy existence. Osiris complains to Atum, "There is no water, there is no air, it is very deep, dark and extensive." (Zandee 10-11) This idea of the chthonic realm bears some similarity to the ancient Greek conception of Hades.

Cosmology and Death Myths

Ancient Egyptian religion was monistic at its core. Its main creation my-thologies demonstrate how we get "many" from "one." One version of the myth comes from Hermopolis, the Ogdoad, or "eight." In this version, pri-meval forces evolved from serpents or frogs into pairings: Nun and Nunette (Water), Hek and Heket (Space), Kek and Keket (Darkness), and Amun and Amunette (Hiddenness). A similar creation myth from Heliopolis is the En-nead, and is the oldest myth; in this version the creator god appears from chaos, impregnates himself, and creates four generations of gods. In a third version the god Ptah creates the world by naming everything in it. (Remler) It is likely that these creation stories influenced their near neighbors. The first two myths bear some resemblance to the Gnostic idea of the Aeons, which will be discussed in Chapter 5; Ptah's role in the latter myth is similar to the role of Adam in the Garden of Eden. But the balancing of male and fe-male in creation is always present. The male as creator in this myth reminds us of the active Yang principle; the masculine takes action to bring the world into a concrete reality.

Important for us are Egyptian mythologies of death. Besides the night-journey of the sun god Ra mentioned above, the most well-known sto-ry is the slaying of Osiris by Seth and his resurrection by the efforts of his sis-ter-wife Isis. Remler notes that there is no complete Egyptian version of this story; the most complete version we have comes from Plutarch. In this ver-sion, Osiris is a great pharaoh who teaches the Egyptians how to grow grain and be self-sufficient. But his brother Typhon [Set] conspires against him; he privately takes Osiris' measurements and builds "a curious ark." (Plutarch 76) Typhon offers it as a gift in a sporting way to whoever could fit into it, and when Osiris climbs into the box, those present "clapped down the cover upon it, and when they had fastened it down with nails and soldered it with melted lead, they carried it forth to the river side, and let it swim into the sea at the Tanaitic mouth, which the Egyptians therefore to this day detest and abominate the very naming of it." (76) Thus begins the saga of Osiris' sister-wife Isis, who goes in search of the ark [sarcophagus], ending up in Byblos, where the sarcophagus lodges in a beautiful but large tree that is cut down by the king Macander to be a pillar in his palace. Isis, like Demeter in the search for Persephone, disguises herself and serves as a nurse to the king's son. She attempts to make the child immortal, until the queen sees her put the child in the flame and cries out. Isis then reveals herself and asks for the pillar containing her husband's body. Horus is already born in this account, and when Isis brings her husband's body with her to see her son and his nurse, Seth finds the body, tears it into fourteen pieces and "thr[ows] them all about" (80). So, Isis goes to recover the pieces, and finds all but her husband's "private part," which has been eaten by certain fish, so she fashions an effigy of one. Osiris then comes from the underworld to train his son Horus, who now intends to avenge his father. Horus goes to battle Typhon and eventually wins; but "Isis, although she had Typhon delivered up to her fast bound, yet would not put him to death, but contrariwise loosed him and let him go." (81) Horus is furious at this, and snatches the royal diadem from her head. In this syncretistic version, Hermes replaces Isis' head with that of a cow. Hermes also appears when Typhon tries to depose Horus as a "bastard," but Hermes serves as his advocate. (81) If this part of the story was believed in Ancient Egpyt, Thoth is a more likely candidate as Osiris' advocate, as he dealt with justice and arbitration among the gods.

Geography of the Underworld

The Egyptian word associated with the underworld is Duat or Tuat, though as Budge tells us, "… it must be distinctly understood that the Egyptian word does not imply that it was situated under our world, and that this rendering is only adopted because the exact signification of the name Tuat is unknown." (Gods 170). Tuat was the place where the sun god Ra passed through during the night, through a process of death and resurrection. (170) It was not located under the earth; it was somewhere beyond the earth, and closer to the gods in the sky. (171) Tuat was separated from the world by a mountain range, and Budge notes that Jews, Christians, and Muslims all have scriptural notions of "[separating the] blessed from the damned" by a wall, mountain, or abyss. (171) In the Egyptian geography of the universe, the realm outside the created world includes the underworld, and dark realms on the edges of creation are seen as having existed before the world and encircling it—"It is thus quite generally the boundary of the ordered world and the limit of the king's rule." [8] (Hornung 169). Just as there are boundaries for the universe, the gods also are limited. As mentioned earlier, there is also the notion of the underworld as the reverse of the earthly world, where the dead walk upside down, drink urine, and eat feces. This latter idea of the underworld as a "shadow" or "reversal" of worldly life suggests that death was seen as the opposite of life.

Gods of the Underworld

The Egyptian afterlife texts associate many deities with the underworld journey. Here are brief descriptions of those deities central to the mythology:

Apophis or Apep: This god was rendered as a giant crocodile or serpent, and it was the main enemy of Ra during his night journey through the underworld. Each night the sun god battles with Apophis, who represents annihilation and non-existence, and defeats him each time. Sometimes Apophis is represented as slain, though other texts and images refer to him as bound; I can't help but notice a similarity between this myth and the defeat of Typhoeus by Zeus.

Seth/Typhon: Seth is the brother of Osiris, and the god of Lower Egypt. He is considered the bringer of storms, and introduces chaos and dissolution into the system. Seth conspires to kill his brother Osiris, and after Isis rescues his body, Seth tears it into fourteen pieces and scatters it all over the world. Later, Seth would dispute Horus' right to accede the throne, claiming he was a "bastard" child. In the mythology of the underworld, judgement is made against Seth in a trial with Horus and Osiris, and he is punished. However, in the version of the myth given to us by Plutarch, a bound Seth (called Typhon) is released by Isis. Contrary to expectation, Seth is not necessarily considered an "evil" deity—this changing of role from Trickster figure and manipulator to an embodiment of evil will be discussed in Chapter 5.

Anubis: This jackal-headed god is said to the be child of Osiris and Nephthys. Osiris lay with his wife's sister by accident, and Nephthys left the child to be exposed, fearing the wrath of her husband Seth. Isis found the child and raised it. Anubis was a protector of the dead in the tomb, but was also involved in the judgement of the dead. On the Papyrus of Ani he is represented as holding the scales that weigh the heart of the deceased against a feather, in the presence of Osiris.

Osiris: As noted, he is the main god of the underworld, represented as an early pharaoh, killed by his brother. We see a great deal of the Egyptian idea of death in the Osiris myth. Gods are not immortal, and humans ultimately

---

[8] See the next chapter on the Latin word "regere" for more on the idea of the king as boundary-setter.

pass through the same trials as Osiris; indeed, it is as if human life is a retelling of the lives of the gods. Osiris lives on in the underworld as its pharaoh, in the "beautiful West". Tobin suggests that Osiris went from "demon to deity" in the Pre-Dynastic period, an idea he may have gotten from Plutarch, which may or may not be accurate (459, Encyclopedia). His son Horus became associated with the sky, and he was considered the living aspect of the pharaoh, while Osiris was the death aspect.

Selket/Nephthys/Neith/Isis: These goddesses are associated with the protection of the dead. Selket or Serket is a scorpion goddess, who has healing gifts, especially against venomous stings. Neith is a war goddess, similar to the Greek Athena in her attributes, and a protector of the royal household. Nephthys is also the sister of Isis and the mother of Anubis, as noted above. Tobin notes that Nephthys and her sister Isis, symbols of the royal throne, did not appear in the earliest versions of the Pyramid Texts (460) Isis and Nephthys are seen as goddesses of lamentation, and it is the text of this that is preserved (Tobin 462). Isis also magically restores her husband, suggesting a feminine connection to death and rebirth, as well as healing and protection.

The act of lamenting the dead and powers of resurrection would be associated with chthonic powers in the Greek system, hence the likely syncretism between Isis and the Great Mother cults. However, these "earth mothers" could also rise to the celestial—Isis could take the form of a kite, and Astarte is often pictured as a dove (Relke 4) The Paraclete also appears as a dove in Christian symbolism, and Jung connects this directly to Astarte and the Old Testament Sophia.[9]

Death Rituals: The Opening of the Mouth

Egyptians had elaborate mummification rituals intended to preserve the body and assist it in the journey to the other world through spells and images, both painted and three-dimensional. These rituals became more or less elaborate over time; however the one ritual that remained consistent from the Old Kingdom through the Hellenistic period was the Opening of the Mouth. "It allowed the mummy, statue, or temple to eat, breathe, see, hear, and otherwise enjoy the provisions offered by the cult." (Roth 605) A cutting tool was touched to the lips of the deceased. While the spells used appear to be a confusion of other spells, Roth suggests that the opening of the mouth is a bit like the clearing of a baby's mouth at birth, and may be symbolic of that action as a rebirth. Fingers were originally used to "open the mouth," with the cutting or shaving tool used in later versions. (606) There are also

---

[9] Sophia will be discussed in Chapter 5.

references in the Pyramid Texts to "Horus opening the mouth of Osiris with his little fingers" (Spells 1329-1330)(606), and the presence of milk jars described as the breasts of Isis and Horus, and five cloves of garlic described as teeth. Another knife used in this ritual (the pss-kf knife) before the opening of the mouth is present to cut the umbilical cord, in Roth's view (606) By the first century CE, there were still variants of this ritual, though their purpose was said to allow the dead person to breathe. (608) The entire ritual from the tomb of Seti I offers details of the ritual. First, a statue of the dead person is placed in the tomb on a platform of sand, the priest garbing himself in the "quenau" garment (Budge Opening 13) as an act of purification to make his spells more effective. He then pours water over the statue to purify it for the *ka*, and puts *qema* incense in its mouth. (20) After further censing rituals, the priests enter the interior room of the tomb, where another priest plays the dead man, wrapped in the skin of a bull or cow, and roused by the words of the priests who enter. Horus is said to cover the deceased with a net, and the formulae spoken mention a mantis and a beetle, two insects associated with resurrection. (33-35) The statue and the mummy are both struck, to represent the murder of Osiris. At this point the priest, saying "I am thy son, I am Horus, I have pressed for thee thy mouth," opens the mouth in the manner described above. (41) The ceremonies finish with several animal sacrifices, the treating of the body, and more purification rituals. The Seth-Osiris-Horus myth re-enacted in these rituals, and the body is purified as a vehicle for the soul, one that is worthy of admittance to the divine pantheon.

Death Attitudes: Immortality, Salvation, Reward and Punishment

The Egyptian idea of "soul" is rather complex, and to use the term "soul" may be misleading. There are five basic components to the idea of the force that bestows life or consciousness in Egyptian thinking:

- *The Ka.* Ka is translated as "double", and is a double of the physical body, known as the Khat. Budge explains: "When the body was born there came into existence with it an abstract individuality or spiritual being, which was wholly independent and distinct from the physical body, whose actions it was supposed to direct and guide, and keep watch over, and it lived in the body until the body died." (Budge Osiris 117) When the person died, the Ka could no longer live in the body, but the Egyptians would create statues in the likeness of the dead person, so that the Ka might reside there if it chose.
- *The Ba.* Ba is often translated as "soul", but this isn't quite accurate. The Ba is paired with the Ka, and is thought of as the "soul of the Ka"

(Budge *Osiris* 128). The Ba was conceived as a bird, usually a falcon. This was very similar to Babylonian belief, and Greek and Roman words for soul either have to do with flight or breath. (Hornung 199)

- *The Akh.* Like the previous two ideas, akh is difficult to translate. It has to do with the vitality or generative life power: that which is able to create and renew. In some ways it is like the primal Greek Eros, who appears at the creation of the universe from Chaos, along with the depths (Tartarus, Erebus), the earth, and the sky. It appears to be the key ingredient in the renewal and regeneration of the deceased, moving them from death back to a renewed life.

- *The Sahu.* The Sahu is translated as "spirit-body", and seems to refer to the mummified body in the tomb, the flesh that was "incorruptible". While the Ka could be kept alive by offerings, it is not clear how the Sahu was revived, or how it moved about after death—or if it was strictly identical with the mummified body (Budge *Osiris* 123) To quote Budge: "As the physical body formed the abiding place of the Ka and the soul [Ba], so the spiritual body was believed to afford a dwelling-place for the soul, for it is distinctly said that 'souls enter into their sahu.' And the spiritual body had power to journey everywhere in heaven and on earth ..." (*Osiris* 124)

- *The Khaibit.* Khaibit means "shadow", and Budge tells us that the resurrection of the spiritual body could not be completed without its shadow (*Osiris* 126). The difference between the sahu and the khaibit was "slight" (127), but it was clear that the sahu was able to cast a shadow, suggesting that this soul-body had something corporeal about it. This may be the origin, or at least an inspiration, for the Greek notions of *psyche* and *eidolon*, with the former being the "breath of life" and the latter being the dim shade of the person. It is the latter that inhabits Hades; more will be said on this in the next chapter.

It is clear that the enemies of Amen-Ra, and the unrighteous, were doomed to punishment after death. But this was not a concept of eternal punishment; it was the total destruction of the soul and the body, and both were required for life after death. Hornung tells us: "Like men, the gods die, but they are not dead. Their existence—and all existence—is not an unchanging endlessness, but rather constant renewal." (Hornung 160) The body was carefully prepared to retain the soul, as the two went together to the afterlife. Annihilation was the threat rather than eternal torture, and prayers or offerings for the deceased had no effect—the deceased passed through the underworld initiations by their own merits or skill. (*Gods* 262)

Those unable to pass might also be devoured by "demons" who then absorb their strength. (Zandee 17) But as Budge tells us:

> We may see, however, that although the Egyptians had no hell for souls in the medieval acceptance of the term, their fiery pits, and fiends, and devils, and enemies of Ra formed the foundations of the hells of later peoples like the Hebrews, and even of the descendants of the Egyptians who became Christians, i.e., the Copts. (*Gods* 265)

A common thread from the Old Kingdom to the New Kingdom was the idea of judgment, though this idea varied over time. The *Pyramid Texts* portray Re or Osiris as judges, and the dead person recites a litany of sins, like a magical formula, that he or she did not commit, and memorization may be more important than one's actual virtue. (Zandee 32). The *Payprus of Ani* shows the dead person's heart being weighed against a feather. Zandee mentions the heart as the carrier of intellectual functions, and there are even spells for keeping one's heart from "complaining" about its owner. (33) Zandee also mentions at least eleven different terms for the notion of "sin" (41-44), including words that translate as "disaster," "misery," "without character," and "disorder."

Role of Magic

Magical formulae were critical in Egyptian rituals, as it is the long litanies that guarantee the rebirth of the dead person, and defend them from their enemies in the afterlife. As noted earlier, ethics had little to do with the judgment of the dead; it was the ability to memorize a litany of charges and refute them before the court of gods.

We discussed the ritual of the opening of the mouth in an earlier section. The body was considered the seat of the soul, which is why it had it be preserved. All Egyptian funerary texts have incantations to secure *heka*, or activation of the *ka*. Coffin Text 261 tells us that *heka*, also translated as "magic," existed at the beginning of the universe, before duality. So, magic appears to be a basic, driving force of life in Egyptian thinking. It may be related to *akh*, the generative force of the universe, though not exactly identical. But all of our attempts to differentiate these terms may be an academic exercise; clearly they are all facets of one idea of life and consciousness.

Amulets were numerous in the tomb, and may have served as protection for the deceased, though the *Book of Coming Forth By Day* suggests that amulets might be used as substitute hearts for the deceased. (Spells 29B and 30, qtd. in Ritner 334). In addition to amulets, curses were written in the tombs against anyone who might disturb the grave or its goods. One of the most famous curses known in popular culture is the one on Tutkankhamen's tomb, but the most extensive one is on the tomb of Amenhotep in the twenty-first dynasty. The curses threaten annihilation of the soul for those who would commit such sacrilege. (Ritner 335) Disturbing the body or breaking up tomb articles threatened the soul, which relied on the body for its housing, and might leave the dead person powerless or impoverished in the other world.

The deceased was represented by a statue that could come to life to receive grave offerings, and an army of little statues were also included in the tomb, to do the work of the deceased. These little statues were known as *ushabtis*, and were also "brought to life" by a series of magical formulae. There is a marked similarity between *ushabti* and the Hebrew idea of the *golem*. *Golem* were images, usually of clay, that had the sacred name of God written on them. They were believed to come to life and do the bidding of their creator. While we don't see this idea developed until Kabbalistic texts appear in the 12th century C.E., there are Old Testament references that suggest the idea is much older. It is unknown if the Jews got this idea from the Egyptians, though it is clear in the Bible that Jews were enslaved by the Egyptians for a period of time, and the cross-adoption of some traditions is not out of the question.

One practice that the Egyptians had in common with the Greeks and Romans was necromancy; the dead had the ability to foretell the future, and could be consulted. The *Book of Going Forth by Day*, Spells 148 and 190 suggest that the deceased can "make known to you what fate befalls it." (Ritner 336) There were also "letters to the dead" requesting favors, suggesting that the dead could still act and intervene on behalf of the living (336). Ritner tells us that some pharaohs had institutionalized necromantic cults, such as those of Imhotep and Amenhotpe I. Amhose had an oracle set up at Abydos, the traditional site of Osiris' burial.

The presence of grave offerings for the deceased is a theme that will be repeated among the Greeks and Romans, and may have been part of the rituals of all their ancestors. For the Egyptians the ka-priests recited a "list of invocation offerings" in which the deceased is "provided with the underworld equivalent or intangible essence of the object named: 'a thousand loaves of bread, a thousand jugs of beer, a thousand oxen, a thousand fowl, a thousand vessels of alabaster, a thousand bolts of cloth, and everything good and pure on which a god lives.'" (Ritner, *Oxford Encyclopedia* 333) The images on the tomb wall that accompanied these spells were just as important; there was a connection between the spoken word and the image, as is the case in sympathetic magic. The images and words have a life-giving energy of their own, and can bring about the desired result. This is notable, especially in light of the fact that these images of daily sustenance disappeared from tomb walls in the late New Kingdom period. In light of later influences of philosophy and "reason" that we read in Plutarch, there certainly seems to be some doubt about the usefulness of these spells, and their erratic maintenance toward the end of Egyptian religion proper and the beginnings of Christianity suggest a clinging to tradition rather than faith in the spells. However, magic did not go away in the Near East; the *Papyri Graecae Magicae* [Greek Magical Papyri] suggest a merging of Egyptian, Persian, Greek, and Roman beliefs in magic spells in the early part of the common era. But we will discuss these in a later chapter.

The Feminine in Egyptian Mythology and Death Beliefs

The primeval god who created the universe was androgynous; all other deities are either male or female. Aten, the "one god" of Akenaten was considered to be "both mother and father" (Hornung 171). From the primeval god a divine couple emerges, Shu and Tefnut, who are male and female respectively, and they conceive other male-female partners in the creation of the world. This is not unusual; creation mythology generally involves a movement into the field of opposites from a unified field. Living in space and time means experience difference rather than unity. When Adam and Eve eat from the Tree of the Knowledge of Good and Evil (i.e., opposites), they suddenly "know that they are naked and cover their shame". Duality is a condition of life, including the duality of life and death. Consistent with this is the Egyptian view that the underworld is an opposite version of this world. Life consists of existence; for the Egyptian, the ultimate tragedy would be to not exist anymore. The wicked are destroyed by flames, like the enemies of Ra. But they are never really destroyed—behind the opposites is a unity, and if you eliminate one, you create an imbalance, or at least a different kind of split. A new "evil" will replace the old one. Space and time exist in the context of the non-existent (179)

Female deities like Isis, Nephthys and Selket protected the dead from what we might consider "evil" entities. In the journey of the sun god, these entities would be the creatures of the outer darkness that threaten to extinguish the sun and bring chaos upon the earth. It is worth noting that Seth/Typhon is one of the deities protecting Ra on his night journey through the "underworld".

Isis as Mother is closer in her attributes to Near Eastern counterparts like Cybele and Ishtar, as opposed to later figures modeled on her, particularly the Virgin Mary. She is the devoted wife of her brother-husband Osiris and takes a long journey to put him back together when he is dismembered. But she also nearly destroyed the sun god Ra. Here is Lewis Spence's retelling of this story:

> Isis, weary of the world of mortals, determined to enter that of the gods, and to this end made up her mind to worm his secret name from the almighty Ra. This name was known to no mortal, and not even to any god but himself. By this time Ra had grown old, and, like many another venerable person, he often permitted the saliva to flow from the corners of his mouth. Some of this fell to the earth, and Isis, mixing it with the soil, kneaded it into the shape of a serpent, and cunningly laid it in the path traversed by the great god every day. Bursting upon the world in his effulgence, and attended by the entire pantheon, he was astounded when the serpent, rising from its coil, stung him ... He called all the gods to come that their healing words might make him well, and with them came Isis, who cunningly inquired what ailed him. He related the incident of the serpent to her, and added that he was suffering the greatest agony. "Then," said Isis, "tell me thy name, Divine Father, for the man shall live who is called by his name." Ra attempted a compromise by stating he was 'Khepera' in the morning, 'Ra' at noon, and 'Atem' in the evening; but the poison worked more fearfully within him than before, and he could no longer walk. ... When [his secret name] was revealed, Isis immediately banished the poison from his veins and he became whole again. (259-260)

Jung equates Isis with the Biblical Sophia and suggests that she was called "'The Black One' because of her association with fate and the mysteries of death." ("Mysterium" 20) Even though she is not the "earth," she is seen by Jung as an earth goddess for this reason: "All these statements apply just as well to the prima material in its feminine aspect: it is the moon, the mother of all things, the vessel, it consists of opposites, has a thousand names ... it is the earth and the serpent hidden in the earth, the blackness and the dew and the miraculous water which brings together all that is divided. The water is therefore called 'mother.'" (21) Jung is referring to aspects of alchemy, and we will see that this mythology of Isis also applies to Greek magical figures like Medea and Circe, and the conception of water and its relation to the earth will be central to the philosophy of Heraclitus.

He mentions Apuleius as a source for the "blackness of her robe," and also associates her with the magical arts, including possessing the elixir of life. ("Mysterium" 20) This may have been part of the ancient Egyptian conception of Isis, or it may represent later syncretism with Greek beliefs. Still the conception of Isis that has survived is this "veiled Isis," who is "the vessel and the matter of good and evil." (20) Jung notes that Isis has a murderous role, as in the story above, but "is also the healer, for she not only cured Ra of the poisoning but put together the dismembered Osiris. As such she personifies that arcane substance, be it dew or the *aqua permanens*, which unites the hostile elements into one." (19-20)

But Isis is also connected to the image of the Black Madonna that is prevalent in many European cathedrals, and the image of Isis with the child Horus on her lap is the model for later artistic renderings of the Madonna and Christ Child. To quote Joan Relke: "The Great Mother delivers and cares for us all, even though in the end, she destroys and subsumes us into her 'thrall.'" (4) Isis is the perfect embodiment of the complex Mother archetype, and her connection to the underworld gives her a chthonic quality.

Other major Egyptian goddesses had various attributes. Nu or Nut is the embodiment of the night sky, with her arched body presented as the starry firmament. Tefnut is the goddess of moist air. Ma'at is the feminine aspect of Thoth, and represents the "living truth." Bastet was a goddess of war, and also associated with cats. Hathor was the goddess of love, joy and motherhood; however she also had a darker aspect as Sekhmet, the "eye of Ra." There is a story of Sekhmet that resembles a story of the Hindu goddess Kali. Ra sends Sekhmet to punish rebellious mortals, and she goes on a such a wild, bloody rampage that she has to be stopped through drunkenness. She is given red beer to drink as a substitute for blood. In the Hindu myth, Kali goes on a destructive rampage, destroying the world, and is stopped when her husband Shiva lays down in front of her, bringing her back to her senses. The method is different, but the idea of a destructive feminine that has to be checked is the same. It is interesting that many female deities are protectors of the sun, and have warlike aspects as well as healing gifts. The archetypal picture presented is one of the Feminine as protector of life, healer of disease, lamenter of the dead, and also destroyer of life. We will see similar characteristics of female deities in ancient Greece, particularly the dual aspect of creation and destruction, as well as nurturing and warrior aspects.

Analysis and Conclusion

In ancient Egypt we see complex ideas about the soul, immortality, and their relationship to the earth and the feminine. The souls of the dead are like birds (i.e., with wings), an idea also articulated in Babylonian myth, but they also require a body after death to survive. We see five different terms representing different aspects of the "soul." There are also complex notions of life after death that change as Egyptian society changes over time. Immortality is initially the domain of the pharaoh, who was viewed as a god, but later became available to everyone. There are two conceptions of an afterlife: one is somewhere between the earth and sky, and is represented in the mythology of Ra's nightly death and rebirth, as his barque travels across the heavens. The resurrected Osiris is also part of this afterlife, where he is king and judge; his son Horus represents his worldly aspect. The second conception is of the "upside down" world, where the souls of the dead walk upside down, drink urine, and eat feces; it is presumed that this is the fate of those who do not achieve immortality. Immortality does require an initiation—there are tests the soul must pass to go through the twelve gates, and these at least superficially require the virtue of the soul. The soul recites a litany of "sins" that he has not committed, and it seems more about memorizing the proper magical formulae than it is about actually living a virtuous life. Later conceptions of the afterlife, particularly in the *Papyrus of Ani*, show the dead person's heart weighed against a feather to determine their innocence or guilt. The Egyptians are very much interested in the idea of divine justice, but their central virtue is Ma'at or Truth. The reciting of formulae in the underworld is remarkably similar to the later Greek mystery cults, whose adherents have been found with gold tablets around their necks, listing special instructions and magical words to allow them control of their destiny in the afterlife. The result is a kind of "conquering" of death, whether this was considered a physical conquering (as the Egyptians did, as they did not separate the corpse from their idea of a "soul") or a psychological one. This initiation of the soul resembles the trial and judgment of Horus and Seth, where the former has to prove himself against false claims of the latter, and Seth is eventually found guilty and bound. Egyptian gods were not immortal; they achieved immortality in the same way that mortals did. There is an obvious class element, as the royal family were eligible for immortality, while the common folk were not. This gradually changed over time, and the Osiris myth was of central importance to Egyptian life and death. When Akhenaten tried to get rid of the Osiris cult in favor of the solar cult of Aten, he failed. Whatever it may have meant politically, it shows that you cannot simply abolish old beliefs by claiming them invalid, especially when the new beliefs are so different from the old ones. We can compare this to the spread of Christianity, which fared better in places where it assimilated the old beliefs rather than forcibly replacing them. You cannot take away the narrative of a culture by force and expect the new one to flourish. There are many arguments against "universalism" when interpreting mythical and religious symbols and stories; however, the successful history of symbolic assimilation suggests that a repurposing of mythical stories and symbols provides some continuity of meaning over long periods of time. We will look at Greek and Egyptian syncretism more closely in a later chapter to demonstrate this point, but the similarities between the Osiris-Seth-Horus myth of succession and the battle of Zeus against the Titans and later against Typhoeus/Typhon allowed these stories to be conflated during Hellenistic rule of Egypt. Diodorus makes Isis a student or daughter of Hermes (Jung, "Mysterium" 20). The older neighboring beliefs become assimilated into the new.

Assmann cites Isis and Nephthys as representing the Feminine in Egyptian myth; Horus is the Masculine principle, Osiris is the deceased, and Seth represents death itself. (67) As we have seen, Isis becomes the embodiment of the Mother archetype, which is both creative and destructive; we will look at other similar mythological figures in the next chapter. The god Geb is almost a Janus-figure—he is two sided, with one side being earthly life, and the other a shadowy reversal. This demonstrates the liminal nature of the earth, and the boundary between life and death, order and chaos. Psychologically this would represent the conscious mind's need to control or at least to understand the visions from the deep unconscious. The edges of the earth were the realms of chaos, and the darkness that lay outside the domain of the sun. The sun god is a central figure—even more central in the Amarna period—and his pantheon consists of these goddesses who act as protectors and saviors. But, as Relke notes, sky goddesses also have destructive aspects. Not only have we seen this with Isis, but it will also be true of the Babylonian Ishtar and the Greek goddesses Athena and Artemis. (Relke 2) If the sun is the "bright light" that gives clarity and form, then goddesses like Isis imply what is hidden and uncertain, and her intervention is required to provide safe passage, much like the goddess Hekate of Greek myth, who lights the way through the underworld with her torches. It is worth observing that the word *occult* means "hidden," and the later unfavorable associations of women with witchcraft come at least partially from this "hidden" nature of the chthonic Feminine.

What this means for our study is not only a complex view of the soul and immortality, but a full and complex view of the feminine in religion. The divine feminine does not lose its connection to the underworld, and the aspects are not considered contradictory. We do not see a divine split between good and evil—Seth/Typhon is released by Isis, not destroyed. The healing goddess can also be a poisoner, and can show the cunning and skill later associated with witches or sorceresses. But there is no concept of eternal punishment; the worst thing that could happen to a soul is annihilation, a "second death". This often occurred because of magical mistakes, not because the person was evil. As we turn to the archaic Greeks, we will see some familiar themes, particularly that of liminality. The death journey was a kind of initiation for the Egyptians, and we will find the same to be true in Hellenistic and Classical Greek thinking, among the mystery cults. The safe passage from one state to another, whether it be the dead soul, a girl or boy on the verge of life changes, or a mystery cult initiate, is the common thread binding underworld beliefs.

Works Cited: Chapter 1

Budge, E. A. Wallis. *The Book of the Opening of the Mouth: The Egyptian Texts with English Translations*. Benjamin Blom, 1972.

Budge, E. A. Wallis. *The Gods of the Egyptians, or Studies in Egyptian Mythology*. Vol. 1, Dover Publications, 1969.

Budge, E. A. Wallis. *The Egyptian Heaven and Hell: The Contents of the Books of the Other World*. Open Court, 1905.

Budge, E. A. Wallis. *Osiris: The Egyptian Religion of Resurrection*. University Books, 1961.

Hornung, Erik. *Conceptions of God in Ancient Egypt: The One and the Many*. Translated by John Baines, Cornell University Press, 1982.

Jung, Carl G. "Mysterium Coniunctionis: An Inquiry into the Separation and Synthesis of Psychic Opposites in Alchemy". *Collected Works*. Translated by R.F.C. Hull, 2nd ed., Vol. 14. Princeton University Press, 1989.

Relke, Joan. The Archetypal Female in Mythology and Religion: the Anima and the Mother of the Earth and Sky. *EJOP: Europe's Journal of Psychology*. Vol. 3, no. 2, 2007. ejop.psychopen.eu/index.php/ejop/article/view/401/html.

Remler, Pat. "Creation Myths, Ancient Egyptian." *Egyptian Mythology A to Z*, Facts on File, 2000, online.infobase.com/HRC/Search/Details/238458.

Remler, Pat. "Myth of Isis and Osiris." *Egyptian Mythology A to Z*, Facts on File, 2000, online.infobase.com/HRC/Search/Details/238784.

Spence, Lewis. *Myths and Legends of Ancient Egypt*. London: George G. Harrap & Company, 1949.

Zandee, Jan. *Death as an Enemy According to Ancient Egyptian Conceptions*. Brill, 1960.

CHAPTER 2: HOMER AND HESIOD: RELATIONSHIP TO THE "OTHER"

What we know about Greek death and afterlife beliefs comes from sources of much later date than those of ancient Egypt. What we know of Archaic Greek belief has some similarities to Egyptian belief, and there are some significant differences between representations of the soul and death in the Archaic period as compared to Greece's Classical and Hellenistic eras. The Greek "Archaic" period is named differently in different disciplines. In terms of language and civilization we see the Greek "Dark Ages" preceding what is formally thought of as the Archaic period in Classical scholarship. The early Dark Ages are preceded by the flourishing Minoan civilization, which is typically dated from about 2000 B.C.E. to 1450 B.C.E. Archaeology then shows a vibrant Mycenaean civilization that lasted until about 1200 B.C.E., when the civilization was suddenly wiped out by an unknown catastrophe (Starr 58-59). Hesiod speaks about ages of Bronze and Iron (Evelyn-White 13-17) and so do archaeologists. The Bronze Age runs from about 3200 B.C.E. to 1200 B.C.E. in the Near East, and ends around 600 B.C.E. in Greece and other known parts of Europe. These periods are primarily associated with the kinds of metals used to make tools and weaponry, but styles of pottery and agricultural developments also play a role in determining these periods of time (Starr 24). The Neolithic period (5th millennium to 3rd millennium B.C.E.) is also important to our early discussion, as the shift from hunting and gathering to agricultural societies and cities had a significant impact.

The earliest civilizations connected with later Greek civilization were the Minoan and Mycenaean civilizations. Minoan civilization thrived on the island of Crete, where Arthur Evans discovered the glorious remains of Knossos, including a palace with brightly painted walls and stunning architecture. Both on Crete and in Pylos across the Peloponnesus we see the earliest evidence of writing in the scripts Linear A and Linear B; the former has not been translated, and the latter was used primarily for record keeping. Linear A is associated with the ancient Minoan language, and Linear B is associated with the Mycenaean language. The earliest Linear B tablets were found at Knossos, dated to about 1450 B.C.E., and later ones were found in Mycenae at Pylos, dating from about 1200 B.C.E. (Violatti). Most of what is written in Linear B takes the form of lists, but we see early examples of names of Greek gods: Zeus is represented as DI-U-JA, Hera as E-RA, Poseidon as POS-E-DO-O, and Dionysus as DI-WO-NI-SO-JO, to name a few (Ventris and Chadwick 463).

So who were these Minoans and Mycenaeans? No doubt they were native people who had been there since the Bronze Age, but the Cretan shore was likely settled by seafarers from Asia Minor, and in fact the coastal areas are the most populated during the Minoan period. The people of the Aegean Sea area were not from one cultural group (Edwards 804), and archaeological data is too sparse to determine the origins of these groups. For our purposes, what matters is that the area was not dominated by a native population and offers at least part of an explanation for Greek deities and religious beliefs, which seem to combine local cult beliefs with foreign deities and practices. From at least 2000 B.C.E. there was evidence in the Near Eastern region of Indo-European language structures that replaced existing languages in some cases. For example, the Sumerian language was replaced by a Semitic one, though Sumerian culture and belief survived (Edwards 824).

Language is important to the study of ideas about masculine and feminine, as both Greek and later Latin language structures contained nouns labeled as masculine, feminine, or neuter. The Greek alphabet is a modification of the Phoenician alphabet, and today Greek is identified as an Indo-European language. The ancient Greek language has some notable features. In English we favor active verbs in our writing; the Greeks made extensive use of the passive and middle (i.e., reflexive) voices. We typically associate the active principle with the masculine and the passive principle with the feminine, and at least in the case of language, our culture prefers the "masculine" mode of direct action in our expression. Corbeill's study of gender in language notes that the Greeks were likely to make ample use of neuter nouns, but the Romans moved away from the neuter to a more definite masculine or feminine word structure (24-25). Here, we merely note this fact, although a later chapter will discuss Roman grammar more thoroughly.

We gather that these early societies survived by farming and perhaps by fishing along the coasts. Some areas were wealthy and some poor, and it seems clear that people lived in houses in towns, some more crowded than others. But the beliefs of these societies are largely unknown. When it comes to afterlife beliefs, we might make guesses about them based on burials, but no literature exists to tell us the mythology or religion of these ancient peoples. All we have are the lists of the Minoans, and they suggest the existence of temples and offerings made to deities.

Nonetheless, it appears that both Bronze Age Minoan and Mycenaean civilizations were quite rich, and they at least had a rich oral tradition if their written materials were scarce. Homer is the first extant writer to touch on this period, with the *Iliad* and the *Odyssey* produced around the 8th century B.C.E. Both are believed to be much older, as the Trojan War depicted in the *Iliad* likely occurred around 1250 B.C.E. We also have Hesiod's *Theogony* and *Works and Days*, as well as the Homeric Hymns and a number of works controversially attributed to Homer, but generally agreed to be from the same time period, including the *Cypria* and the *Aethiopia*.

Notably, these poetical writings may tell us things about Archaic Greek belief and history, or they may not. The writings of the poets do not necessarily reflect the attitude of the general populace, as both Ian Morris (296-320) and Jon D. Mikalson (178) have pointed out. But we can still get a sense of the zeitgeist of the period. We can reasonably assume widespread beliefs and values from these writings; as Erwin Rodhe writes, "He [Homer] does not offer his pictures of God, the world, and fate as anything peculiar to himself; and it is natural, therefore, to suppose that his public recognized them as substantially the same as their own" (26). Still, Rodhe tends to take certain views of Homer, such as the notion of the Elysian Fields, as the result of poetic imagination (62). Plato excludes poets, citing Homer in particular, from his ideal Republic because of their tendency to tell "falsehoods" (*Republic*, 462-465).

If we cannot trust the views of Hesiod and Homer on this early period, who can we trust? The main primary non-poetic sources are the historians Herodotus and Thucydides, who did not write until the fifth century. Vincent D'Arba Desborough notes the unreliability of their accounts, because they try to connect their contemporary kings to the age of heroes as a means of establishing credibility (322). What we can meaningfully glean from these accounts is that various groups moved through different parts of Greece during the "dark ages"—that period between the end of Mycenaean civilization and the beginning of the Archaic period of Homer and Hesiod.

Desborough sums up the assumed movement of groups at this time:

> The Dorians, from their Peloponnesian strongholds, chiefly Laconia and the Argolid, spread across the southern Aegean to Melos (its set-

tlement placed by Thucydides as still within the late twelfth century) and Thera, to certain parts of Crete, to the Dodecanese, and eventually to the Asiatic mainland opposite. The northern island bridge was the route taken by the Aeolians, both from Thessaly and Boeotia, and they settled mainly in north-west Asia Minor, though they claimed the important island of Lesbos. The central Aegean and especially the adjacent coasts of Asia Minor were occupied by Ionians. Herodotus is our fullest witness for these last two, and it will be seen that, according to him, the Ionian move, though originating from Athens and consisting largely of Ionians, included many others, from Achaea and Arcadia, from north-west Greece (the Molossi), from Boeotia, Phocis, and Euoboea, and even Dorians from Epidaurus in the Argolid. (323)

Herodotus does discuss this Greek pre-history, but only in vague mythical terms. He relates the account of the Persians, who hated the Greeks for invading Asia Minor. He sees early Greek history as αρπαγας—grabbing, theft, or robbery. This refers to the abduction of Europa, allegedly carried away by Zeus disguised as a bull, which he attributes to Cretans instead. He also refers to the abductions of Io and Helen, and even treats the story of Medea in the *Argonautica* as another example of an abduction without reparation by the Greeks. But he attributes these accounts to "Persians and Phoenicians," and "will not say that this or that story is true" (8-9).

Thucydides speaks more generally about Greek pre-history, suggesting that the frequent migrations of tribes had to do with the quality of the land (3-5). There were no "Hellenes" before the Trojan War; he cites the people of Achilles of Phthiotis as the first Hellenes, though Homer refers to them in the *Iliad* as "Danaans and Argives and Achaeans" (6-7). There was a great deal of mistrust between the tribes, and they never traveled without their weapons. Piracy was also common and respectable in his account, with Minos of Crete having the first fleet for such expeditions.

We can observe from this account that the post-Mycenaean period was not dominated by one particular tribe. Rodhe cites the Ionians as having the most influence on Greek writing and thought:

> In this narrow sense it can be truly said that Homer's poems represent the popular belief of their time; not, indeed, the belief of all Greece, but only of the Ionian cities of the coasts and islands of Asia Minor in which the poet and his songs were at home. In a similarly restricted sense may the pictures of outward life and manners that we find in the *Iliad* and the *Odyssey* be taken as a reflection of the contemporary life of the Greeks with particular reference to that of the Ionians. This life must have differed in many respects from that of the 'Mycenaean civilization', and there can be little doubt that the reasons for this difference

are to be sought in the long-contained disturbances which marked the centuries that divide Homer from the age of Mycenae, more especially in the Greek migrations, both in what they destroyed and what they created. (26-27)

Rodhe's point is well taken; however, if we can believe the ancient writers, there were continual migrations among the Greek tribes, and it is hard to say if Homer's ideas are therefore purely "Ionian." Thucydides does suggest that the Attic region of Greece, due to the thinness of its soil, had fewer quarrels over land and tended to be inhabited by the same people (4-5). Even so, many tribes moved through these lands, and the Ionians themselves traveled to other places, which probably brought new ideas to the region. We know this for sure about the Orientalizing period, which we will discuss later on in this chapter.

What of our other Archaic bard, Hesiod? In *Works and Days*, he says his father came from the city of Kyme (43). Translator Stanley Lombardo tells us that Kyme is part of Aeolia, a northwest Greek settlement that included the Isle of Lesbos, but that Kyme itself was farther to the South, and its inhabitants tended to speak Ionian (2). Hesiod's case serves to prove the earlier point; here is an Aeolian living among Ionians. There is a notable difference between the styles of Hesiod and Homer. The Homeric hymns take a very positive view of the gods and their exploits, while Hesiod's tone is world-weary and tinged with bitterness. For instance, the *Homeric Hymn to the Muses and Apollo* says "Happy is he whom the Muses love; sweet flows speech from his lips." (Evelyn-White 450-451). By contrast, Hesiod's Muses in the *Theogony* tell us, "Shepherds of the wilderness, wretched things of shame, mere bellies, we know how to speak many false things as though they were true; but we know, when we will, to utter true things" (Evelyn-White 81).

Our picture of the early Aegean area is thus complicated by matters of local identity. Even after the city-state replaced tribal movements, many Greek regions were still on the outside. For example, Thrace is considered part of Northern Greece, but it was part of Macedon at the time and was treated as "foreign" by the early Archaic writers. Dionysus, one of the oldest deities worshipped in this area, was considered to be from Thrace, and the mythical stories about him always associate him with "foreignness."

The concept of the "foreign" is interesting, because here is one place where geography and psychology intersect. In human psychology the "other" is that which is unfamiliar and therefore suspect. Religion was xenophobic when it came to neighboring tribes; strangers in their midst represented a threat. If we can believe Thucydides, this was certainly true of the Greek tribes. And yet, the ancient Greeks clearly held ξενία [xenia, guest-friendship or hospitality] in the highest esteem; even in wartime hospitality was considered a high virtue.

ξενία went hand-in-hand with δικε [*dike*, justice] as the core values of Archaic Greece. In the *Iliad*, there is a scene in which Glaucus and Diomedes meet on the battlefield. Diomedes recalls that his grandfather hosted Glaucus' grandfather, so in a gesture of hospitality they exchange gifts and agree not to fight (*Iliad* 199-203). One of the main plots of the *Odyssey* deals with the gross breach of hospitality by the suitors for Odysseus' wife Penelope; they remain in her house, eating and drinking, for years. But because Penelope is a woman of high virtue, she observes the rules of *xenia* even in these circumstances. A final example comes from the Euripides play *Hecabe*; Hecabe's son Polydorus was sent to King Polymestor in Thrace for safekeeping during the Trojan War. Polymestor kills the boy and takes his wealth, another grievous breach of hospitality. Hecabe and her attendants blind Polymestor as punishment for his transgression, and the Greek warriors do not support his protests (Euripides 75-77).

Thomas R. Martin writes about the identification of Zeus with justice:

In his poem Works and Days, Hesiod identified Zeus as the fount of justice in all human affairs, a marked contrast to the portrayal of Zeus in Homeric poetry as primarily concerned only with the fate of his favorite warriors in battle. Hesiod presents justice as a divine quality that will assert itself to punish evildoers: 'Zeus ordained this law for men, that fishes and wild beasts and birds should eat each other, for they have no justice; but to human beings he has given justice, which is far the best'(48).

Zeus is the patron of justice and hospitality, and his actions, particularly in the *Iliad* and the *Odyssey*, can be understood in light of these values. He demands that all of Penelope's suitors die because of their violation of hospitality (*Odyssey* 413-414). When Hektor is doomed to die in the *Iliad*, Zeus is moved to sympathy, but still upholds the ruling of Fate (546). Burkert notes that Zeus could have overstepped the bounds of his position, but "the other gods do not applaud this, and therefore he does not do so, just as the good and wise ruler does not use his real power to encroach on the limits set by custom" (Burkert, *Greek* 130). The ruler is the king, and Zeus is king of the gods. Beneviste writes on *rex*, the Latin word for king:

In order to understand the formation of *rex* and the verb *regere* we must start with this notion ... *Regere fines* means literally "trace out the limbs by straight lines." This is the operation carried out by the high priest before a temple or town is built and it consists in the delimitation on a given terrain of a sacred plot of ground ... The tracing of these limits is carried out by the person invested with the highest powers, *rex*. (qtd. in Guénoun 63)

The word "ruler" also implies this when we refer to the object used to measure things. The king sets the boundaries, the limitations; therefore Zeus, as king of the gods, must enforce the boundaries set. These boundaries are very important, whether dealing with invading tribes or the underworld itself. He represents a protection against the Other. As noted earlier, the ancient Egyptians' value system also centered around justice, with the vindication of Horus against Seth eventually mirroring the vindication of the soul of the dead individual, who recites his litany of just behavior when he comes before Osiris for judgement.

Dike and *xenia* also influenced Greek thinking about the afterlife. Δικε, in particular, affects Socrates' philosophical views of life after death, assuming that if there is justice in this world, it must also be in the next one (Plato, *Republic* 484-485). ξενια is bound up with ideas of the "Other"; as Greek culture became dominant in the Aegean region, we also see an increased fear of the Other which is also reflected in later afterlife beliefs. Rohde (26-27) and Morris (307) both argue that we cannot read Greek epics and simply assume they represent the attitudes of the average Greek tribal member or citizen on matters of life after death. Yet one belief clearly operates even through the Greek Hellenistic period: mortals and gods are separate, and the upper and lower worlds do not interact except in rare cases. We do hear of mortals being swept away without being affected by death; Amphiaraus is swallowed up at the end of the Theban war before dying (Rohde 89-93), Ganymede is taken away by Zeus to be the cup-bearer of the gods on Olympus (Rohde 58), Menelaus is "transported" to the Elysian Fields (59). The latter case may have been post-*Odyssey*, as it does not make sense for a hero like Achilles to end up in the gloom of Hades (*Odyssey* 265) while Menelaus enjoys the Isles of the Blessed (Rohde 58). This curious escape from death, as well as the presence of chthonic versions of Olympian deities (e.g., Zeus Chthonios, Hermes Chthonios) suggest a carry-over from ancient cults of the dead. Rohde supports this idea with the fact that certain sites are said to be the "graves" of deities. For example, on Mount Ida, the mythical birthplace of Zeus, there is also said to be the grave of Zeus. These underground deities suggest local worship in caves or similar dwellings, which may also have been sites of oracles. The "graves" of older deities may also represent the triumph of newer ones (96-97). Whatever the origin, there is no contradiction with Homer's idea that men and gods are separate.

It's not surprising that Greek religion doesn't resemble our modern conceptions of religion in many ways. Roger Beck has referred to the "package deal" approach to religion that "was never appropriate to ancient paganisms" (2); it is not a matter of "faith" or a "belief system". There are no sacred scriptures, no churches or temples where worshippers met regularly, and no set dogmas. There were temples of various gods and sacrificial rituals, and these occurred throughout the calendar year. No two Greek cities, even at the beginning of the *polis*, had the same calendar (Burkert, *Greek* 225-227). These rituals initially were family or tribal events that became part of a religious life meant to insure prosperity in the city. It is tempting to think of these as part of an agricultural cycle of rituals, but Burkert does not think there is sufficient evidence to make this claim:

> It is remarkable how little the calendar takes account of the natural rhythm of the agricultural year: there is no month of sowing or harvest and no grape-gathering month; the names are taken from the artificial festivals of the polis. This is also true of the other Greek calendars (*Greek* 226).

On the subject of *xenia*, the rules of hospitality in a tribal society relate to concerns about the "Other" or the "foreign." It is a form of appeasement; if one approaches in friendship bearing gifts, the other might not be a threat. The reverse would also be true; a member of the tribe would hope for hospitable treatment by foreigners. Even when conflict ensued, there were behavioral boundaries, and mythology tells of serious consequences for those who breached those boundaries, as we saw in the *Hecabe* example.

The "Other" is also the central concern when dealing with the dead. Sarah Iles Johnston has a chapter in her book on ancient ideas about the dead entitled "To Honor and Avert" (Johnston 36-81). All evidence points to an Archaic belief that whatever remained of the dead was weak and could not contact the living except through extreme intervention. Odysseus' visit to Hades to speak with the ghost of Tiresias the prophet is a good example of this. The underworld portrayed in Book 11 of the *Odyssey* is a sad and gloomy place; the most frightening thing about it is seeing great queens, kings, and heroes wandering around as ineffective shadows. The dead can speak to the living, but only by drinking blood, the symbol of life. The Greek word for soul, *psyche*, seems to refer to life at the moment of death, or, as John Casey writes, "the breath of life:"

> When a person dies, the psyche is the breath that has left the body. From the moment someone dies, the psyche becomes an *eidolon*, a phantom image 'like the image in a mirror which can be seen, but not grasped'. The psyche in its apparition as eidolon had special relation to dreams—the dead, through these images, come to the living in dreams. (69)

Casey also notes: "Throughout the *Iliad* we have warriors who are reduced to nothing as their soul flees to Hades. It is as though human greatness must include the sense of nothingness that awaits us, and that the hero has a clear sense of this nothingness" (71).

In the *Odyssey*, Odysseus encounters his mother, and reaches out to embrace her three times, but she "fluttered through my fingers, sifting away like a shadow, dissolving like a dream" (256). He asks if Persephone sends him this torment as a hallucination; his mother responds:

> My son, my son, the unluckiest man alive!
> This is no deception sent by Queen Persephone
> This is just the way of mortals when we die.
> Sinews no longer bind the flesh and bones together—
> The fire in all its fury burns the body down to ashes
> Once life slips from the white bones, and the spirit,
> Rustling, flutters away ... flown like a dream." (256)

The Greeks are not alone in this belief; many of their neighbors in early times shared the same idea. In the previous chapter we saw that ancient Egypt had at least 5 different conceptions of the "soul," in what seems an attempt to portray the complexity of human cognition and consciousness. The oldest source we have on ancient afterlife beliefs besides the Egyptian Pyramid Texts is from the Babylonians, the *Epic of Gilgamesh*, estimated to have been written about 1750 B.C.E. After Gilgamesh, we don't see writings until the 10th and 9th centuries B.C.E., with early Greek and Biblical literature.

In Babylonian beliefs, Casey explains that "Those who go there—all the dead—immediately become terrifying and malevolent ghosts, unless they are appeased by constant offerings at their tombs" (45). In the Gilgamesh epic, Gilgamesh crosses the waters of death, and meets a female tavern-keeper who denies the possibility of immortality, telling Gilgamesh to cherish his life:

> O, Gilgamesh, where are you wandering?
> The life you seek you will never find:
> when the gods created mankind
> death they dispensed to mankind
> life they kept for themselves.
> But you, Gilgamesh, let your belly be full,
> enjoy yourself always by day and by night! (50)

Not all shades had to be malevolent in all views, but certainly among Babylonians, Greeks, and early Hebrews, the assumption was that the afterlife was miserable, and that the dead might be unhappy about being dead. Many of the cults of the dead revolved around continual offerings to the dead ancestors to keep them satisfied and away from the realm of the living. The Homeric view of the dead was less fearful of living and dead interaction, but this would change during the course of classical Greek history.

In Hebrew belief we compare the idea of *nefesh met*. The *nefesh* is the life energy of the person. The living person is referred to as *nefesh hayyah*, and is a "vital, psychophysical entity" (Raphael 56). The dead person is the *nefesh met*, the individual in the world of the dead. Raphael explains: "After the energy to sustain life dissipated to an extreme, the individual claimed a place in Sheol [the Hebrew underworld] where existence undeniably continued, but in a weakened, faded condition" (57). The exact meaning of Sheol is unknown, though Rivkah Scharf Kluger suggests the term is associated with depth, or with a cavity, giving it a Feminine (i.e., vaginal/uterine) association that is also monstrous. (153) This is supported by its description in Isaiah 5:14 "Therefore She'ol hath enlarged herself, and opened her mouth without measure ..." (qtd. in Scharf Kluger 154). The beings in Sheol were called *rephaim*, which literally means "weak ones" or "powerless ones" (55).

There is another idea about "soul" in ancient Hebrew thought that is usually associated with the Kabbalah, but has its roots in ancient scriptures. This is the notion of the *golem*, "a creature, particularly a human being, made in an artificial way by virtue of a magic act, through the use of holy names." (Encyclopedia Judaica 735) The *golem* is often mentioned as a clay figurine brought to life or given the power of speech by putting letters on its forehead. In some Kabbalistic sources Adam is referred to as golem before Yahweh gives him a soul, in his first 12 hours of existence. Indeed, the Talmudic use of the term refers to something unformed and imperfect. The only mention of the *golem* in the Old Testament is in Psalms 139:16:

> Thy eyes beheld my unformed substance:
> In thy book were written, every one of them,
> The days that were formed for me,
> When as yet there were none of them. ("Psalms" 716)

The translator of this passage, which comes from the NSV, suggests that the term "unformed substance" means "embryo". There is no written evidence suggesting the ancient Israelites viewed the *golem* in the same way as the later Kabbalists, who saw the *golem* as a being created to do the bidding of its master. However, it is possible that there was an ancient view of this kind; the Israelites kept figurines called *teraphim*, often associated with divination, which may be related to the idea of the *golem*. Jan Assmann notes the similarity between the *golem* and the *shabty* or *ushabty* of the ancient Egyptians; these were artificial clay figures created to do labor on behalf of the dead person in the tomb, and were allegedly animated by writing certain magical formulae on them, or reciting certain spells. (110-111) In any event, the Hebrews seemed to share with the Egyptians the idea of a being created through magical spells that could speak and act, and there is some kinship to the consciousness of humans. Perhaps this is why there is no uniform concept of a "soul" in archaic belief; the ancient Egyptians had the *ba* and the *ka* among other nuances, the ancient Greeks had the *psyche* and *eidolon*. There is a sense that part of the person survives in different forms, and that those forms could be manipulated by human intervention (i.e., a priest or magician).

The similarities between the Hebrew, Babylonian, and Greek beliefs provide food for thought, especially for scholars who believe these groups did not influence each other in this early period. All these beliefs suggest the afterlife is nothing but the shadow of the lived life, and the Near East seems unanimous on this point, with the exception of the Egyptians.

Rohde's view is that the beliefs represented by Homer in the *Odyssey* pointed to a cult of the dead or ancestor worship that gradually weakened in influence, and hence the importance of the dead waned as well. He refers to the alternate practices of cremation and burial, and relates them to possible Neolithic ancestor worship; later, for the migrant Greek, death outside the homeland became the norm, and so practices of dealing with the dead changed accordingly.

> It may well be that the origin of this new form of funeral rite lay, as has been suggested, in the wish to dismiss the soul of the dead man as quickly and completely as possible from the realm of the living; but it is beyond doubt that the result of this practice was to cut at the root of the belief in the near presence of the departed ... (28)

This may be part of the story about Greek afterlife beliefs; yet it is curious that other major groups of the Levant and Asia Minor held similar convictions. Most scholarship is doubtful about a connection between the East and the Greeks, but later evidence suggests otherwise. Burkert states that the "borrowing from the Semitic" of Greek script is "beyond all doubt" (*Orientalizing* 25). The Greek letters come from Semitic words; *alpha* and *beta* are the words for bull and house in the Semitic language, but have no such meaning in Greek (28). The transmission of language suggests contact with these cultures. Greek craftsmanship also suggests contact with the Near East; Burkert cites the appearance of lions in craftwork, as well as a female figure motif known as "The Mistress of the Animals," Eastern robes on Greek goddess sculptures, and Greek gods portrayed hoisting weapons in their right hand as examples of Eastern influence (19-20). If writing and artwork from the East could influence Greeks, why not their myths and belief systems as well?

It is difficult to say if the archaic Greeks believed in another Eastern belief, the idea of restless spirits or angry dead. Evidence for this is scarce at best in the period, though we can't be certain that later works aren't referring to earlier beliefs. We shall see in later chapters that the dead were perceived as more dangerous as time went, so, in the late Archaic period we start to see evidence of the *goes*, the magician who dealt with raising the dead or calming them down. Most scholars believe that what is known as goetic practice in Greek was around long before the Archaic period, but there is no evidence of it in the area we know as Greece at this time, with the exception of Odysseus' journey to the edge of the underworld. The *Odyssey* indicates that Heracles made that journey long before Odysseus (269-270), so the lack of written or archaeological evidence doesn't mean the idea didn't exist. But Sarah Iles Johnston points out that Odysseus and Heracles are heroes; they are closer to the divine, and do not belong to the class of average men (Johnston 12).

In the case of Heracles, he becomes immortal, but also ends up in Hades:

> And next I caught a glimpse of powerful Heracles—
> His ghost, I mean: the man himself delights
> In the grand feasts of the deathless gods on high,
> Wed to Hebe, famed for her lithe, alluring ankles,
> The daughter of mighty Zeus and Hera shod in gold.
> (Homer *Odyssey* 269)

Fagles translates the word εἴδωλον [eidolon] as "ghost," as opposed to ψυχὴ [psykhe] in Odysseus' conversation with his mother, translated there as "spirit," though "phantom" and "soul" respectively would be better, since "spirit" in particular has a different connotation. This passage suggests that the true "spirit" of Heracles is now immortal and among the gods, but that a phantom shade, associated with the Greek word *eidolon*, still remained in Hades. This suggests that the divine "spirit" of the person was separate from a "ghost" and that one had the potential to be immortal, while the other did not. However, this did not seem to be a common belief about heroes in the afterlife. Heracles is a unique example, closer to a god than a human. Common mortals were not united with the gods at death. Lars Albinus states:

Nothing in the Nekuia implies on a general level that a person who might act in a certain way was entitled to look forward to a better fate in the afterlife, let alone that the enterprise of Heracles represented a model for imitation. Quite the contrary: the Homeric mythologem of Heracles represented an exceptional fate as regards the afterlife, an exception which proves the rule, since even as an exception it was represented in a way that only underlined the Olympian and Panhellenic dimension of the epics. (81-82)

The example of Heracles and the fates of semi-divine heroes of ancient Greece remind us of early Egyptian beliefs from the Old Kingdom, in which the pharaoh is the only one eligible for something like immortality after death, as he is considered a god.

Just as immortality was reserved for the gods, the miraculous and magical was strictly divine in origin; the average person had nothing to do with such events, as far as we know. Odysseus' going to the edge of the underworld is a heroic act undertaken by an extraordinary individual. Goetia and magic were foreign practices that eventually became common in Greece and later in Rome, as evidenced by curse tablets found in ancient cemeteries. These practices were thought to come from the North and East, most notably from Persia. As Johnston notes, foreign practices don't become part of the mainstream unless there is a good reason (83). There had to be a greater fear of the "Other."

In Jungian psychology, the "Other" is represented by the idea of the Shadow. The Shadow is sometimes seen as an archetype, but it really represents the underdeveloped part of our consciousness. The Jungian psyche is made up of opposites; therefore, whatever we think we are, we are also its opposite. Social convention, tradition, and many other life factors make us repress certain parts of ourselves; there are also parts of our consciousness that we may never experience except perhaps in dreams. Robert Bly uses the excellent metaphor of a big bag we drag around, and start filling from the first time someone tells us to be ashamed of something we are doing (Bly 17). Because we don't like to acknowledge this part of ourselves, it becomes invisible to our conscious life. But just as a mirror shows us what we look like, others show us what the shadow looks like. What we fear or dislike in others tends to be an aspect of our own Shadow.

In a society dominated by masculine associations, the feminine falls into shadow even for women. Our evidence for the archaic period of Greek history suggests that women may have had more status at this period in time, though the separation of roles was still apparent; a woman's destiny was to marry and have children. But the centrality of the οικοσ [*oikos*, household] before the rise of the polis was likely to make the female role more important. Johnston remarks: "Before the rise of the polis, whatever security, wealth, and honor an individual possessed depended not on him alone but on his *oikos*. A strong *oikos* was also the building block of larger, informal confederations of *oikoi*, established by means of marriage and *xenia*" (194). Before the rise of the city-state, the family unit guaranteed survival and expansion; in our modern world of secular individualism, allegiance to the family does not have the same importance it would have had in Archaic Greece. Even without individualism, the family became subordinate to the society.

This is an important consideration for our discussion of the feminine. Carol Gilligan's famous work on the psychology of young girls demonstrated the tendency of men and boys to think logically and legalistically, while women and girls tend to think in terms of relationships and community.[10] Jung's discussion of the Animus does correspond with Gilligan's Freudian perspective; he tends to see the Animus as the woman's weaker part:

> [T]heir Logos is often only a regrettable accident. It gives rise to misunderstandings and annoying interpretations in the family circle and among friends. This is because it consists of *opinions* instead of reflections, and by opinions I mean *a priori* assumptions that lay claim to absolute truth. (Jung, "Syzygy"14-15)

Women are naturally more relationship oriented, and this is their strength from Jung's perspective; men have more difficulty coming into adult relationships with women:

> I use *Eros* and *Logos* merely as conceptual aids to describe the fact that woman's consciousness is characterized more by the connective quality of Eros than by the discrimination and cognition associated with Logos. In men, Eros, the function of relationship, is usually less developed than Logos. (14)

For years, this feminine connective quality was interpreted as immaturity by mainstream psychology. This may not be surprising in a society that

---

[10] Gilligan gave the example of an old psychological test given to 11-year-old boys and girls known as "Heinz's Dilemma". Heinz is a man with a wife dying from a disease. He does not have enough money for medicine. The question posed is whether he should steal the medicine or let his wife die. When a boy was asked this question, he suggested that Heinz steal the medicine, because he could not simply "get" another wife, and a judge would probably understand if he was arrested. By contrast, Amy, a girl the same age, was less decisive. She felt that perhaps the community could raise money to get the medicine. She did not answer the question definitively, and was judged to be "immature". Gilligan concludes that she is thinking about the question in terms of relationships rather than in terms of legalistic decision-making. (Gilligan 25-29)

values individuality; was it different in a society where community was important?

The Feminine in Greek (and Babylonian) Religion and the Afterlife

Our discussion of the feminine refers to female deities, girls and women in the Greek ritual cycle, and liminal deities including Dionysus and Hermes. With regard to ritual, we are specifically looking at the transformation from *kore* [young girl] to *parthenos* [married woman] to *gyne* [woman with child]. In archetypal terms, this deals with the complex relationship between the Anima and the Mother. The liminal is important because it has to do with birth and death, two attributes of the archetypal feminine. The other aspect of the Feminine addressed here relates specifically to the "mother goddess" and the sorceress—Cybele and Ishtar, Circe and Medea. These equally complex figures represent a direct threat to the Masculine. Rather than separate each of these factors, we will look at some of the major relevant deities and discuss their role in life, ritual, and archetypal psychology.

Circe and Medea: I will treat these two in one section, as they both are characterized as witches or sorceresses. Circe and Medea are both treated in Greek literature as goddesses, though they are distinguished by their practice of magic, notably making potions. The concept of "magic" was not well formed in Greek society prior to the 5th century B.C.E. (Stanley Spaeth 42), and it is likely that they were not viewed as "witches" until after that time. In the *Odyssey*, Homer refers to Circe in Book Ten:

> We reached the Aeaean island next, the home of Circe
> the nymph with lovely braids, an awesome power too
> who can speak with human voice,
> the true sister of murderous-minded Aeetes [King of Colchis].
> Both were bred by the Sun who lights our lives;
> their mother was Perse, a child the Ocean bore. (Odyssey 234).

We see, then, that Circe is a nymph or a goddess; certainly she has a divine origin. Her brother is Aeetes, the King of Colchis, which links her to the *Argonautica*; Aeetes holds the golden fleece sought by Jason, and Medea is his daughter, and therefore Circe's niece. Medea is a priestess of the goddess Hekate; as we noted earlier, Hekate's role also changed over time, metamorphosing from beloved Titan to a goddess of ghosts, monsters, and witchcraft. Both women claim lineage from the Sun and one of the Oceanids. Both women also have great powers, and can help or harm those who seek their aid. In the Odyssey, Odysseus' men are first turned into pigs; Odysseus escapes her spell with the help of Hermes. She then tries to seduce him, and succeeds after she swears an oath not to harm him, and she restores his men to their former condition. Hermes warns Odysseus not to let Circe "unman you, strip away your courage." (Odyssey 239) Once Circe becomes an ally, she is able to aid him in the task of getting home by instructing him in necromancy. Odysseus owes his descent to the underworld and his meeting with Tiresias to Circe. Later she advises him further regarding the Sirens, Scylla and Charybdis, and the cattle of Helios. She demonstrates the ability to make potions (*pharmakeutria*) and to contact spirits for the purpose of telling the future (*goete*).

Medea is an equally powerful figure; while Circe is outwitted by a clever Odysseus and Hermes, Medea's powers are tamed by Hera and Athena indirectly, and Aphrodite directly, when she falls in love with Jason:

> Come, let us go find Cyprian Aphrodite
> and tell her that she must approach her son
> and pressure him to sink a shaft into
> Aeetes' daughter, drug-adept Medea,
> so that the girl is struck with lust for Jason.
> I am quite certain that, with her assistance,
> Jason will bring the fleece back home to Greece. (Apollonius 101)

The speaker in this scene is Hera, and she is speaking to Athena. It is notable that Athena and Hera work toward the Greek victory in the Trojan War, and now they contrive to help Jason in his quest to be a Greek king. Medea here is referred to as "drug-adept", which also makes her a *pharmakeutria*. She does Jason's bidding through lust, but in the end he betrays her by becoming engaged to Glauce, a princess of Corinth. However, Medea gets her revenge by giving Glauce the gift of a robe that burns her alive when she puts it on, and also kills Creon, her father, when he tries to pull the robe from her body. She then kills the two sons she bore with Jason, and leaves on the chariot of Helios with the bodies. The account of Jason's betrayal and Medea's revenge is detailed in Euripides' play *Medea*, and also in a later *Medea* written by Seneca in the early Roman Empire period. Seneca's play is more detailed in describing Medea's magic, and she invokes the Furies to assist her in revenge. It is hard to know if audiences had sympathy for Medea, as she was portrayed as a "barbarian" princess from Corinth.

Both Circe and Medea are powerful women, and are allied with the powers of nature. They are nymphs or related to nymphs, which are water divinities. Both of them live in the woods, away from civilization; this was also true of another Hekate priestess, the Sibyl of Cumae in the *Aeneid*. They are daughters of the Sun god, but it is the Titan Helios who is their father. We will discuss the Titans in the next chapter, but it is sufficient for the moment to note that the Titans were associated with the untamed and uncivilized, and the Orphic cosmogony suggests that they are actually evil or debased. This is pure speculation, and perhaps an unconvincing assessment, as the Sun clearly gained prominence in later Greek and Roman religious thinking. But there is a "wildness" to them; they are powerful in their own right, but their own sexual desires become their downfall, or at least serve to tame them to some degree. There is a masculine tempering of the feminine wildness in these narratives. The talents of both women are related to the earth and the chthonic: magic potions made from knowledge of herbs, raising the dead. This is not accidental; as Barbette Stanley Spaeth writes, "Witches are not merely associated with nature, they are identified with it . . . The witch's control of the natural world is an inversion of the 'natural' order of things, whereby men through their association with culture have control of the world." (45) Though Circe and Medea become prototypes for future literary renderings of witches, they are benign compared to later Roman literary witches. (44) While we still see the idea of masculine control over the wildness of the "natural" woman, the portrayals of these two suggest that they are not good or evil by nature—they can help or harm.

A psychoanalytic reading of these stories suggests that Circe and Medea are anima figures; they may present a challenge to men, but they are also integral to male development. Neither Odysseus nor Jason could have completed their journeys or tasks without the help of the anima. In Odysseus' case, the anima sends him on the nekyia, the underworld journey that allows him to confront forces opposite to his own nature. Odysseus is a more complete man in the end because of his encounter. The story of Jason is not as straightforward; the story reads more like a pact with the Devil, in which Medea allows him to achieve his goals, but not without cost. Many innocents are slain along the way, and while Medea is responsible, Jason's own lack of heroic initiative is certainly part of the problem. The *Argonautica* reads as an almost anti-heroic story. As J.F. Carspecken states:

> [He is] chosen leader because his superior declines the honour, subordinate to his comrades, except once, in every trial of strength, skill or courage, a great warrior only with the help of magical charms, jealous of honour but incapable of asserting it, passive in the face of crisis, timid and confused before trouble, tearful at insult, easily despondent, gracefully treacherous in his dealings with the love-sick Medea... (101)

It is hard to ignore the lack of character displayed by Jason in Apollonius of Rhodes' text. His passivity leads to a domination by the feminine, to the point that he is destroyed by it later when he tries to make a "civilized" marriage.

Ishtar: Ishtar was a Mesopotamian goddess of love and fertility, but also of war, combat, and political power. She is related to the Sumerian goddess Inanna, and the Semitic goddess Astarte or Asherah, originally a consort of the Hebrew Yahweh. She is a seductive yet deadly goddess, which makes her a quintessential anima figure. In the Gilgamesh epic, she attempts to seduce Gilgamesh when he returns from his successful exploit against Humbaba. But Gilgamesh does not fall for her charms:

> What lover of thine is there whom thou dost love forever?
> What shepherd of thine is there who can please thee for all time?
> Come, and I will unfold thee the tale of thy lovers.
> For Tammuz, thy youthful husband,
> Thou hast decreed wailing year after year. (qtd. in Scharf Kluger 114)

Tammuz is an ancient vegetation god, who dies from the heat of Ishtar's passion (i.e., the summer heat), and is mourned as part of a Babylonian ritual. Gilgamesh points out all of Ishtar's "stinking deeds and rotten acts" (128). She responds in rage by sending the bull of heaven to destroy him, but Gilgamesh and his friend Enkidu kill the bull and sacrifice it to the sun god, Shamash.

Rivkah Scharf Kluger observes that the "bull of heaven" is actually a negative Feminine manifestation, Ishtar's rage at being insulted for having her "rotten deeds" pointed out. There is a similar motif in Mithraism, in the image of the tauroctony, in which Mithras (the Sun) slays the bull (the Moon) (Beck 197-99). The aggressive force of the bull suggests that unconscious rage has now been made conscious. (Kluger 134-135) She compares this to Odysseus' encounter with Circe, who turns his men into pigs. Gilgamesh's encounter with the anima in the form of Ishtar suggests his own disconnect with the Feminine—he is unable to handle her, so he turns her away. On the other hand,

> The hero Odysseus, in a different position, as was said, accepts Circe's invitation; but he has the divine help of Hermes, who gave him the miraculous herb Moly to foil her drugs, and who instructed him to charge her with his sword when she tried to bewitch him. What would it mean that he has his sword with him? The sword is a symbol of discrimination. So he has a certain awareness of the situation. (119)

Odysseus is said to be the grandson of Hermes, and his name is sometimes translated as "trouble". He is well known for his cunning, and he is as much a master of deceit as he is of combat. This gives him a "liminal" character: he can operate directly or he can move behind the scenes. He is comfortable moving between the Masculine and Feminine, and this gives him an awareness of the Feminine that other heroic figures may lack. In Greek mythology, his rival Ajax of Telemon is a notable example. Ajax rejects the Feminine; he rebuffs Athena when she comes to help him on the battlefield, and in the end he is driven to suicide.[11]

Similarly, with Gilgamesh, his rejection of Ishtar and the destruction of her bull (which is then offered to the sun god—the symbol of rational, conscious intelligence) leads to the death of his close friend Enkidu, and now the hero must struggle with death. This does happen later, when he searches for his ancestor Utnapishtim, the "Noah" who survived the Flood before the Biblical Noah, and who found eternal life. On his night journey, Gilgamesh fights lions with an axe, a sword, and an arrow. (162) Scharf Kluger tells us that the lion is the animal of the underworld, as the underworld goddess Erishkigal has a lion head. Gilgamesh fights the lions with the weapons of discrimination—just as Odysseus did by charging at Circe with his sword.

Ερις [Eris]: She is the goddess of Strife or Chaos, though she should not be confused with χάος [Kaos], the personification of the Void that brought forth the universe. It is notable that Eris is a feminine noun, while Kaos is neuter. We learn about both deities from Hesiod. The *Theogony* mentions Chaos as the Abyss from which Erebus (Gloom) and Night are born. After his invocation of Zeus, Hesiod suggests there are two Erises as he discusses the "two kinds of Strife" in *Works and Days*:

> So, after all, there was not one kind of Strife alone, but all over the earth there are two. As for the one, a man would praise her when he came to understand her; but the other is blameworthy: and they are wholly different in nature. For one fosters evil war and battle, being cruel: her no man lovers; but perforce, through the will of the deathless gods, men pay harsh Strife her honour due. But the other is the elder daughter of dark Night, and the son of Cronos who sits above and dwells in the aether, set her in the roots of the earth: and she is far kinder to men. She stirs up even the shiftless to toil: for a man grows eager to work when he considers his neighbor, a rich man who hastens to plough and plant and put his house in good order; and the neighbour vies with his neighbor as he hurries after wealth. This Strife is wholesome for men. (Evelyn-White 3-5)

---

[11] See: Sophocles. "Ajax." *Sophocles II*, translated by David Grene and Richmond Lattimore, University of Chicago Press, 1957, pp. 2–62.

Hesiod portrays Eris as a necessary evil; if humans were not besieged by strife, they would be lazy and unproductive. If we consider the modern cliché "idle hands are the Devil's workshop," we get an idea of this "good" Eris. Comparing Eris to the Devil and calling her "good" may seem strange, but it makes perfect sense if we consider the Jungian archetype of the Trickster. Tricksters are described by Jung as "pre-conscious" figures and he believes the Trickster may be one of our most archaic archetypes:

> He [i.e., the Trickster] is obviously a 'psychologem', an archetypal psychic structure of extreme antiquity. In his clearest manifestations he is a faithful reflection of an absolutely undifferentiated human consciousness, corresponding to a psyche that has hardly left the animal level. (Jung "Trickster" 260)

Eris is an obvious symbol of this undifferentiated psyche. World mythologies are full of Tricksters, and Eris is only one of them in Greek mythology. Even a female goddess as dignified as Hera can function as a Trickster, as we shall see later on. Tricksters engage in childish behavior and manifest in our everyday lives as upsets to our carefully laid plans. The Biblical tricksters of the Old Testament are angels, and are described by the Hebrew word שָׂטָן, [Satan]. In the Bible, we see Satan in two ways as well; there is the Old Testament way when the Satan is sent to either test or obstruct a human being, and there is the New Testament Satan, who tests Jesus. The most obvious example is the Satan of the Book of Job, who pushes Job to his limits with God's blessing. This has been one of the most difficult books for Western monotheists, but it is not so difficult if we take Hesiod's view of Strife: the gods have ordained it, and it can make us better humans.

Tricksters are also associated with the liminal; they push our personal boundaries and often appear as creatures that have conflicting characteristics. The "wise fool" is one such character. The discomfort experienced from this archetype relates it to the human Shadow. Our everyday lives are affected by psychological "tricksters" when our carefully laid plans go wrong:

> Since the personal shadow, in fact, is nothing more than an odds-and-ends collection of traits that we have failed to fuse into our conscious persona, the tricks played by this prankster are likewise disorganized ... We are beset by one trifling difficulty after another. ... At such times all phone calls connect to busy lines, the car needs gas, the weather is terrible and the umbrella is at the office, and the traffic lights are all red. It is just this variety of bad luck that evidently inspired Murphy's Law, which states that anything that can go wrong will go wrong. There are numerous correlates; for instance, if a slice of bread falls on the floor, it will always land butter-side down. One of the authors likes

to refer to such coincidences as 'perverse synchronicity.' (Combs and Holland 106-107)

Ignoring the Trickster can be dangerous; our other story of Eris from Greek myth concerns the wedding feast of Peleus and Thetis. The oldest version of this story comes from the *Cypria*, a work of eleven books controversially attributed to Homer (Evelyn-White 488-505). All the gods are invited except Eris, and she gets her revenge by tossing a golden apple into the group with the words "to the fairest" inscribed on it. The three Olympian goddesses at the feast—Aphrodite, Athena, and Hera—all want to claim the apple, and they call upon Paris, son of King Priam of Troy, to judge which one of them is the fairest. Each bribes him with different gifts: Athena will make him a great warrior, Hera will make him a great King, Aphrodite will give him Helen, Queen of Sparta, who is the most beautiful woman in the world. Paris judges in Aphrodite's favor and Helen's abduction by Paris brings about the Trojan War. Eris does not need to act directly to create conflict; she only has to plant the seeds in the ego. She tests the other female goddesses, and brings out their worst trait: vanity.

The role of the feminine in the Trojan War is quite interesting. While Helen is the cause of the war, the opening lines of the *Iliad* tell us: "Rage— Goddess, sing the rage of Peleus' son Achilles, murderous, doomed, that cost the Achaeans countless losses, hurling down to the House of Death so many sturdy souls ..." (77). Agamemnon has taken Chryseis, daughter of Chryses, as part of the spoils of war for himself. Her father, who is a priest of Apollo, comes begging Agamemnon for his daughter and brings a ransom. When Agamemnon refuses, Chryses prays to Apollo to avenge him and Apollo attacks the Achaean armies with plague. The argument of Book One is between Agamemnon and Achilles; Achilles tells him to give up Chryseis, and Agamemnon eventually agrees, but takes Achilles' concubine Briseis as a consolation prize. Infuriated by this humiliation, Achilles refuses to fight; we don't see him involved in the war again until his friend Patroclus is killed in battle. We have a war over Helen, but we also have a war over Chryseis and Briseis. Vanity, pride, and anger among both gods and humans all cause bloodshed and the destruction of Troy.

Such emotions and the "irrational" are associated with the Feminine, *Eros* rather than *Logos*. The moon, more often than not a feminine symbol in mythology due to its connection with fertility, is a symbol of the irrational.[12]

---

[12] For a discussion of the moon and the irrational see: Harding, M. Esther. *Woman's Mysteries: Ancient and Modern*. New York: G.P. Putnam, 1971. Print, Chapter 5.

The light of the moon is reflected from the sun, and things appear shadowy in the moonlight, as opposed to the clear view we get from the sunlight. Here in the *Iliad* we see Achaean warriors, the very embodiments of masculinity, behaving in an irrational and childish manner. This brings us back to the Shadow; whatever is underdeveloped in our psyches will cause problems for us. Achilles and Agamemnon do not have a balanced sense of the Feminine; they are warriors and operate consciously in a world of rules, fighting skills, and physical strength. They are not developed emotionally, and therefore their emotions become their downfall. Emotions and even "irrationality" are not "bad"; sometimes our irrational impulses, especially our intuition, clue us in to something that is not apparent logically. But if dealing with emotions is not our strength, it can cause trouble until we get it right. As Esther Harding noted, both men and women in the modern world have difficulty with these aspects of the feminine:

> For if a woman is out of touch with the feminine principle, which dic-
> tates the laws of relatedness, she cannot take the lead in what is after
> all the feminine realm, that of human relationships ... Many women
> suffer seriously in their personal lives on account of this neglect of the
> feminine principle. (16-17)

Hesiod has much more to say about Eris in the *Theogony*; she is listed as the mother of Toil, Forgetfulness, Famine, tearful Sorrows, Fightings, Battles, Murders, Manslaughters, Quarrels, Lying Words, Disputes, Lawlessness, and Ruin. Here he describes her as "abhorred" [στυγερε] (Evelyn-White 96-97). The *Theogony* was written earlier than *Works and Days*, and it is interesting that Hesiod's attitude towards Strife becomes more accepting in the later work. Scholars believe *Works and Days* was written in the midst of an agricultural crisis; Hesiod addresses his brother Perses, who has manipulated the law to take away most of his land. He not only censures his brother and the judges who awarded him the land, but he resigns himself to the difficulties of life. Joseph Campbell said we should participate in the pain of life (65), and Jung would agree:

You open the gates of the soul to let the dark flood of chaos flow into your order and meaning. If you marry the ordered to the chaos you produce the divine child, the supreme meaning beyond meaning and meaninglessness ... I have had to recognize that I must submit to what I fear; yes, even more, that I must even love what horrifies me. We must learn such from that saint who was disgusted by the plague infections; she drank the pus of plague boils and became aware that it smelled like roses. The acts of the saint were not in vain. (Jung, *Red* 139)

῞Ηρā *[Hera]:* Hera is the wife of Zeus, and Queen of the gods of Mount Olympus. She is also Zeus' sister, born of the Titans Kronos and Rhea. "The name of Hera, the queen of the gods, admits a variety of mutually exclusive etymologies; one possibility is to connect it with hora, season, and to interpret it as ripe for marriage" (Burkert, *Greek* 131). She is the patroness of traditional marriage and family; the Greek myths are full of irony about this very civilized role. Zeus tricks her into marrying him by appearing to her as a helpless, bedraggled bird. She feels sorry for the bird and takes it to her breast. When she does so, he changes into his own form and ravishes her. Her mortification at this turn of events leads her to marry Zeus; it would be undignified for her to not marry him after being intimate with him.

More will be said about virginity in our discussion of Persephone; however, the connection between marriage and sexual intimacy is interesting here. A woman who is unmarried and not a virgin is considered undignified; this attitude hasn't changed much in over 2,000 years. We don't know if there is love between Zeus and Hera; we do know that he was attracted to her in the way that men are attracted to women who resemble the unconscious Anima archetype. Once she became his wife, he ran around constantly with other women, both divine and mortal, who attracted his interest. Hera never opposes her husband; instead, she gets her revenge on the women he sleeps with, and their children (*Greek* 134).

We may be puzzled by this marital drama, especially from the King and Queen of the gods. When "god" is defined in modern times, we always equate the term with positive virtues. It is hard to imagine a god who is unfaithful and capricious. But if we recognize the Greek gods as metaphorical of psychological processes, we can see the drama of the Anima and Animus played out here:

> [W]hen animus and anima meet, the animus draws his sword of power and the anima injects her poison of illusion and seduction. The outcome need not always be negative, since the two are equally likely to fall in love (a special instance of love at first sight). (Jung, "Syzygy" 15)

The Anima/Animus drama is a recurring one in anyone's life, and it is hardly uncommon to think of the bored spouse who cheats. The spouse takes on the attributes of the Mother or Father archetype; they no longer have the mysterious allure of the Anima or Animus. The story of Eros and Psyche is probably the best mythical illustration of the mature notion of marriage; we shall look at that story in our discussion of Aphrodite.

We associate the Greek gods with Greek humanism; we assume that the gods are like ordinary mortals. This is true to a certain extent; the behavior of the gods often represents both the rational and irrational aspects of human interaction. However, the gods are archetypes; archetypes do not individuate—human beings do. Zeus and Hera represent the complexity of the marriage relationship and the positive and negative challenges faced by those who take it on.

In the *Iliad*, Hera and Zeus are initially on opposing sides in the Trojan War. Hera favors the Achaeans; Zeus favors the Trojans. Thetis, Achilles' mother, has asked Zeus' help in avenging the humiliation Achilles suffered when Agamemnon took Briseis away. Zeus has agreed to make the Achaeans realize how much they need Achilles, but he vows that Achilles' best friend Patroclus will not live through the battle as a result. When Achilles joins the war, Zeus switches his allegiance to the Achaean side. But Hera does everything in her power in the meantime to help the Achaeans. There is a scene in the *Iliad* that Walter Burkert calls "The Deception of Zeus" (*Orientalizing* 91). Zeus has forbidden any intervention by the gods in the battle, and the Achaeans are losing. Hera, desperate to help them, enlists the aid of a reluctant Hypnos, the god of Sleep. She takes Zeus to Mount Ida, where she seductively entices him to make love, and he falls asleep afterward. She takes advantage of his sleep to send help to the Achaeans. When Zeus awakens, he realizes he has been deceived. (Homer, *Iliad* 243-250). Burkert likens this scene to another one from Akkadian mythology, which he believes may be the source of the story, and views it as an alternate creation myth (*Orientalizing* 88-92).

Significantly, whatever the source of the myth, we only hear of Hera making love to her husband when she is trying to trick him. Clearly they have had relations; this is how they ended up married, and in most myths the pair have four children: Hebe (youthful bloom), Eileithyia (childbirth), Hephaestus (blacksmith of the gods) and Ares (war). The three children seem to mirror the story of their relationship; Zeus loves Hera in her youthful bloom, their marriage becomes the embodiment of civilized marriage, which includes bearing children, but they are also very contentious, hence the symbolism of war. Hephaestus is ugly and lame, but he is valuable for his metalworking skills, suggesting a certain practicality over appearance. What is clear is that marriage is not mythically portrayed as a sexual relationship; once the work of bearing children is done, there are no more relations; Zeus looks elsewhere for his gratification.

The contradictory virginal/mother nature of Hera may have had to do with her social role or may be tied up with her pre-Greek role as a mother goddess (*Greek* 131). In the *Homeric Hymn to Pythian Apollo*, Hera is listed as the mother of the monster Typhaon (Evelyn-White 345-347), while Hesiod lists the Earth Mother Ge as Typhaon's mother (138-139). This is likely an ancient Minoan form of the goddess Hera; we do see her name on the Linear B tablets found at Knossos on Crete and in Mycenae. This relates to the Jungian Kore archetype; the "young girl" is both the virginal child and the mother at the same time:

> Demeter and Kore, mother and daughter, extend the feminine con-
> sciousness both upwards and downwards. They add an 'older and
> younger', 'stronger and weaker' dimension to it and widen out the nar-
> rowly limited conscious mind bound in space and time, giving it inti-
> mations of a greater and more comprehensive personality which has a
> share in the eternal course of things. (Jung, "Kore" 188)

Hera also has aspects of the Trickster; we see her deceiving Zeus in the *Iliad*, but the Trickster role is more pronounced in the *Aeneid*, a much later Roman epic. Her determination to keep Aeneas from fulfilling his destiny by founding a city in Latinum is baffling, until one considers her archetypal role:

> Like Virgil's Juno [i.e., Hera], Satan both sets the plot in motion and
> then tries to delay its inevitable, ordained end. Juno and Satan are
> both associated with confusion, transgression, and boundary breaking
> (Satan is quite a bounder in every sense). They thus oppose the figures
> of Jove [i.e., Zeus] and Jesus, who, as the Son's appearance in Paradise
> Lost book 6 also indicates, are both connected with order, closure, and
> the setting of limits through discrimination and differentiation. (Kil-
> gour 654)

However she is revered, it is clear that Hera does not always sit by pas-
sively and submit to her husband; she ultimately bows to his will in many
cases, but she has a strong will of her own, and he often does not oppose it.
The Feminine has a strong and almost equal place in the mythological marriage bond.

Αφροδίτη *[Aphrodite]*: Aphrodite is the goddess of love and beauty and is
one of the most powerful Olympians. Certainly all the male deities fall victim
to her powers, especially Zeus, who resents the power Aphrodite has over
him. The name Aphrodite means "foam born," and refers to the castration of
Ouranos. In the *Theogony*, Hesiod tells us about the union of Ouranos (Sky)
and Ge (Earth) and their constant production of children. Ouranos becomes
ashamed of Ge's monstrous offspring, and refuses to allow them to come to
the surface. Ge gets tired of this treatment, and asks one of her children to
help her. Kronos (Time) obliges her by taking a sickle and castrating his father, thus separating the earth and the sky. When Ouranos' genitals fall into
the ocean, various monstrous beings are born, but so is Aphrodite; most of us

are familiar with Sandro Botticelli's painting "The Birth of Venus," showing a blonde and naked Aphrodite standing on a conch shell. However, Homer's *Iliad* claims she is the daughter of Zeus and Dione, the latter being a feminine appellation of Zeus (Burkert, *Greek* 154). Whatever her true origins, Aphrodite has the potential to cause the most trouble on Mount Olympus, so Zeus marries her to Hephaestus, the ugliest of the gods. Yet Aphrodite never consummates her relationship with her husband; instead, she has many other lovers including Ares, the god of war. Eros is said to be her son, and again, this Eros is distinct from Hesiod's Eros in the *Theogony*, who represents the drive and desire to create that was present in early creation. Aphrodite's son Eros, like the Hindu god Kama, shoots his arrows of desire to make humans fall in love. Aphrodite has a rather scandalous relationship with Eros; in Apuleius' story of Eros and Psyche, we see her kissing her son in a rather shocking manner (Apuleius 106). In Jungian theory, the manifestation of the Anima archetype is dependent on the manifestation of the Mother archetype; the Anima image comes from the Mother image (Jung, "Kore" 183). The relationship of Eros and Aphrodite suggests this unconscious erotic relationship of Mother-Son that was central to Freud's Oedipus complex. The maturation process requires the movement from Mother to Anima, and in spite of any illusions created by the manifestation of the Anima, it is a necessary step to any kind of adult marriage.

The story of Eros and Psyche is a late one in the literature—Apuleius writes *The Golden Ass* in the second century C.E. I will make an exception and discuss it here as it illustrates Jung's idea of the mature relationship that can lead to individuation. According to Jung: "Whenever we speak of a 'psychological relationship' we presuppose one that is conscious, for there is no such thing as a psychological relationship between two people who are in a state of unconsciousness" (Jung, "Marriage" 189). Psyche is a beautiful young girl whisked away to a palace, where she is supposedly married to a monster. She lives a charmed life but never sees her husband, and is forbidden to look at him. Her sisters come to visit her, reminding her that her husband is supposed to be a monster, and they tell her to kill him before he kills her. This is often interpreted as a jealous act on the part of the sisters, but they really represent the archetype of the wise woman, and they alert Psyche to the unconscious nature of her relationship. She does not know her husband—in this way he is a monster, moving about in the darkness of the unconscious. She brings a knife with her and a lamp when he goes to sleep, and when she leans over to look at him, she realizes he is Eros. But she then spills oil from the lamp and burns him accidentally. Feeling betrayed, Eros leaves her, and her trials of love begin.

Neumann argues that the minute Psyche enters into a conscious relationship, her pain and suffering begins, because this is a condition of growth and transformation:

> The knowing Psyche, who sees Eros in the full light and has broken the taboo of his invisibility, is no longer naïve and infantile in her attitude toward the masculine; she is no longer merely captivating and captivated, but is so completely changed in her new womanhood that she loses and indeed must lose her lover. (79)

She and Eros are eventually reunited after she has numerous encounters with the negative masculine in the form of Aphrodite's tasks. Her marriage to Eros is a real one at the end, because they are two lovers who are fully aware of each other, and who have suffered the conflicts that real relationships bring.

Αθηνα [Athena]: Athena is quite the opposite of Aphrodite; she is a virgin goddess who represents wisdom, skilled craft and strategy in war. Ares represents brute force on the battlefield; Athena is a strategist, and in the *Iliad*, she beats Ares in combat (Homer, *Iliad* 523). She is Zeus' favorite daughter, and she is said to have sprung fully clothed from his forehead. This is often interpreted as a kind of "virgin birth" through the male, but her mother is actually the goddess Metis. Metis was the Titaness of wisdom, and there was a prophecy that any child she bore would be greater than his father. Zeus swallowed her, and Athena is said to be her offspring through Zeus. Hesiod comments on this birth: "But Zeus himself gave birth from his own head to bright-eyed Tritogeneia [i.e. Athena], the awful, the strife-stirring, the host-leader, the unwearying, the queen, who delights in tumults and battles" (Evelyn-White 146-147).

Athena is a prominent figure in Greek mythology; she becomes the patroness of the city that bears her name, Athens, after winning a contest with Poseidon. She is involved with much of the action in the *Iliad* helping the Achaean side, and she is the primary director of all the action in the *Odyssey*, appearing to Telemachos and Odysseus in various guises in order to bring Odysseus home and rid his house of the suitors. Athena is a strategist, which means she has an element of the Trickster herself. She represents the need for cleverness and planning rather than taking a direct approach to a situation. For this reason she loves Odysseus, whose chief talent is his cunning, and acts on his behalf.

Athena is the archetypal feminine in the Greek warrior. Those who embrace the aid of Athena, such as Odysseus and Diomedes, are rewarded.[13] Those who reject her, including Locrian Ajax (the Lesser) and Telamonian

[13] For Odysseus, see Homer, *Odyssey* 296 ; for Diomedes see Homer, *Iliad* 168.

Ajax (the Greater), end up meeting an ignoble death.[14] In Sophocles' play about Telemonian Ajax, a messenger in the play tells us, "...Queen Athena, as she spurred him on to turn his reeking hand upon his foes, He spake a blasphemous outrageous word, 'Queen, stand beside the other Greeks: where I am posted, fear not that our ranks will break'" (64-65). Both men rejected their feminine instincts in favor of brute force, and paid the price of imbalance.

This may seem like an odd concept, but the Jungian Shadow relates to ignored or underdeveloped parts of our psyche. The Trickster often acts as the catalyst for bringing these imbalances to our attention. We shall see later on that this was also a concept in ancient necromantic practices; a frightening trickster figure often acts as the agent that brings the service of the dead from the underworld. These figures will also be important in the mystery cults that developed in the late Archaic period; they are figures of initiation and transformation.

Αρτεμισ [*Artemis*]: Artemis is another ancient and complex goddess, similar to Athena in her virginity, and is the goddess of the hunt, forests, and hills. It is notable that these female figures are the divinities of very masculine activities. She is the child of Zeus and Leto and is the twin sister of the god Apollo. Homer mentions her in the *Iliad* (535-536) where she upbraids her brother for not taking part in the battle. The Artemis of the *Iliad* comes across as almost childish; when Hera strikes her, "the arrows fall scattered on the ground and Artemis runs off in tears to be comforted by her father Zeus, leaving Leto, her mother, to pick up the arrows" (Burkert, *Greek* 150). But the Artemis of myth has a gruesome side; so does her brother. She is paradoxically a patroness of childbirth and of violent death in children. Niobe brags that she is better than Artemis and Apollo's mother Leto because she has six sons and six daughters. The twins avenge this slight to their mother by killing all of Niobe's children, and according to Homer, leaving them unburied. Niobe is then turned to stone and placed on Mount Sipylus (*Iliad* 608).

Artemis is also merciless toward men who see her naked and to her female followers who break their vows of chastity. Actaeon accidentally sees the goddess bathing, and she turns him into a stag. He ends up hunted and killed by his own dogs (Apollodorus 322-325). Similarly, when Callisto is tricked by Zeus and ravished by him, Artemis punishes her by turning her into a bear. She is almost killed by her son, Arcas, but Zeus stops him. Callisto is placed in the sky as the constellation Ursa Major, and in some versions

---

[14] For Locrian Ajax, see Homer, *Odyssey* 140; For Telemonian Ajax, see the Sophocles play: Sophocles. "Ajax".   *Sophocles*. Translated by F. Storr. Vol. 2. Heinemann, 1913.

of the myth, Arcas is changed into a bear and placed next to her in the sky as Ursa Minor (Apollodorus 394-397).

Artemis has a role as a moon goddess, and the temple of Artemis at Ephesus was considered one of the Seven Wonders of the World. The Artemis represented there had many breasts, making her more of a mother figure. It is hard to separate the feminine and masculine aspects of her character, and this may suggest that the natural world reflects a combination of masculine and feminine elements working together, and there is a bit of each in the other. The Chinese Yin-Yang symbol is an older representation of this concept, and it appears to be part of ancient Greek mythical thinking. The contradictory collection of associations may also indicate the ancient nature of Artemis; like Demeter and Hera, she is a form of an older, pre-Greek deity, and her various associations may come together in one figure. However, the fact that the Greeks accepted these contradictions suggests they were accepting of the complex nature of the Feminine, consciously or not.

Ἑκάτη [Hekate]: Hekate is one of the most complicated ancient goddesses, represented very differently in the Archaic period compared to later times. She has been called the Artemis of the underworld, as she is also associated with the moon and runs with her hounds at nighttime. The Homeric Hymn to Hekate shows her as honored and respected by Zeus, who allowed her to keep all of her dignity and fortune when the Titans lost the war with the Olympians. She is the granddaughter of Phoebe (the moon) in this version, and daughter of Perses and Asteria:

> And she conceived and bare Hecate whom Zeus the son of Cronos honoured above all. He gave her splendid gifts, to have a share of the earth and the unfruitful sea. She received honour in starry heaven, and is honoured exceedingly by the deathless gods. For to this day, whenever any one of men on earth offers rich sacrifices and prays for favor according to custom, he calls upon Hecate. Great honour comes easily to him whose prayers the goddess receives favourably, and she bestows wealth upon him; for the power is surely with her (Evelyn-White 108-109).

This is very different from the later conception of Hekate as the goddess of crossroads, death, and witchcraft. She is sometimes viewed as a goddess of the moon, and has a strong connection to Artemis. In the Archaic period, Hekate is mentioned by Homer in the Hymn to Demeter, as the goddess who helps Demeter find her daughter Persephone and later dedicates herself as Persephone's companion in the underworld (Evelyn-White 292-293, 320-321). But the most interesting story comes from another Hesiod source, The Catalogue of Women, and relates to the sacrifice of Iphigenia. During the Trojan

War, the Achaeans had unfavorable winds for sailing to Troy. They sent an emissary to an oracle and were told that Artemis was angry and causing the problem; they would need to sacrifice a virgin girl in order for the winds to be favorable again. Odysseus suggests Agamemnon's daughter Iphigenia; they deceive her mother Clytemnestra by saying she will be married to Achilles. However, in the Hesiod story, "Iphigenia was not killed, but, by the will of Artemis, became Hecate" (Evelyn-White 204-205). Sarah Iles Johnston suggests that Hekate was an older, foreign deity whose role in marriage and childbirth was taken over by Artemis during the rise of Greek civilization (*Restless* 246-247).

This appears to be a case of an older deity becoming subordinate to a newer one. However:

> Unlike the other virgins we have discussed, Hecate neither dies nor is transformed. Instead, in both versions of the story, Hecate is what *emerges* from the virgin's death. She is the vengeful ghost uniquely created for the role, the divine prototype of all vengeful ghosts, as befits the goddess who is expected to control them. (*Restless* 247)

And thus we see how the Hekate of the *Theogony* with her universal powers becomes a queen of ghosts. We can also connect her with the monstrous figures Gello, Mormo, and Lamia, feminine creatures who take children because they were deprived of their own motherhood. The Iphigenia story is strange, but what figure in Greek mythology is more justified as a model of the "angry dead"? She is a virgin girl whose life is cut short when she is about to be married and fits the pattern of the liminal *aorai* [ghosts of those who died young].

Hekate develops into a different kind of figure for the Neoplatonists in the Chaldean Oracles, which sought to marry Greek philosophy with religion. Hekate is the only deity from the Greek pantheon who survives in their system, and she becomes an intermediary figure between gods and mortals, bringing a whole new meaning to the liminal nature of this goddess. She is in fact split into two goddesses, Hekate and Physis, with the former ruling "good" spirits who bring truth and salvation, and the latter dealing with "evil" daemons who deceive humans into following the wrong paths. This "split" Hekate will be discussed at length in Chapter 5.

Ἐρῑνύες *[The Erinyes (Furies)]*: The Erinyes are called "the helpers of justice" by Heraclitus (Johnston, *Restless* 265). They are very old deities; they are named on the Linear B tablets found on Knossos as ERINU, which seems to refer to a single goddess. Their role in avenging wrongs done to blood-kin suggests a role as divine ancestor guardians; we also have Heraclitus' assertion "the sun is the length of a foot, and if it steps one foot out of place, the

Erinyes will force him back" (265). Heraclitus' views are considered contro-versial, and not the norm with regard to Greek thought (266); nonetheless, we recognize that they are responsible for maintaining the celestial order created by the gods, whether it be at the family level or on a broader spec-trum. The most famous story involving the Erinyes is the *Oresteia*, in which Orestes is pursued by the Furies for the crime of matricide; he kills his moth-er, Clytemnestra, to avenge the murder at her hands of his father, Agamem-non. In the Euripides play *The Eumenides*, the Erinyes stop pursuing Orestes after a trial is held by an Athenian court at the temple of Apollo at Delphi. Athena soothes their anger by making a pact with them—they will receive worship in Athens as the Semnas Theas (honorable goddesses), and they will protect young girls from dying: "...they specifically promise to prevent young girls from becoming *aorai*" (Johnston, *Restless* 263).

This is a rather remarkable assertion, though we hear Penelope in the *Odyssey* talk about the Pandareids, a group of sisters beloved of the gods and given many gifts but snatched away by the Harpies and doomed to roam with the Erinyes (412). We don't know why they were snatched away, but it is a clear reference to girls dying before they are married—they become like the unmarried Erinyes who look after family affairs, particularly moth-er-child relationships.

Johnston notes the curious example of Demeter Erinyes, a characteriza-tion of the goddess Demeter while she is searching for her daughter and is raped by Poseidon who takes the form of a horse. Her anger at losing her daughter and being raped in this story gives her the title "Erinyes," as if to demonstrate the angry mood of the goddess (259-260). They have also been related to the maenads, those followers of Dionysus, women out of control who destroyed their families. While Hindu mythology is not the subject of this writing, I cannot help but note the similarity between a goddess in an "angry" mood and the appearance of the goddess Durga as *Chandi* (angry) in the *Srichandipath*. Chandi appears when there is an imbalance between "too much and too little" (Saraswati 18). This is strikingly similar to Heraclitus' view of the Erinyes, who "stop either one of a pair of opposites (day and night, for example) from 'exceeding its limits' and overriding the other complete-ly" (Johnston, *Restless* 267). Froma Zeitin has suggested that the Erinyes are defenders of feminine power against males (Johnston, *Restless* 264); if this is so, then they are very similar to deities like Durga, Chandi, and Kali, who are all aspects of the same angry goddess. Kali has been associated with death, the afterlife, and black magic—but also with "raw" consciousness. She is the pure energy of consciousness and the universe and can be a loving mother as well as a destroyer. Hinduism has many manifestations of the feminine, and sometimes there are contradictory characteristics within the same deity. There is no evidence that this view had any influence on Greek thinking at this time; however, it seems to be part of an archaic worldview that the gods had both positive and negative attributes; they could protect you or destroy you as they pleased. This is an important point, and one to remember in the context of the good and evil "split" that is a theme of this work. The pre-philosophical Greeks did not believe "the gods are good" by default.

This is certainly evident in the attributes of the goddess Artemis, who is both the protector and destroyer of children. Artemis may be related to the Erinyes in this sense; when young girls become women, there were rituals to appease Artemis, who would become angry at their loss of virginity. Artemis, like the early Hekate, had a special role as wedding attendant; a marriage was not considered blessed if Artemis did not attend. Stories like the one of Artemis turning Callisto into a bear shows the anger of the goddess when a young woman was at a critical stage in life, like pregnancy (Johnston, *Restless* 216). Johnston believes that these stories were told to young girls at these critical periods to frighten them into maintaining the social norm by marrying and having children. That might be the reason for the transitional rituals at the Temple of Artemis at Brauron, in which young girls "acted like bears" (Zaidman 343). This would give the girls an occasion to "wander" and to engage in aggressive play before submitting to marriage and motherhood.

There is also the rite of Aletis, in which young girls sing a song called Aletis [The Wanderer], and it was likely a dance that accompanied the song. The idea of girls as "wanderers" is reminiscent of the unburied dead, who can neither return to life nor enter the underworld. They are in a liminal place, and the liminal is dangerous. There was a belief that the ghosts of virgins who died before bearing children would try to steal children from the living, or try to kill virgin girls before they could marry (Johnston, *Restless* 221-223). We mentioned Gello, Marmo, and the Lamia, whose stories were frequent in Greek folklore, and all of them destroyed young mothers and their children out of envy. Protections were sought in the form of proper rituals, amulets, and Hekation (statues of Hekate placed at entries to the home) to protect the young girl or the unborn child (Johnston, *Restless* 209-210).

The myths of these female monsters represent the fears of being caught "in-between" this world and the underworld. Gello was "the tormented soul of a girl who had died young, and who keeps returning to earth to steal children" (Purkiss 21). There is a vicious cycle of being denied motherhood and trying to deny motherhood to others. Undoubtedly infant death was attributed to monsters like herself, Marmo, or Lamia. Diane Purkiss writes:

> These stories about child-demons are very complex. They are about
> the parents' simple fear that the child will die young, but also about
> more tangled fears of loss of identity in the darkness of death, of being
> forgotten, of being absolutely lost in the sense of never having been
> known. (22)

The transition from womb to birth is dangerous, and surviving infancy
can also be dangerous. If Greek culture did not believe in immortality, then
"never having been known" would be a particularly horrible fate.

Another transition is from girlhood to womanhood. This leads us to the
Hanging Virgins. There are a few notable examples of this story, including
the myths of Erigone and Carya, among others. There are several versions of
the Erigone story; one makes her the daughter of King Icarius, who is killed
by his people after allowing Dionysus to introduce wine into the kingdom.
Another version makes her Orestes' sister, who is distraught when he is ac-
quitted of his mother's murder by Athena and the court. In both cases she
hangs herself. Carya falls in love with Dionysus but her family will not allow
her association with him, and so Dionysus turns her into a nut tree. Later,
young girls were said to be driven to suicide by hanging themselves from
that nut tree. Johnston suggests that this is metaphorical of the tension between the girl's family and the "stranger" who would take her away from her
family (*Restless* 226-227). Dionysus, as we noted earlier, has the attribute of
"foreignness," which would make him the frightening "other." It is also noted
that the priestesses of Artemis were called caryatids, and in all likelihood the
association of the virgin girl encountering Dionysus goes back to the "angry"
Artemis who would kill young girls who did not retain their virginity (*Restless* 216-218).

That dangerous transitional time is discussed by Carl Jung in his essay
on the Kore archetype:

> As a matter of practical observation, the Kore often appears in a wom-
> an as an *unknown young girl*, not infrequently as Gretchen [from Dr.
> Faustus] or the unmarried mother. Another frequent modulation is the
> *dancer*, who is often formed by borrowings from classical knowledge,
> in which case the 'maiden' appears as the *corybant, maenad*, or *nymph*.
> An occasional variant is the nixie or water-sprite, who betrays her
> superhuman nature by her fish-tail. Sometimes the Kore-and-mother
> figures slither down altogether to the animal kingdom, the favourite
> representatives then being the cat or the *snake* or the *bear*, or else some
> black monster of the underworld like the crocodile, or other salaman-
> der-like, saurian creatures. The maiden's helplessness exposes her to
> all sorts of *dangers*, for instance of being devoured by reptiles or ritually

slaughtered like a beast of sacrifice ... Oddly enough, the various tortures and obscenities are carried out by an 'Earth Mother.' ("Psychological" 184)

Jung does not mention hanging, but it fits into the class of dangers described. Johnston mentions the transition away from the family to "wander" to a new place, leaving girls in a dangerously liminal state (221). However, the transition is necessary; they cannot stay young girls forever unless they die. It is worse if they do not make the transition, painful and bloody as it is.

This leads us to the story of Persephone, Hades, and Demeter. The story is well-known; Persephone is a young virginal girl carried off by Hades to the underworld to be his wife. Demeter searches desperately for her missing daughter, and when she finds out what happens, she makes the earth barren, prompting Zeus to negotiate with Hades for the return of Persephone to her mother. But Persephone has eaten some pomegranate seeds in the underworld; the Fates have decreed that anyone who eats the food of the underworld must stay there. Still, a deal emerges in which she spends half the year with her mother, and half the year in the underworld.

This myth is loaded with meaning on many levels. The point of interest for us is the pomegranate. John Myres observes that Hades could not have fed the pomegranate to Persephone (51). Instead,

> What Hades did, then, was to put in effective contact with his person the pomegranate, whose general efficacy in respect of marriage and potency was common knowledge. Thereby he gave to it, literally, a personal application, making of it a love-charm to bind Persephone to himself ... Persephone knows, by now, that a spell is upon her; she 'feels like that'; 'her desire is to her husband.' (52)

Persephone tells her mother that she was tricked into taking the seeds, but is that really so? The pomegranate seed doesn't just bind her to the underworld; it is a symbol of sexuality and love. Persephone has fallen in love with her husband and has given her mother a plausible lie about how it happened. And it is a lie, for isn't it shameful to admit that someone who abducted and raped you is someone you love? How would you admit that to your own mother? Beneath the surface issue of rape lay the psychological facts of the transition from girlhood to womanhood; the young girl falls for the dangerous Animus figure. Her parents will worry and tell her to stay away; they will not approve of the relationship. There is a desire to keep the budding young woman chaste. There is an element of the "star-crossed lovers" archetype in this type of story. Carya kills herself when she cannot have Dionysus;

Persephone is taken against her will but tells her mother she is "tricked" into falling in love. The motif is the same.

Ἑρμῆς *[Hermes]*: It is impossible to talk about life transitions and crossing boundaries without discussing Hermes, the god of boundaries. Hermes is the ultimate Trickster; just a few hours after his birth he stole the god Apollo's cattle, cleverly walking them backward into a cave so that their footprints could not be detected. Apollo discovers Hermes' treachery and brings him to Zeus, where the boy god continues to lie about his theft. Zeus is charmed by his deception, and eventually Hermes returns Apollo's cattle and they exchange gifts. In the exchange, Hermes gains the gift of prophecy and Apollo's golden staff used for herding cattle. Zeus makes Hermes the messenger between himself and his brother Hades in the underworld (Evelyn-White 362-405). We can already see the liminal nature of his role as he moves between the sky and under the earth. At the end of the *Odyssey*, Homer depicts Hermes as a psychopomp, a leader of souls into the land of the dead (*Odyssey* 397); thus, Hermes is the bridge between life and death.

Hermes also sets boundaries. The Greeks set up piles of stones or individual cairns, sometimes carved with bearded heads and male genitalia, known as *herma* or E-MA-A in Mycenaean Linear B (Burkert, *Greek* 156). These cairns marked the midway points between Attic villages starting from approximately 520 B.C.E. (*Greek* 156). This makes Hermes akin to Zeus, as he is associated with the setting of boundaries, the role of the king or ruler. But Hermes always lurks in shadow; he is frequently sent to "steal," rescuing the war god Ares when he was chained in a brazen barrel and taking Priam to Achilles to plead for Hector's body at the end of the *Iliad* (*Greek* 157). He is associated with magic, giving Odysseus the magical moly plant to ward off Circe's spells (Homer, *Odyssey* 166). No figure in Greek mythology embodies the Trickster more completely than Hermes.

[Dionysus]: Hades, Zeus, and other male gods tend to ravish their lovers; Dionysus is the one deity who is respectful of women. He is the mysterious Animus, the forbidden lover who, desired by young girls, does not meet parental approval. As we noted earlier, Dionysus is a foreign god; he is allegedly from Thrace and may be one of the oldest deities in the Greek pantheon. Dionysus is the god of wine and is associated with the madness and frenzy that comes with drinking it. There are two accounts of his birth: the first makes him the son of Zeus and a mortal woman, Semele. An angry Hera tricks Semele into asking Zeus to show himself to her as a god, and she burns up as a result of seeing his true form. Zeus saves the child in her womb and sews it into his thigh; this child is born as Dionysus. His madness, like that of Heracles, is said to come from Hera. The other story is connected with Orphic re-

ligious beliefs; in this story, Dionysus is the son of Zeus and Persephone. The Titans want to kill him, so they lure him away from his mother with toys. They then boil him and intend to eat him, but Athena saves his heart, and the god is reborn from that part. Indeed, there is a connection with mortals, as the attempt to kill Dionysus results in the need to give tribute to Persephone once every ten years for the crime.

Dionysus is a difficult deity to define, as Walter Burkert explains:

> Dionysus eludes definition and for this very reason his relations to the other Olympian gods are ambivalent and indeed paradoxical: proximity becomes the secret of the mysteries, antithesis turns into identity. Thus Dionysus may belong with Demeter as the fruit of the tree with the fruit of the field, as wine with bread; but behind the facts of nature lurks the dark myth of Persephone's dismembered child (*Greek* 222).

The epic battles of the gods mentioned in Hesiod's *Theogony* (Evelyn-White 124-139), in particular the Titanomachy, suggest a movement from the brutal chaos of the Titans to the civilized order of the Olympian reign. Dionysus comes from Thrace, and brings chaos with him. His followers are satyrs and maenads, known for wild fits of drinking, dancing, and tearing humans and animals apart. Yet the Greeks celebrated Dionysus in the three-day Anthesteria festival. The festival was celebrated in the Spring, and involved the opening of the wine jugs from Autumn. Each day of the festival had a name: *Pithoigia* (jar-opening), *Choes* (wine-jugs), and *Chytroi* (pottage). Dionysus is honored with the first libations on the first day; the second day consists of the sharing of mixed wine among all, including slaves, and there was a wine drinking contest. Even children as young as three years old were given wine to drink (Burkert, *Greek* 237).

But the day of Choes was also a day of defilement:

> The doors of the houses are freshly painted with pitch, and buckthorn leaves are chewed first thing in the morning to keep away the ghosts. All the sanctuaries are closed, roped off ... access to the gods is interrupted; business dealings requiring the swearing of oaths are forced to halt as well. The city is peopled by uncanny guests, but not even the tradition of antiquity can agree on who or what they are – Carians or Keres, foreigners or destructive spirits, who are later interpreted also as souls of the dead. (*Greek* 238)

With the Choes we return to the idea of the "foreign," or the Other. As time goes on, Greek culture becomes the center of Western and Near East civilization. Why would the Anthesteria be so important? Before we answer that question, we need to consider other rites related to Dionysus. The *Bacchae* of Euripides provides us with a view of Dionysian ritual and the problems it could cause:

> Pentheus seeks to suppress the Dionysos cult forcibly, but is unable to prevent the women of Thebes from swarming into the mountains, among them his own mother Agaue and her two sisters. The king has Dionysus arrested, but the god easily frees himself from his bonds and entices Pentheus to steal into the wilds to spy on the revels of the maenads. It is particularly uncanny to see how Pentheus, already lost, arrays himself in Dionysian attire with the long, womanly robe, the very image of the effeminate Dionysus himself. Thus adorned he is led as victim to the maenads; with their bare hands they tear him limb from limb, his own mother tearing out his arm and shoulder (Burkert, *Greek* 165).

Humans are always in an uneasy relationship with the Other, and Dionysus as the foreigner and bringer of chaos becomes a symbol of the Other. When Dionysus worship ended in the Christian era, it was replaced by other festivals, such as the *festum stultorum* (fool's feast). Jung tells us:

> In vain did Pope Innocent III inveigh against the 'jests and madness that make the clergy a mockery' and the 'shameless frenzy of their play-acting.' Two hundred and fifty years later (March 12, 1444), a letter from the Theological Faculty of Paris to all the French bishops was still fulminating against these festivals, at which 'even the priests and clerics elected an archbishop or a bishop or pope, and named him the Fool's Pope (*fatuorum papam*). ("Trickster" 257)

The modern festival we know of that had a similar purpose is Halloween, though our modern celebrations have lost much of that original meaning. Jung identifies such festivals and deities like Dionysus with the Trickster archetype:

> Considering the crude primitivity of the trickster cycle, it would not be surprising if one saw in this myth simply the reflection of an earlier, rudimentary stage of consciousness, which is what the trickster obviously seems to be ... We are no longer aware that in carnival customs and the like there are remnants of a collective shadow figure which prove that the personal shadow is in part descended from a numinous collective figure. ("Trickster" 261)

Encountering this shadow figure is part of the initiatory process that we see in the Greek mystery cults. Not surprisingly, the two main cults were those of Demeter and Dionysus. From the little we know about the rites of these cults, both included an ordeal that involved an encounter with frightening figures and an enacted journey to the underworld. It is also worth looking at Apollodorus' observation that Dionysus went to "Cybela in Phrygia," the Mother Goddess Cybele, whose rites were as frenzied as those of Dionysus. "And there, after he had been purified by Rhea [i.e., Cybele] and learned the rites of initiation, he received from her the costume and hastened through Thrace against the Indians. (Apollodorus 327). The purification was meant to cure his madness, as Hera had driven him mad. The idea of madness cured through purification and initiation by a chthonic mother, whether the primal Cybele or the Greek Titan Rhea, may be unintentionally instructive. Turning to the Mother as a cure for madness and to be transformed is an archetypal event as well as a religious one. The rites of Dionysus are usually connected with Orpheus, whom we shall discuss in the next chapter. Orpheus, if he was a real person, wrote in the 6th century or later, judging from the Orphic hymns; the discovery of the *Derveni Papyrus* sets his dates later, around the 4th century (Betegh 59). In any event, the usual assumption is that these rites were designed to guarantee a better place in the underworld. The main sources for this idea are the Bacchic gold tablets, a series of tablets found in Greek cemeteries from about the 4th century B.C.E. onward.[15]

This is of interest to us, as we try to discover how the Greeks moved from the idea of the dead as shadowy, weak phantoms to the idea of the dead having conscious and possibly immortal souls. With regard to Demeter's Rites of Eleusis, Rohde notes:

> We often see it asserted that the belief in a future state of compensation for the good and evil deeds of this world was obtained by the Greeks from the Eleusian mysteries. In reality, the opposite is true; if and in so far as the Greeks ever received or entertained such a belief in future rewards and punishments, the mysteries of Eleusis had nothing whatever to do with the matter ... Not political or moral worth but 'spiritual' merit alone is decisive. (239)

However, with regard to the mysteries of Dionysus, Rodhe sees the ecstatic trances and fevered dancing of the rituals as an example of Greek mysticism, particularly in the 5th century and later:

> Greek religion never indeed (so long at least as the independence of the Greek life lasted) went to the extravagant lengths of Oriental mysticism ... But for all that, on Greek soil, in the ecstatic Cult of Dionysos, under the influence of Greek reflexion upon God, the world, and mankind, the seeds which previously lay undeveloped in the womb of that cult were unfolded in a mystical doctrine, whose guiding principle

[15] For the text of the gold tablets, see Graf, Fritz, and Sarah Iles Johnston. *Ritual Texts for the Afterlife: Orpheus and the Bacchic Gold Tablets.* London: Routledge, 2007.

was the divinity of the human soul and the infiniteness of its life in God. It was from this source that Greek philosophy found the courage to advance a doctrine of the immortality of the soul. (266)

It is worth backing up for a moment. Rohde embraces a progressive view of religion, seeing Western monotheism as a mature development from ancient religion. I do not make that assumption here. What is clear from his assessment is that the combination of early philosophy and the Dionysian mysteries were instrumental in developing the notion of immortality for the soul. The rational mind attempts to take on the chaos of the Trickster, and ends up with conclusions about human participation in the divine. It is an attempt to find the "goodness" in a form of worship that could be dangerous.

The irony here is that the seed for notions of immortality come from a deity that represents what modern Christians would think of as demonic, or even as the Devil himself, though Dionysus does have attributes similar to those of Jesus Christ.[16] Jung demonstrates that this "demonic" element is in fact the seed of the "divine"—by giving the chaotic element a place we move towards wholeness, something often represented as the marriage of opposites: sun/moon, dark/light, male/female:

The Dionysian element has to do with emotions and affects which have found no suitable religious outlets in the predominantly Apollonian cult and ethos of Christianity. The medieval carnivals and *jeux de paume* in the Church were abolished relatively early; consequently the carnival became secularized and with it divine intoxication vanished from the sacred precincts... [I]ntoxication, that most direct form of possession, turned away from the gods and enveloped the human world with its exuberance and pathos. The pagan religions met this danger by giving drunken ecstasy a place within their cult. Heraclitus doubtless saw what was at the back of it when he said, 'But Hades is that same Dionysios in whose honour they go mad and keep the feast of the vat.' For this very reason orgies were granted religious license, so as to exorcise the danger that threatened from Hades. Our solution, however, has served to throw the gates of hell wide open. ("Dream" 136)

Burkert notes the "antithesis" between Dionysus and Apollo, used by Frederick Nietzsche as the essence of Greek history and art: "There, Apollo and Dionysus are not only brothers, but they also always have other gods beside them. Nevertheless, the two were often set in relation to each other. Several black-figure vases place Apollo on one side and Dionysus on the other" (*Greek* 224). There is a similar antithesis between Dionysus and Hera, but

---

[16] For the Dionysus-Jesus connection, see: Taylor-Perry, Rosemary. *God Who Comes: Dionysian Mysteries Reclaimed*. Algora Publishing, 2003.

her hostility toward Dionysus "betrays a curious intimacy: to send madness is the peculiar domain of the god himself" (*Greek* 223). Our "civilized" deities need to have a chaotic, polar antithesis. If there is a light, there must also be a shadow—in the literal sense and the figurative Jungian sense. Jung says above that our solution throws open the gates of Hell; what he means is that by disavowing the shadow and all the chaos that goes with it, it becomes unconscious. We are no longer aware of that side of ourselves, and instead we can only see it in others through psychological projection. Dionysus reminds us that the Other is also ourselves.

The potent mixture of emotions and the dangers of the Other are clear in the relationship of Greek myth to beliefs about the underworld. The place between life and death represents the transitional spaces of women's lives, and is a notable theme in ancient Greek rite-of-passage rituals for girls. There is more of an acceptance of death for what it is; there is no attachment of morality to the otherworld. If Rodhe is correct and earlier societies engaged in ancestral worship, then the dismissal of most humans after death is curious. The realm of the dead is certainly the realm of the Other, and there is no evidence of an overwhelming fear of the "Other," in spite of Thucydides' comment on the distrust between neighboring tribes (3-5). The uncivilized and frightening parts of our nature had an outlet; the Greeks recognized the necessity of chaotic revelry, even as the Dionysian rituals became more controlled in subsequent centuries. While ancient life no doubt had its difficulties and traditional roles for women, we see a collective psychological landscape in which the feminine, the earth, and the chaotic have a place. Even the mystery cults, which would plant the seeds of belief in the immortal soul, served only to remove the fear of death at this time. By the end of the 6th century B.C.E., as Greek society was less tribal and more urban, all of this would begin to change.

Works Cited: Chapter 2

Albinus, Lars. *House of Hades: Studies in Ancient Greek Eschatology.* Aarhus University Press, 2000.

Apollodorus. *Apollodorus, The Library.* Translated by James George Frazer. Vol. 1, W. Heinemann, 1965.

Apollonius of Rhodes. *Jason and the Argonauts.* Translated by Aaron Poochigian, Penguin Books, 2014.

Apuleius. *The Golden Ass.* Translated by Jack Lindsay. Indiana UP, 1962.

Beck, Roger. *The Religion of the Mithras Cult in the Roman Empire: Mysteries of the Unconquered Sun.* Oxford University Press, 2010.

Betegh, Gábor. *The Derveni Papyrus: Cosmology, Theology, and Interpretation.* Cambridge UP, 2004.

Bly, Robert, and William C. Booth. *A Little Book on the Human Shadow.* Harper & Row, 1988.

Burkert, Walter. *Greek Religion.* Harvard UP, 1985.

Burkert, Walter. *The Orientalizing Revolution: Near Eastern Influence on Greek Culture in the Early Archaic Age.* Harvard University Press, 1992.

Campbell, Joseph, and Bill D. Moyers. *The Power of Myth.* Doubleday, 1988.

Carspecken, J. F. "Apollonius Rhodius and the Homeric Epic." *Yale Classical Studies,* vol. 13, 1952, p. 33-143.

Casey, John. *After Lives: A Guide to Heaven, Hell, and Purgatory.* Oxford UP, 2009.

Combs, Allan, and Mark Holland. *Synchronicity: Science, Myth, and the Trickster.* Paragon House, 1990.

Corbeill, Anthony. *Sexing the World: Grammatical Gender and Biological Sex in Ancient Rome.* Princeton UP, 2015.

Desborough, V. R. D'A. *The Greek Dark Ages.* St. Martin's, 1972.

Edwards, I. E. S. *The Cambridge Ancient History.* Vol. 1, Cambridge UP, 1970.

Euripides. *Electra and Other Plays.* Translated by R. B. Rutherford. Penguin, 1998.

Euripides. *Medea and Other Plays.* Translated by Philip Vellacott. Penguin, 1963.

Evelyn-White, Hugh, translator. *Hesiod, the Homeric Hymns, and Homerica.* Harvard UP, 1964.

Gilligan, Carol. *In a Different Voice: Women's Conception of the Self and of Morality.* Harvard UP, 1977.

Graf, Fritz, and Sarah Iles Johnston. *Ritual Texts for the Afterlife : Orpheus and the Bacchic Gold Tablets.* Routledge, 2007.

Graziosi, Barbara. "Theologies of the Family in Homer and Hesiod." *Theologies of Ancient Greek Religion,* edited by Julia Kindt et al., Cambridge University Press, 2016, pp. 35–61.

Guénoun, Denis. *About Europe: Philosophical Hypotheses.* Trans. Christine Irizarry. Stanford UP, 2013.

Harding, M. Esther. *Woman's Mysteries: Ancient and Modern.* G.P. Putnam, 1971.

Herodotus. *Herodotus.* Trans. A. D. Godley. Vol. 1, Harvard UP, 1971.

Hesiod. *Works and Days ; and Theogony.* Trans. Stanley Lombardo. Hackett Pub., 1993.

Homer. *The Iliad.* Trans. Robert Fagles. Penguin, 1998.

Homer. *The Odyssey*. Trans. Robert Fagles. Penguin, 1996.

Jacobi, Jolande. *The Psychology of C.G. Jung: an Introduction with Illustrations*. Yale UP, 1973.

Johnston, Sarah Iles. *Restless Dead: Encounters between the Living and the Dead in Ancient Greece*. University of California, 1999.

Jung, Carl G. "Dream Symbolism in Relation to Alchemy." *Collected Works*. 2nd ed. Vol. 12, Routledge & Kegan Paul, 1952, pp. 41-213.

Jung, C. G. "Marriage as a Psychological Relationship." Translated by R. F. C. Hull. *Collected Works*. Vol. 17, Pantheon, 1954, pp. 189-201.

Jung, C. G. "On the Psychology of the Trickster Figure." *The Archetypes and the Collective Unconscious*. Translated by R.F.C. Hull. Pantheon, 1959, pp. 255-72.

Jung, C. G. "The Psychological Aspects of the Kore." *The Collected Works of C. G. Jung*. Translated by R.F.C. Hull. Vol. 9.1, Pantheon, 1959, pp. 182-203.

Jung, C. G. *The Red Book = Liber Novus. a Reader's Edition*. W.W. Norton, 2012.

Jung, C. G. "The Syzygy: Anima and Animus." *Aion: Researches into the Phenomenology of the Self*. Princeton UP, 1959, pp. 11-22.

Kilgour, Maggie. "Satan and the Wrath of Juno." *ELH*, vol. 75, no.3, 2008, pp. 653-71.

Knox, Peter, and J.C McKeown, editors. *The Oxford Anthology of Roman Literature*. Oxford University Press, 2013.

Martin, Thomas R. *Ancient Greece: From Prehistoric to Hellenistic Times*. Yale UP, 1996.

Mikalson, Jon D. *Ancient Greek Religion*. Blackwell Pub., 2005.

Morris, Ian. "Attitudes toward Death in Archaic Greece." *Classical Antiquity*, vol. 8, no. 2, 1989, pp. 296-320.

Myres, John L. "Persephone and the Pomegranate (H. Dem. 372–4)." *The Classical Review*, vol. 52, no. 2, 1938, pp. 51.

Neumann, Erich, and Apuleius. *Amor and Psyche; the Psychic Development of the Feminine; a Commentary on the Tale by Apuleius*. Pantheon, 1956.

Neumann, Erich. *The Great Mother: an Analysis of the Archetype*. Princeton UP, 1974.

Plato. *The Republic*. Translated by Paul Shorey. Vol. 2. William Heinemann, 1956.

Purkiss, Diane. *At the Bottom of the Garden: A Dark History of Fairies, Hobgoblins, and Other Troublesome Things*. New York UP, 2000.

Raphael, Simcha Paull. *Jewish Views of the Afterlife*. 2nd ed. Rowman & Littlefield, 2009.

Rohde, Erwin. *Psyche; the Cult of Souls and Belief in Immortality Among the Greeks*. K. Paul, Trench, Trubner, 1925.

Saraswati, Satyananda. *Chandi Path*. Devi Mandir, 2002.

Scharf Kluger, Rivkha. *The Archetypal Significance of Gilgamesh : a Modern Ancient Hero*. Daimon Verlag, 1991.

Sophocles. *Sophocles*. Translated by F. Storr. Vol. 2. Heinemann, 1913.

Stanley Spaeth, Barbette. "From Goddess to Hag: the Greek and the Roman Witch in Classical Literature." *Daughters of Hecate: Women and Magic in the Ancient World*, edited by Kimberly B. Stratton and Dayna S. Kalleres, Oxford University Press, 2014, pp. 41–70.

Starr, Chester G. *The Origins of Greek Civilization: 1100-65 B.C.* Alfred A. Knopf, 1961.

Thucydides. *Thucydides*. Translated by Charles Foster Smith. Vol. 1. W. Heinemann, 1930.

Ventris, Michael, and John Chadwick. "Document 172 from Pylos." *Documents in Mycenaean Greek*. Cambridge UP, 1973.

Violatti, Cristian. "Linear B Script." *Ancient History Encyclopedia*. 26 Jan. 2015, www.ancient.eu/Linear_B_Script/.

Zaidman, Louise Bruit. "Pandora's Daughters and Rituals in Grecian Cities." *A History of Women in the West*. Edited by Pauline Schmitt Pantel. Belknap of Harvard University, 1992, pp. 338-77.

CHAPTER 3: ORPHEUS, PYTHAGORAS, ZOROASTER, AND PLATO

We shall now examine the late Archaic through the Hellenistic period of Greek history, covering the 600s through about 146 B.C.E. The late Archaic period was the beginning of what scholars call the "Orientalizing Period" of Greek history. The influence of art and culture from Syria, Assyria, Phoenicia and Egypt becomes apparent, as well as early dealings with the Etruscans in Italy (Burkert, *Orientalizing* 12). This revolution meant new technology and new skills, and the Greeks were eager to put these into practice (128). As noted in the previous chapter, this led to influences on Greek language as well. When the language changes, consciousness also changes; language and its associations are the ultimate symbols in our interpretation of consciousness, as well as the symbolism seen in art. As Jung tells us, "Interpretations make use of certain linguistic matrices that are themselves derived from primordial images. From whatever side we approach the question, we find ourselves confronted with the history of language"(Jung, "Archetypes" 32-33). Such changes are gradual, but nonetheless influential.

This time period was also marked by many political and social changes. The law of Solon was instituted in Athens, which replaced Draconian law and laid the framework for democratic government. We see democracy in Athens from about 510 B.C.E., just a few years before the start of the Persian Wars, which began when Cyrus the Great conquered Ionia in 547 B.C.E., and a series of tyrants ruled in Athens. The Persian Empire, also known as the Achaemenid Empire, affected not only the Greeks, but the Jews, who saw the reign of Persian emperor Cyrus II as positive because he allowed them to keep their religion and their temples. Cyrus was believed to be a Zoroastrian;

we shall discuss the Zoroastrian religion later in this chapter. This religion would have an effect on Judaism, though there is some disagreement about this impact; the evidence does not suggest Zoroastrianism as the primary Iranian religion until the time just before the rise of Islam (Bremmer 47-48). But the Ionians were much more independent-minded and revolted against the Persians, who struggled to maintain peace there. Pesistratos overthrew the democracy founded by Solon temporarily, but he was overthrown by his son, and democracy was re-instituted. The main effect of the democratic laws was that every free male and female citizen of Attica was registered as a citizen, and eventually the men could participate in government. This was in contrast to the laws of Draco, that essentially made the Athenians slaves to the aristocracy. With Solon, we see the beginnings of democratic society; invasions from the East would conflict with these efforts for a number of years. After the battle of Marathon in 490, the Persians led by Darius were defeated; 10 years later Xerxes would march on Athens and burn the Acropolis, but he was also ultimately defeated. The continual unwanted invasions by the Persians led to a very negative attitude towards Persian culture; the only positive portrayal comes from the Aeschylus play *The Persians*, which shows a surprising amount of sympathy for the Persian queen and her subjects at the defeat of Xerxes (Benardete 216).

Perikles became the ruler of Athens in 460 B.C.E., which began Greece's "Golden Age." This era not only gives us the rise of philosophy, but also the drama of Sophocles, Aeschylus, and Euripides. However, this era was also marred by the continuing Peloponnesian Wars with Sparta. A peace treaty was signed around 446 B.C.E., but the wars resumed again in 418. Democracy was restored, but eventually Athens became part of the League of Corinth in the Macedonian Empire.

By the 4th century B.C.E., Alexander the Great created an empire, which lasted until about 323 B.C.E. at his death. Greek philosophy was firmly established, but Greece as a world power was beginning to decline. In addition to the Macedonian Wars, there were invasions from Gaul, and finally, in 146 B.C.E., Rome conquered Greece.

We can see that the Classical and Hellenistic eras incorporated a lot of change—Eastern influence, empire building, war, and the flourishing of Greek intellectual culture. The state of religious and eschatological belief at the end of the Archaic period and its state at the beginning of the Roman period are quite different, and we need to examine the contributing factors to that change in thinking. For this we need to look at Orphism, Pythagoras, and the "Oriental" influences.

Orphism

The term "Orphism" is very controversial. Scholars have difficulty agree-ing on what "Orphic" and "Orphism" really meant to the ancient Greeks. Scholars run the spectrum of opinions, from Radcliffe Edmonds' assertion that Orphism is a catchall phrase for anything out of the Greek mainstream, similar to the term "New Age" in modern times (5), to W. B. Guthrie's de-fense of Orphism as a stream of religious thought that modified existing Greek religion, even if there were no specifically "Orphic" communities. (9) The truth may lie somewhere in between.

What do we know about "Orphism"? Its alleged founder was Orpheus, a mythical figure who is given various divine parentages but is generally agreed to be a son of Apollo. Orpheus was a skilled musician; he was so skilled that he could affect nature with his melodies. He is among the crew of the Argo in the *Argonautica*, brought along because he could out-sing the Sirens (Guthrie and Chambers 28). A famous myth from the Roman period has him descend-ing into the underworld to fetch his deceased wife, Eurydice. He is able to make the dead momentarily forget their woes with his music, and he even charms Persephone and Hades, who allow him to take his wife back to the upper world with the condition that he doesn't look back. In the most well-known version, he does look back and loses her forever, but in other versions he is successful. But if we stick with the canonical version, he returns to the upper world, and when he encounters the maenads of Dionysus, he refuses to participate in their rites, and they tear him to pieces. All that remains is his head, which continues to sing. There are variations of this story as well as various motives for dismembering him. Guthrie even suggests that Orpheus is a misogynist—the maenads tore him apart because he despised women and refused to initiate them into the rites of Dionysus, which he is credited with inventing. In this same vein, Orpheus is also credited with introducing homosexuality into the mystery rites. (Guthrie and Chambers 49) Guthrie also reminds us that when Orpheus begins to follow Dionysus, Dionysus is enraged at the singer's connection to Apollo and has him torn apart. (32) In the Archaic period and even later, the worship of both Apollo and Dionysus would not have been contradictory, since the moralistic separation between deities with opposing attributes had not developed. Guthrie theorizes that any human who may have been the basis for the mythical Orpheus might have been a priest of Apollo. Later, when taking mystical initiation into the Dionysian cult, he may have reformed that cult to make it more "Apollonian" in nature. (29)

It is certainly curious that someone with as gentle a disposition as Orpheus, yet with possible misogynistic tendencies, should be the founder of the rites of a god with many female followers associated with chaotic frenzy. It is worth exploring this connection, which is an important one in our study of the psychology of myth. The theogonies of Greek myth show the Olympian gods, those champions of civilization, overthrowing the Titans, often represented as brute natural forces. We saw this in our previous discussion of "Great Earth Mothers". The dragon-slaying hero in almost any Western myth has an element of overcoming the shadowy, chaotic parts of the psyche. They are part of the trials we pass through to become fully mature adults who may benefit our society through our experience. Because Apollo is associated with the civilized world, the sun god and god of music, poetry, and the "higher" arts, he also provides enlightenment in the form of prophecies at his oracle. Apollo does have a dark side, as a bringer of plagues and violent death to children. As we noted in the previous chapter, the god or goddess who threatens death to a young person often represents the dangers of transition from one phase of life to another, and it is notable that Artemis is his twin sister, with similarly dangerous characteristics regarding children. Still, Apollo is primarily associated with the sun and the achievements of civilization.

Dionysus has the curious status of being an Olympian with highly chaotic tendencies: the madness that comes from drunkenness and ecstatic episodes is his. Guthrie has already suggested that Orpheus, who is very "Apollonian" in nature with his disposition and gift as a musician, may have taken over and modified the rites of Dionysus to make them more palatable to "civilized" Greeks. We don't know if this is true; however, it makes psychological sense for the Apollonian hero to encounter the wild "foreigner" Dionysus and incorporate his rites meaningfully into Greek consciousness. Dionysus is functionally a chthonic god; his domain deals with fruits of the earth, and he is a bringer of madness, representing the dark places of the mind. Walter Burkert connects the notion of *theos* with Dionysus, a word that has its roots in the idea of divine ecstasy (*Greek* 271-272). Hence, Dionysus is not only chthonic, but individual: he represents the personal and direct connection to the god as opposed to the supplication of distant Olympians or denizens of Hades. The Orphic myth connects Dionysus to Zeus as appointed successor of the king of the gods; the Titans are treated as evildoers interfering with the plan of Zeus, who takes on the role of creator. The *Odes of Horace*, published about 23 BCE, contain a hymn to Bacchus (Dionysus) that clearly mixes the legends of Bacchus with those of Apollo (Horace 69-70). What we see in the Greek and later Roman writings is the recasting of Dionysus in the light of the masculine sun god; his chthonic, earthy and foreign/"other" tendencies diminish in the public sphere. This is the best example from this era of a chthonic deity that is made celestial. It has the negative effect of "watering down" or sanitizing the reality of the archetype represented by Dionysus, and sets the stage for the repression and demonizing of our naturally chaotic instincts, though it seems the original intent was to make them conscious. This is a natural consequence of taking private ritual and making it public; the larger the group, the greater the attempt to contain the "shadowy" part of human nature in the name of law and order. On the positive side, it still represents some kind of an outlet for the darker, more chaotic nature of humans in a relatively safe environment. The mystery rites address the ultimate fear of what will happen to us after death. Death anxiety and the fascination with this less civilized part of us may have contributed to the popularity of the Dionysus cult right up until Christian times.

The Orphic cosmogony provides a different view of creation, the soul, and death. The versions we have of this myth come from a collection of texts called the *Rhapsodies*, as well as the writings of Hieronymos and Hellanikos.[17] In this cosmogony, the first principle is Chronos (Time), who bears Aether, Chaos, and Erebos (Gloom). Chronos then creates an egg in the Aether, which breaks open, giving birth to Phanes, the creator god. Phanes creates the universe and the gods with Night as his partner, and he eventually hands over control of the universe to her. Zeus then becomes ruler of the universe, but consults with Night for advice. At her bidding, he swallows Phanes and creates a second universe. Metis is sometimes substituted for Phanes, and Zeus does swallow Metis in Hesiod's *Theogony*. The *Derveni Papyrus* tells the story in fragmented form, interspersed with commentary.

> And when Zeus took from his father the prophesized rule / And the strength in his hands and the glorious daimon (19) ... [?She] [possibly Night] proclaimed an oracle about all that was right to him to hear (25) ... so that he may rule on the lovely abode of snowcapped Olympus (27) ... He swallowed the phallus of [...], who sprang from the aither first (29).

The *Derveni Payprus* equates Time with Olympus (27), and equates both Kronos and Zeus with Mind (185). The field of time is the field of creation— we don't know anything outside of time and space. This is similar to Hesiod, whose *Theogony* has Kronos (Time) castrate Ouranos (Sky), thus separating Earth and Sky, and then Kronos becomes the ruler until he is overthrown

---

[17] For a full analysis of these writings, see Guthrie, William Keith Chambers. *Orpheus and Greek Religion: A Study of the Orphic Movement.* Princeton, NJ: Princeton UP, 1993. 73-87. Print.

by Zeus. What are different in the whole Orphic cosmogony are the dual creations by Phanes and then by Zeus, and this rather celestial conception of creation. In Hesiod's story, Ge or Gaia (Earth) is the creative deity.

There are a couple of things to note from the *Derveni* text in particular. First, the *Derveni* writer makes the comment:

> It has been made clear above [that] he called the sun a phallus. Since the beings that are now come to be from the already subsistent he says: [with?] the phallus of the first-born king, onto which / All the immortals grew (or clung fast), blessed gods and goddesses / And rivers and lovely springs and everything else / That had been born then; and he himself became solitary. (35)

The sun is equated with a phallus, and is thus given a masculine characteristic. Heraclitus saw the sun and other celestial bodies as bowls of fire (West 176), whereas earth was associated with water, and human souls were said to come from the water of the earth. (151) Fire has a divine association. The sun, and also Zeus, are considered responsible for creation. Though Night also plays a central role in this cosmogony, she becomes a passive advisor. The Earth is not central as a creator in this myth. This is a departure from both Hesiod and the Homeric hymns, and can be considered different from the Archaic view by the dating of the texts. Other comparative myths of the Near East with male creators come from Judaism and Zoroastrianism.

Zorastrianism becomes a factor again when we consider the resemblance between Chronos (Ageless Time) and the Persian deity Zrvan Akarana (Endless Time). Chronos is described as "a serpent having heads growing upon him of a bull and a lion, and in the middle is the face of a god; and he has also wings upon his shoulders" (Guthrie and Chambers 86). The image of Zrvan Akarana is very similar in detail. Zrvan Akarana would later become known as Aion in the Greek world, a term initially introduced to Greek thought by Heraclitus. (West 159) Whatever else it may mean, there seems to be clear Persian influence on Orphic thought and image.

In the *Rhapsodies* and other later Orphic texts, the theogony continues when Zeus ravishes Demeter and produces Persephone. He then ravishes Persephone and produces Dionysus. Zeus intends to hand over the throne of the universe to the child Dionysus. However the Titans become jealous and lure the child Dionysus to their dwelling with toys. There they dismember him and boil him for eating. His limbs are collected by Apollo, and Athena saves his heart. At Delphi, Zeus causes Dionysus to be reborn. Because the Titans had tasted Dionysus' flesh, Zeus hurled a thunderbolt at them, and they burned to ashes; mortal men rose from the smoking remnants. Humans, therefore, have both the divine spark of Dionysus in them, but also the wickedness of the Titans. In the Orphic view, humans must purify themselves of their "Titanic" tendencies in order to become immortal and transcend the sorrows of Hades (Guthrie and Chambers 83).

In this cosmogony there is an implied dualism that is not present in other Greek cosmogonic writings. Jeffrey Russell writes:

> Iranian dualism posited a conflict between two spiritual powers, one of light and one of darkness. Orphic dualism posited a conflict between the divine soul and the evil, Titanic body that imprisoned it. ... To the extent that Dionysus was good and the Titans evil, which is assumed, to that extent the soul is good and the body evil. This interpretation grew steadily throughout the Hellenistic period when, influenced by Iranian dualism, matter and the body were assigned to the realm of the evil spirit, and soul to that of the good spirit. (139)

Guthrie and Chambers cite F.M. Cornford: "Whether or not we accept the hypothesis of direct influence from Persia on the Ionian Greeks in the sixth century, any student of Orphic and Pythagorean thought cannot fail to see that the similarities between it and Persian religion are so close as to warrant our regarding them as expressions of the same view of life, and using the one system to interpret the other" (Cornford qtd. in Guthrie and Chambers 87). We begin to see the overlap between these systems, and from our survey of the Archaic period, we know that the influence of Persian religion on Greece prior to Alexander the Great is far from implausible.

At this point it would be wise to consider our chronology. Though Orphism is sometimes portrayed as an ancient religion, no writings that could be classified as "Orphic" in character exist before the 5th century B.C.E. The *Derveni Papyrus* is the oldest extant writing containing what we think of as Orphic cosmogony and doctrine, and that is dated approximately to the early part of 4th century B.C.E, but even this is uncertain. Greek papyri from these periods are rare, due to the humid conditions in Greece that usually contribute to their decomposition. There is not much to compare to the *Derveni Papyrus*; the only reason it is so well preserved is because it was burned on a funeral pyre, which removed the humidity (Betegh 59-61). Still, it is one of the few documents that are consistent in narrative with later Orphic works and actually mentions Orpheus by name.

There is also disagreement about what constitute "Orphic" texts; most texts labeled as "Orphic" are from at least 500 years after the Greek Hellenistic period. The same problem exists with ancient writers speaking of things happening hundreds of years before their time, such as the Trojan War: they might have some truth, but the time distance makes them unreliable. But even texts like the *Derveni Papyrus* did not have "Orpheus" as their author;

Orphic writings have been attributed to Onomakritos and even Pythagoras (Guthrie and Chambers 13-14), but much of what have been described as the poetry or *hieros logos* of Orpheus is only described secondhand. Herodotus tells us of the Egyptians:

> They wear linen tunics, with fringes hanging about the legs, called 'calasiris', and loose white woolen mantles over these. But nothing of wool is brought into temples, or buried with them; that is forbidden. In this they follow the same rule as the ritual called Orphic and Bacchic, but which is in truth Egyptian and Pythagorean; for neither may those initiated into these rites be buried in woolen wrappings. (366-367)

We also have Diodorus Siculus's account from first century B.C.E.:

> Orpheus brought from Egypt most of his mystic ceremonies, the orgiastic rites that accompanied his wanderings, and his fabulous account of his experiences in Hades. For the rite of Osiris is the same as that of Dionysus and that of Isis very similar to that of Demeter, the names alone having been interchanged; and the punishments in Hades of the unrighteous, the Fields of the Righteous, and the fantastic conceptions, current among the many, which are figments of the imagination—all these were introduced by Orpheus in imitation of the Egyptian funeral customs. (327)

We should take this interpretation with a grain of salt, as Diodorus is writing in a period of frequent syncretism, and local practices merged with foreign ones as different cultures meshed during the various conquests in the region. Still, as noted in Chapter 1, Egyptian influence cannot be discounted, and here it may be most evident. Martin Nilsson suggests that even if the myths of a dismembered Osiris and a dismembered Dionysus have a later connection, the connection cannot be denied (39-40).

It is clear that even the ancients differed on the origins of the Orphic. Still, if we are to define "Orphism," and particularly Orphic afterlife beliefs, we need to have some consensus on what this means. Edmonds cites Alberto Bernabé, who suggests there are 3 agreed-upon "Orphic" ideas: belief in body-soul dualism, the idea of an original "sin" from which purification can be sought to attain "salvation," and the notion of a cycle of reincarnations over which this process occurs (Edmonds 249). Edmonds believes only the body-soul dualism may be considered truly unique to Orphism, but we do not want to be sidelined with interpretative controversies. We are interested in the ideas, whether fully Orphic or not, of body-soul dualism and immortality of the soul.

On the idea of body-soul dualism, Plato says:

> Now some say that the body (σῶμα) is the tomb (σεμα) of the soul, as
> if it were buried in its present existence; and also because through it
> the soul makes signs (σεμα) of whatever it has to express, for in this
> way also they claim it is rightly named from σεμα. In my opinion it is
> the followers of Orpheus who are chiefly responsible for giving it the
> name, holding that the soul is undergoing punishment for some reason
> or other, and has this husk around it, like a prison, to keep it from run-
> ning away. (*Craytlus* 62-63)

There is a pun here, linking the word *soma* (body) to *sema* (tomb). *Sema*
also means "sign," and is the root of the English word "semantic". Hence,
we have Socrates' explanation of the body as the tomb of the soul that gives
"signs." The idea of the body as a tomb or prison led Orphics to an ascetic,
vegetarian lifestyle. Another means of purification came through initiation
into the Dionysus cult. Orpheus was connected not only to the cult of Dionysus, but also of Demeter at Eleusis and of the wandering priests offering
initiation and magical services to the people (Burkert, *Greek* 297). Most initiations were criticized by Plato and also by Aristophanes as being nothing
more than a device to make money for the priests. All one had to do was
make the right sacrifices and say the right magical formulae, and they were
guaranteed a blessed spot in the underworld. In the Aristophanes *Peace*,
when Hermes tells Trygaeus that he must die, Trygaeus says, "Oh then, I
prithee, lend me half a crown. I'll buy a pig and get initiated first" (86-87).
However, Guthrie and Chambers suggest that the Orphic initiations were
more serious—they may have involved ritual drama, but Orphics were also
required to read *hieros logos* (sacred stories) that explained the mysteries behind the rites. The *hieros logos* appear to be the first type of dogmatic writing
in the ancient world, as they explain the reasons for certain beliefs or rituals.
We see an ascetic, intellectual system designed to purify mortals of their
evil tendencies. This seems a curious thing when we consider the nature of
Dionysus.

Bernabé's second assertion of "original sin" and "salvation" has been partially discussed to some degree above. I do not like the term "original sin,"
as the crime of the Titans is a false comparison to the episode of the serpent
and the forbidden fruit in the Garden of Eden from the Biblical Genesis story.
Perhaps Bernabé and others are trying to find a modern parallel to the crime
of the Titans. Nowhere in the Orphic writings is "sin" mentioned; we don't
see sin as a concept until we get to the Common Era, in New Testament
writings. The idea of Orphism as espousing original sin comes from an interpretation of Plato. In Plato's *Laws*, he discusses the lawlessness that can

come from certain types of liberty and speaks of "the Titans of story, who are said to have reverted to their original state, dragging out a painful existence with never any rest from woe" (1:248-249). Edmonds suggests that this is not a reference to the Orphic myth, but to the evil of the Titans, who felt they were beyond the gods (Edmonds 329). But Edmonds also cites Olympiodorus, who claims that man has a dual nature, Dionysiac (divine/good) and Titanic (evil) (Edmonds 327) . Whatever the case, it is clear there is an interpretation of Titanic nature as somehow lesser or evil. "Titan" may have its origins in the word for "clay", and this part is similar conceptually to the Genesis I myth, in which Yahweh makes Adam out of clay, emphasizing the earthly and mortal nature of the body. If anything, the Orphic myth is more "Gnostic" in character, as humans are meant to recognize their greater "divine" nature.

The word "salvation" is also a loaded one. We think of "salvation" as being saved from something, usually punishment or the fires of Hell. Perhaps that is what is meant here, even in the context of reincarnation. One may eventually be freed from the bondage of being reborn as punishment, but this sounds more like the Eastern idea of liberation. In Western religious parlance, salvation is the intervention of a deity to save one through an act of grace; this does not occur in the Orphic religious idea or in the Hindu and Buddhist notion of liberation. What is similar is the notion of a cycle of birth, death and rebirth that eventually ends. In fact, it is easy to see why some authors see the Orphic system as "Asiatic"—it has a distinctly Hindu flavor, though I would not go so far as to claim it is derived from Hinduism. (Russell 137)

This idea of salvation, tied in with the third element of reincarnation, is certainly different from other writings on the afterlife in ancient Greece, and it is also different from Hindu conceptions because it is dualistic. There is an ethical notion of good overcoming evil. Burkert notes that polytheism has great difficulty maintaining moral religion, as gods representing opposite qualities are presented as defending their own territory. The worshipper seeks to appease the god that influences his personal life or his community (*Greek* 248). Dualism is the minimum requirement for ethical religion as we know it; there has to be a divine and doctrinal sense of right and wrong. In order for there to be "salvation" from death or fear, there has to be a divine "goodness" that will intervene on one's behalf.

We do not know if there was a human "Orpheus" that served as the basis of the Greek myth. We also don't know the age of Orphic ideas; the fifth century is the farthest back that we can date Orphic-themed writings. There was never any formal "cult" of Orpheus, nor is he mentioned on any of the

Bacchic gold tablets found in Greek burial sites from the 4th to 2nd centuries B.C.E. Many scholars believe that Orphism, whatever form it took, was a 6th century phenomenon that gradually faded out. However, based on the sudden surge of writings about Orpheus during the late Hellenistic and Roman Republican period, I'm inclined to agree with Guthrie that an underground movement suddenly gained some level of mainstream popularity.

It is worth noting that Orpheus was also associated with magic and magic spells; there are several mentions of Orphic tablets with magical spells. Graf and Johnston point out that γοητεία (goetia or necromancy) was part of archaic song-culture, and it is the song that connects the living with the dead. Euripides speaks of Orphic spells in his plays *Cyclops* and *Alcestis* (170). This is of interest to us, as the practice of magic and necromancy appears in Greek literature during the fifth century, and only seemed to surge in popularity after that. If it tells us nothing else, we see a Western society that is increasingly insecure about its future, both in this life and the next.

Pythagoras

We now move from Orpheus to Pythagoras, and there are enough similarities between the two for scholars and ancient writers to think that one was influenced by the other, or that one wrote the writings of the other. Pythagoras is a name we tend to associate with mathematics. Indeed, mathematics was an integral part of Pythagoras' philosophical system. Greek philosophers focused on all the "big questions" of life, and sought not only to look at human behavior and morality, but the natural world and the entire universe, and Pythagoras was no exception. Burkert suggests that Pythagoras' philosophy had two parts: the mathematical, and the mystical (299). We are focused on the latter of these, and particularly in Pythagoras' ideas about the afterlife.

A brief word about Pythagoras himself is in order. He lived from about 570 to 495 B.C.E. According to Iamblichus, Pythagoras spent 22 years in Egypt studying with the priests, and also studying the wisdom of the Chaldeans (Diogenes 322-323). There are also claims that he studied with Zoroaster, but these are doubtful at best. After his studies he returned to his home on the island of Samos and opened up his school of philosophy. He left Samos at the age of 40, when Polycrates became king, and moved to Croton. He established a secret brotherhood there, which may have religiously centered on Apollo. In fact, Diogenes Laertius tells us his disciples "held the opinion about him that he was Apollo come down from the far north" (330-331). The connection of both Orpheus and Pythagoras to Apollo is notable.

When a conflict broke out between Sybaris and Croton, it was Milo, a Pythagorean, who led the charge against Sybaris successfully. However, when Croton decided to establish a democratic government after that, the Pythagoreans were opposed. They lost their popularity with the people, and eventually Milo's house was burned down, killing its inhabitants, among them Pythagoras himself. Some stories claim Pythagoras escaped and continued his philosophical and religious teachings elsewhere, but there is little evidence for this. No writings of Pythagoras himself survive; everything we know comes from other philosophers, including Plato, Xenophanes, and Heraclitus among others. Most of these writings do not refer to the writings of Pythagoras, but of the "Pythagoreans." Diogenes mentions three books by Pythagoras that were extant in his lifetime: *On Education*, *On Statesmanship*, and *On Nature* (326-327). None of these remain today. So, like Orpheus and Zoroaster, the truth about the actual man is shrouded in mystery and myth.

According to the sources we have, Pythagorean doctrine was similar to that of the Orphics; they were said to live a strictly ascetic lifestyle, and had a belief in reincarnation. According to Burkert, "The Pythagoreans share with the Orphics the view that life is trouble and punishment: 'Good are the troubles, but the pleasures are evil at all events; for whoever has come in for punishment must be punished'" (*Greek* 303). There was an emphasis on learning, and Pythagoreans are credited with advances in mathematics, astronomy and medicine.

With regard to our question of the afterlife and the feminine, the following Pythagorean passages from Timaeus of Locri are worth noting. The first is on the nature of the universe:

> Of all the things in the universe there are two causes: Mind, of things existing according to reason; and Necessity, of things [existing] by force, according to the power of bodies. The former of these causes is the nature of the good, and is called God, and the principle of things that are best, but what accessory causes follow are referred to Necessity. Regarding the things in the universe, there exist Form, Matter, and the Perceptible which is, as it were, the offspring of the two others. Form is unproduced, unmoved, unstationary, of the nature of the Same ... Matter, however, is a recipient of impressions, is a mother and a nurse, and is procreative of the third kind of being; for receiving upon itself the resemblances of form, and as it were remoulding them, it perfects these productions ... These two principles then are opposite to each other, of which Form is analogous to a male power and a father, while matter is analogous to a female power and a mother. (Guthrie and Fideler 287)

The second quotation of note is on "human destiny":

> Now he whom the deity has happened to assign somewhat of a good fate is, through opinion, led to the happiest life. But if he be morose and indocile, let the punishment that comes from law and reason follow him, bringing with it the fears ever on the increase, both those that originate in heaven or Hades, how that punishments inexorable are below laid up for the unhappy, as well as those ancient Homeric threats of retaliation for the wickedness of those defiled by crime. For as we sometimes restore bodies to health by means of diseased substances, if they will not yield to the more healthy, so if the soul will not be led by true reasoning, we restrain it by false. These are unusual since, by a change, we say that the souls of cowards enter into the bodies of women who are inclined to insulting conduct ... On all these matters, however, there has at a second period been delivered a judgment by Nemesis, of Fate, together with the avenging deities that preside over murderers, and those under the earth in Hades, and the inspectors of human affairs to whom God, the leader of all, has entrusted the administration of the world, which is filled with Gods and men, and the rest of the living beings who have been fashioned according to the best model of an unbegotten, eternal and mentally-perceived form. (Guthrie and Fideler 296)

So, we have a philosophical/religious school of thought that separates good from evil, associates "God" with the "good," and associates Hades with punishment. The reference to "ancient Homeric threats of retaliation" might come from the assertion that Pythagoras had been to Hades, and saw "Hesiod bound fast to a brazen pillar and gibbering, and the soul of Homer hung on a tree with serpents writhing about it, this being their punishment for what they said about the gods" (Diogenes 338-339). Not only do we see the idea of punishment, but the implication is that Greek religion up to that point has "gotten it wrong" regarding the gods.

We see in Timaeus of Locri that abstract form is treated as masculine (and capitalized by the translator, consciously or not) and matter is treated as feminine. If we follow the assertion that Pythagoreans saw life in the material world and in human bodies as a kind of punishment, then it also follows that matter and the material world would be seen as inferior by Pythagoreans, if not totally evil. Timaeus does not go so far as to declare matter "evil." But avoiding the pleasures of life is an indirect way of saying the same thing, for the pleasures of life are the pleasures of the flesh, and involve partaking in the pleasurable things of our material life. In Eastern thinking, these pleasures are avoided because they are temporal, not eternal. There is a similar idea here—the body passes away, but the soul, or whatever you call the divine or immortal substance in humans, continues on. Some writers credit twentieth-century Theosophist Madame Blavatsky with the idea of "karmic lessons" for the reincarnated soul (Goodrick-Clarke 222), but clearly this idea existed long before she was born.

I am not making a value judgment on the pursuit of a "good" or "pure" life. Certainly there are benefits to avoiding excesses and having greater goals than material gain. I want to point out that with the idea of spiritual discipline there is an unconscious denigration of matter, the earth, and the feminine. In both Orpheus and Pythagoras, the bad/filthy/Titanic/material must be rejected in favor of the pure/good/spiritual/divine. Apollo and Dionysus may have co-existed in the worlds of the Orphics and the Pythagoreans, but ultimately the Apollonian that wins out. Dionysus becomes acceptable when he assumes a more Apollonian or Olympian role in the Orphic tradition.

Heraclitus

Carl Jung said of Heraclitus, "He is singularly Chinese in his philosophy and is the only Western man who has ever really compassed the East. If the Western world had followed his lead, we would all be Chinese in our viewpoint instead of Christian." (Analytical 77) As we noted in the discussion of the Erinyes, Heraclitus' cosmology was not fully embraced. Nonetheless, he was an influence on Plato and Aristotle's thought, particularly in conception of matter and spirit in relation to fire and water, dryness and wetness. His ideas about the balancing of opposites are very much like those of Taoism, hence Jung's comment about the "Chinese" nature of his philosophy. Of great importance to this study is the relationship of his thought to Zoroastrianism; while it is difficult to prove a direct Persian connection to Pythagoras or the Greek mystery cults, there is much in Heraclitus' writings that suggest more than an accidental connection: "Heraclitus must have been somewhat aware of the nature of the wide-spread mazda-worship with which his successors were so familiar. For the Persian forces which looked to Auramazda for victory and hated Angra Mainyu as the author of defeat, surged for years up to the very gates of Ephesus when Heraclitus was in his prime. ... What we have found in Heraclitus seems to presuppose a deeper intercourse with a more learned class of person." (West 202)

The argument for an "Eastern" Heraclitus doubtlessly comes from his view that apparently dual things are really one, and that a correct "apportionment" of opposites is the desirable state of the world (West 138). He was not absolute about the tension of opposites, and opposites could be experienced simultaneously; for instance, day and night are not separate, they are one thing that changes, and he identifies that "one thing" with God. (139-140) This idea that difference is illusory is similar to the Eastern idea of *maya*, the illusion of separateness. His most famous quote relates to this idea, and is generally translated as "you never step into the same river twice." (121) As West indicates, "It had probably been intended to illustrate that a thing's substance can be changing without affecting its shape and measurements." (121) Jung's notion of *enantiodromia* comes directly from this view, and it is the idea that an overabundance of any force will produce its opposite. The term is used in analytical psychology to represent the tension between the conscious and unconscious mind, "the view that everything that exists turns into its opposite." (Jung, *Psychological* 426) Whatever our values, beliefs, and narratives, the opposite of those also exist in shadow, and if we repress the unconscious forces, they translate into threatening projections. In psychology, enantiodromia can accompany a neurotic conflict or breakdown. To quote Jung: "The grand plan on which the unconscious life of the psyche is constructed is so inaccessible to our understanding that we can never know what evil may not be necessary in order to produce good by enantiodromia, and what good may very possibly lead to evil." (Phenomenology 215)

Plato associated this Heraclitean idea with the current of the river, an alternating "up and down" (άνω και κάτω) flux.[18] This implies two separate forces or substances that alternate, rather than a single force or substance that changes. So, it appears that Heraclitus was not a dualist in spite of his theory of opposites; there is difference within unity.

On the other hand, there is a dualistic element to Heraclitus' thought that resembles Platonic ideas that would take hold in the Classical Greek period and during the Roman Empire. Heraclitus believed that "dry" souls were wise, and rose to celestial heights, to the region of the sun and stars. The moon was lower than the sun, and in a less "pure" region. "Damp" souls clustered around the moon, weighted down by the moisture. The dictates of dike confined their gatherings to the nighttime and to winter. This is why there are so many souls and *daimones* in the world (West 187-188). The most "Zoroastrian" part of Heraclitus' death idea may be in his conception of a conflict between Zeus and Hades (158). The conversion of the soul to water is in the agency of Hades, who is thought of as present in the world of men (188-189) "The Greeks, besides identifying Ahura Mazdah with Zeus, identified Angra Mainyu with Hades" (189). This conflation is first implied in Heraclitus' thought, and may be the first instance of Hades as an evil god. We also seen an association between evil and the formation of the soul, and this is an early instance of a celestial cosmology that allows righteous and

---

[18] Phaedo 90C and Philebus 43 a are examples given by West, p. 121-122.

wise souls to ascend to the region of the sun, and banishes inferior souls to the earth, or leaves them to cluster around the moon. As we will see in Middle Platonic and Neoplatonic thought, this aspect of Heraclitus' cosmology will become standard, and will be part of Christian cosmology until the Renaissance period. The non-dualistic aspects of Heraclitus' philosophy were rejected, but the Zoroastrian ideas were incorporated in subsequent philosophical and religious thinking about cosmology and death. Perhaps this is why Jung also says, "We can think of Heraclitus as making the switch between East and West." (Analytical 77).

Other Greek Philosophers

Ancient Greek philosophy is generally understood as a movement away from "mythological" thinking to attempts at understanding the world and the cosmos through reason and logical deduction. The earliest philosophers were the Pre-Socratics: such figures as Anaximander, Democritus, Empedocles, Heraclitus of Ephesus, Xenophanes, Parmenides, and Pythagoras, among others. These philosophers and their contemporaries sought the origins of the material world, and often referred to the traditional elements of fire, air, water, and earth to explain the visible world and the universe. They also had opinions on the nature of the gods and the nature of the soul and its destiny.

Xenophanes was the first to reflect on the nature of the gods in an ethical way: "Homer and Hesiod attributed to the gods all things which are disreputable and worthy of blame when done by men; and they told of them many lawless deeds, stealing, adultery, and deception of each other" (69). Xenophanes also noted the tendency of humans to assume the gods are like themselves, implying that their standards are different from ours and cannot be compared (67). Gods were not like humans; anthropomorphism was, therefore, indefensible. Xenophanes also spoke on the nature of god: "God is one, supreme among gods and men, and not like mortals in body or in mind. The whole [of god] sees, the whole perceives, the whole hears. But without effort he sets in motion all things by mind and thought" (67). Empedocles follows Xenophanes in suggesting that god has no form but is the purity of "Thinking alone." In Burkert's words, "A god had to be "ungenerated, sufficient to himself, and not in need of anything; this is his strength and his bliss. God acts through spirit, omniscient and guiding everything; but whether he cares for the individual remains a problem" (*Greek* 317-318).

Burkert goes on to cite Euripides' play *Heracles*, in which the myth of Heracles being driven mad by Hera and murdering his wife and children is no longer acceptable. "The god, if he is truly a god, requires nothing. The rest of the world is wretched singers" (*Greek* 318). Heracles takes responsibility for his own actions, and separates his will from that of the gods.

It is worth pausing here for a moment. Jungian psychology tells us that the gods themselves are archetypes. They are rather complex metaphors used to make sense out of what is irrational yet universal in human nature. The ancient Greek projected his or her consciousness onto the gods, who were neither good nor evil by nature; like any natural force or quality, they could be destructive or creative. This intellectual shift fosters the rise of humanism, where the gods are separated from the affairs of man. In some sense they were always separate—they were immortal, we were mortal, and they only care about us insofar as we show them proper reverence. The statement of Heracles implies an even greater distance between humans and gods, and suggests that humans can stand on their own. This seems perfectly reasonable on the surface; however, this is the beginning of a psychological separation in which the gods now become part of what is unconscious, and not part of human life. What is important is human reason and action. These are certainly critical, and this action appears progressive. In the process, however, something is lost—the connection with our deeper selves.

If we move from the gods to the soul, we see a different conception of the *psyche*. The philosophers saw the soul as a substance, like the elements, and attempted to understand its nature. Parmenides thought the soul was a special kind of matter belonging to the category of fire, air, or aether (Burkert, *Greek* 319), similar to the Orphic idea of being "wind-born" (Guthrie and Chambers 94). Parmenides seems to have been influenced by Pythagoras when he says "Nothing dies of everything that arises" (Burkert, *Greek* 319). "The association of soul and heaven, which had probably received some impulse from Iranian eschatology, could easily be combined with this: soul is heavenly matter" (Burkert, *Greek* 319-320). Once again, we see a possible Persian connection to philosophical thought. Empedocles writes:

> The coming together of all things brings one generation into being and destroys it; the other grows up and is scattered as things become divided. And these things never cease continually changing places, at one time all uniting in one through Love, at another each borne in different directions by the repulsion of Strife. (Empedokles)

Here we see the idea of soul as a substance that is never destroyed; it comes together or is scattered by Love or by Strife respectively.

When we move from the Pre-Socratics to Socrates himself, we see a further development of these ideas. In Plato's dialogues, we see the idea of a divine soul that his held down by matter and the temptations of the material world. This is most evident in the myth known as the "Vision of Er," found in Book 10 of the *Republic*. Socrates tells the story of a Pamphylian warrior called Er, who is thought dead but comes back to life just before his funeral pyre is lit. He has returned to give an account of the afterlife, which includes a congregation of souls that comes before two judges. Those who have led righteous lives head upward on a celestial pathway; those who have led wicked lives are led down to the depths of Hades for punishment. After a period of years, both groups of souls return and come before the Fates, where lots are cast and they are able to choose their next life (*Republic* 2: 492-521). This new mythology of Plato's certainly falls in line with what we know about Pythagorean teaching. Additionally, in the *Phaedo* Socrates speaks about death as something welcome for the righteous man:

> 'But now good sirs,' Socrates continued, 'there is a further point on which we should do well to reflect: if the soul is immortal, it certainly calls for our attention, not only in respect of this present period which we call our lifetime, but in respect of all time; and now, if not before, the danger of neglecting it may well seem terrible. For if death were the end of all things, it would be a heaven-sent boon for the wicked when they die, to be at one stroke released both from the body and, with the death of the soul, from their own wickedness; but now that we have found the soul to be immortal, there can be no other escape from evil, no other salvation for it save by becoming as good and intelligent as possible ... (*Phaedo* 167).

The marriage of religious thought to natural philosophy and logical reasoning laid the groundwork for a separation of body and soul, and for the idea of immortality for the soul after the body is discarded:

> The ground had been well prepared. A piety directed towards an afterlife existed in Orphic circles; the philosophy of Parmenides had placed true being in contrast with illusory reality; and the Pre-Socratics had set the stage for a synthesis of religion and natural philosophy to a greater extent than Plato's polemics would allow. Then again there was the crucial progress in mathematics and astronomy from which Plato took method and model in order to reach a new level of discussion. (Burkert, *Greek* 322).

We have only looked at a few examples of ancient philosophy on this topic, and there are many others. The core ideas regarding life after death of the Orphics, the Pythagoreans, and these other Greek philosophers of the period are immortality and the divinity of the soul. This is what marries the mystery cults and their quest for a happy afterlife living "as a god" to the rational speculation of the natural philosophers. This is the beginning of Greek humanism, which gives humans attributes of the divine. Like any other mode of thinking, this has both positive and negative consequences.

Zoroaster, the Persians, and the Jews

Zoroaster, or Zarathustra, was the prophet of the religion that bore his name. Some scholars doubt he existed; most assume that he did live, but he belongs to the realm of prehistory (De Jong 7183). The body of Zoroastrian texts is known as the *Avesta*, and the writing of the *Gathas* (songs) is often attributed directly to Zoroaster, even though there is little direct historical evidence for his existence (De Jong 7183). Bremmer distinguishes between old Avestan texts and young Avestan texts, the latter being written a half a millennium later, and the older ones "perhaps not" written by Zoroaster (48). The earliest extant copy of the Avesta is from 1288 C.E., so the dating of an original text is difficult. Iranians did not write their religious texts, and yet the *Avesta* makes reference to geographical places in Eastern Iran (De Jong 7183). If there was a historical Zoroaster, no one knows his birth or death dates, and even the founding date of Zoroastrianism as a religion is controversial. Afnan places Zoroaster in the 6th century B.C.E., and gives Media as his birthplace (16), but that is widely disputed. Jan Bremmer suggests that Zoroastrianism was only known with certainty as an established religion during the Sassanian Empire (3rd century to 7th century C.E.), which immediately predated the founding of Islam, and that the dating of the religion to 1000 B.C.E. is "uncertain" (47-48). And yet, we see writers from the 5th and 4th centuries B.C.E. referencing Zoroastrianism and its influence on Greek practices. The chronology of Zoroastrianism is difficult to untangle.

The *Avesta* only tells us the history of the Zoroastrian religion; it is not rich in mythology. The religion is dualistic; the mythology tells us that before the world was created, there was a pact between two gods, Ahura Mazda (also known as Ormazd), the Wise Lord, and Angra Mainyu (also known as Ahriman), the Evil Spirit. Ahura Mazda created the world, but Ahriman, who lived in darkness, was not aware of it. Once he became aware of Ahura Mazda and the world he created, he started a war with Ahura Mazda, which was then stopped by a pact sealed by Mithra, lord of contracts. The contract stated that they would wage war for 9,000 years in the limited space of creation. Humans were not created as either good or evil, but they were free to choose their side. The observant Zoroastrian sided with Ahura Mazda, and most rituals and practices were aimed at purification (De Jong 7184). Jan Zandee observed the relationship between Zoroastrian and Egyptian views of the afterlife, in particular the idea that death is a journey. The just and unjust follow roads and have to cross the Chinvat Bridge, which appears narrow as the edge of a knife to the unjust. (Zandee 25) "Sinners" who fall will land in *druj-demana*, the House of Lies, a place of punishment. It is interesting that the term "Chinvat" refers to "sifting, "which is reminiscent of the Dionysian liknon, an agricultural tool used for sifting corn from chaff. The liknon became a symbol in later Dionysian mysteries for purification. (Nilsson 22) It is also hard to avoid thinking of Matthew 3:12, "His winnowing fork is in his hand, and he will clear his threshing floor, gathering his wheat into the barn and burning up the chaff with unquenchable fire." ("Matthew" 266)

Our main sources on Zoroaster from Greece and Rome range from the 5th century B.C.E. to the 2nd century C.E. Most of these writers lived toward the end of the peak of Greek civilization, but they refer to earlier writings that are no longer extant. Mithraism, a religion contemporary with an influence on early Christianity, was a Zoroastrian mystery cult, though fraught with syncretism. Most of these references are fragmentary. Joseph Bidez and Franz Cumont's study of Zoroastrian texts places most of the Greek references in the category of "Pseudo-Zoroastre"; Pliny the Elder tells us that "Hermippus... de tota ea arte (magice) diligentissime scripsit et viciens centum milia versuum a Zoroastre condita, indicibus quoque voluminum eius positis, expanavit" (Bidez and Cumont 85-86).[19] Hermippus had created an entire catalog of these pseudo-Zoroastrian writings, attributing thousands of lines of verse to Zoroaster, but

> Il est donc infiniment probable que l'indication d'Hermippe ne se rapporte pas seulement a certains hymnes et codes sacres du mazdeisme, mais a toute la litterature que, des l'epoque hellenistique, on attribuait aux Mages et a leur maitre Zorastre, et qui avait probablement ete au moins partiellement, traduite en grec des le regne de Ptolemee Philadelphe"(Bidez and Cumont 88).[20]

Ptolemy Philadelphus was the son of Cleopatra, putting the Greek translations indexed by Hermippus near the beginning of the common era (36-29 B.C.E.), though undoubtedly some version of these had been in circulation throughout the Classical era.

---

[19] "Hermippus wrote carefully of the whole of this art (magic) [attributing it to Zoroaster] and putting together one hundred thousand lines from Zoroaster, with information that also explains his arrangement of the volumes." Translation and bracketed notes are mine.
[20] "It is now infinitely probable that Hermippe's indication [of one hundred thousand lines] was not only reporting certain hymns and sacred books of Mazdaism [Zoroastrianism], but of all the literature that, in the Hellenistic era, would have been attributed to the Magi and their master Zoroaster, and which probably had to be at least partially translated into Greek during the reign of Ptolemy Philadelphus." Translation and bracketed notes are mine.

Aside from mentioning Zoroaster as the prophet of the Persian religion, much of Greek belief about Zoroaster combines their own traditions with their fragmentary understanding of the Zoroastrian religion. Beck tells us:

Even if the Greeks had wished to reconstruct a historically accurate Zoroaster, the task would have been impossible. The distance in space, time, and language between Zoroaster and them was simply too great. Furthermore, the only possible intermediaries, Iranian magi, were themselves historically distanced from Zoroaster; and, at least after Alexander and the Greeks had humiliated their religion by bringing down their empire, they were not particularly interested in educating the Greeks about that religion or its founder. Culturally and politically, circumstances did not favor the easy communication of religion, as they did, for example, in Hellenistic Egypt. (Beck "Zoroaster")

Zoroastrian priests were referred to as Magi; in Greece, the term *magoi* was associated with the idea of magician. Thus, Zoroaster himself and the Magi became associated with the Greek *magoi* and *goes*, who practiced divination and magical works through astrology, herbal lore, and necromancy. Astrology is believed to be Chaldean in origin rather than Persian, but the two Eastern beliefs became conflated in Greek thought.

Scholars differ when it comes to the reception of magical practices from the East by the Greeks. We do not see reference to such practices in the early Archaic period, with the exception of Odysseus' *nekyia* in the *Odyssey*, and yet they likely existed in some form, just not in what we think of as "Greece." Bremmer notes: "It has been repeatedly observed that the digging of a pit with a sword, the sacrificing of a black sheep and the sprinkling of groats in the Odyssean ritual closely parallel Hittite purification rituals, in which deities of the underworld, not the dead, are summoned up. Here Oriental influence seems likely and was perhaps meant to contribute to the creation of a frightening atmosphere" (73). What does seem to be clear is that magic is a largely foreign practice that came into Greece from another country, and that it gained a broader reputation and wider practice through the Classical and Hellenistic eras, though mention of It falls off after Plato's time (*Laws* 2: 454-457) until the Roman era (Bremmer 74). Sorceresses like Medea and Circe were considered foreign (see previous chapter). Johnston suggests that the rise of the polis created a distancing from the dead, as burials were placed outside the city walls as early as the eighth and seventh centuries BCE. As noted earlier, this proximity tells us about the cultural response to death. Heroes were venerated collectively, as there was a move away from the local *oikos* to the broader *polis* influenced by its involvement with neighboring countries (Johnston 97-98). But as the Greeks distanced themselves from the dead in their larger society, the individual and his or her distinct personality became more important, especially as ideas about immortality of the soul and punishment after death became a more dominant part of Greek culture, and led to the popularity of the mystery religions (Johnston 98). This curious mixture of public and private changes in Greek culture were fertile ground for these new religious ideas.

We return to Zoroaster. The combination of Greek and Zoroastrian elements are most clearly seen in the Greek understanding of Ahura Mazda and Ahriman. The Greeks referred to both gods as *theoi*, rather than referring to the "l'esprit du Mal" as a *daimon* or spirit. The Greeks did not then associate the word δαίμων (*daimon*) with its later meaning, "demon". Like the gods, *daimons* could be good or evil. Socrates attributes his own philosophical reasoning and intuition to a *daimon* (*Dialogues* 1:356). But a *daimon* is not a god, and the Greeks saw Ahriman as another deity and made sacrifices to him if they wished to harm or curse another. This is something true Zoroastrians would never do; the faithful do not have dealings with Ahriman (Bidez and Cumont 61-62).

Later philosophical writings view the Zoroastrian dualism as "le Feu et l'Eau" [the Fire and the Water], and these were often identified with the marriage of Zeus and Hera. Plato's ideas about the natural world and the cosmos become intertwined with Zoroastrian beliefs, which maintained their influence in the writings of later Neoplatonists (Bidez and Cumont 73-74). Like many of the musings of the early philosophers, there was an attempt to marry the existing Greek traditions with these newer ideas.

Still, the influx of Persian ideas was not well-received in Athens, even though leaders such as Pericles were clearly influenced by them (Afnan 35-36). Afnan suggests that the Attic legal prosecution of "impiety" came from a desire to keep Persian beliefs from overtaking Greek culture, and even the trial of Socrates was part of this movement (24). Much of this had to do with the political hostility against Persia during the Achaemenid Empire period. There was a certain pride in Greek nationality, and they did not want to be taken over by foreign religion and culture, particularly not by their enemies at war.

There was another group that had a relationship to Zoroastrianism that would have an effect on afterlife beliefs in the later Roman period, and this group was the Jews. Bremmer has his doubts about Zoroastrian influence on the Jews, particularly in regard to the notion of resurrection, an idea frequently assumed to come from the Zoroastrians (47). Nonetheless, the Bible is clear in its accolades for a particular Persian of the 6th century: Cyrus II, or Cyrus the Great. The book of Ezra starts with a discussion of Cyrus, and

Yahweh is said to have "aroused the spirit" of the Persian conqueror (Ezra 1:1), allowing the Jews build their temple and maintain their own kingdom. Isaiah refers to him as Yahweh's "anointed ... whom he grasps by his right hand" (2 Isaiah 45:1), a phrasing usually reserved for Messiah figures. None of this proves that Cyrus influenced Jewish religion. However, his sympathy for the Jews seems to come from his admiration of their worship of Yahweh as the central god of their people. This is attributed to the assertion that Cyrus was a Zoroastrian, and his notion of worshipping one "good" god resonated with the Jewish people.

Though I had always assumed that Cyrus was a Zoroastrian, a review of primary sources made me question that idea. The *Cyrus Cylinder* suggests that Cyrus saw himself as chosen by the Babylonian god Marduk:

> I am Cyrus, king of the universe, the great king, the powerful king, king of Babylon, king of Sumer and Akkad, king of the four quarters of the world, son of Cambyses, the great king, king of the city of Anshan, grandson of Cyrus, the great king, ki[ng of the ci]ty of Anshan, descendant of Teispes, the great king, king of the city of Anshan, the perpetual seed of kingship, whose reign Bel (Marduk) and Nabu love, and with whose kingship, to their joy, they concern themselves. When I went as harbinger of peace i[nt]o Babylon I founded my sovereign residence within the palace amid celebration and rejoicing. Marduk, the great lord, bestowed on me as my destiny the great magnanimity of one who loves Babylon, and I every day sought him out in awe. (Finkel 5-6)

Within the *History of Persia*, Ctesias says Cyrus "had the god's assistance" (161), though he doesn't say which god. In his battle against Astyages, Cyrus says "So then, you didn't realize the power of the gods, Astyages, if you don't realize now that it was *they* who stirred the goatherds into performing these actions — which *we* will see through to the end" (167). Xenophon declares that Cyrus prayed to "ancestral Hestia, ancestral Zeus" (87). The rituals and beliefs attributed to Cyrus seem to relate to the old Babylonian gods or Greek equivalents, not to the Zoroastrian Ahura Mazda, if these sources are credible at all. There is more evidence for the Zoroastrianism of his successors:

> With Darius there is a wealth of monuments and inscriptions as evidence. Among the former the most striking from the religious point of view are his tomb-carvings. The tomb itself, cut high in the cliff of Naqš-e Rostam, kept the embalmed corpse even more sequestered from the good creations than the chamber-tomb of Cyrus. In the sculpture above the tomb's door Darius is shown standing in reverent attitude before a fire-holder of Pasargadae type, on which flames leap up.

Overhead is the figure in a winged circle, which here appears to have dual significance, a symbol of both the royal xvarənah and the sun; behind it is the Akkadian moon-symbol, a disk with crescent along its lower rim. In Zoroastrian orthopraxy prayers may be said before a terrestrial fire or facing sun or moon. Darius thus appears to have had himself portrayed at prayer according to the widest Zoroastrian prescriptions. (Boyce)

No such evidence exists from the reign of Cyrus II, though there are still scholars who look for indirect evidence of a Zoroastrian link. The Greek authors may be unreliable on this point, perhaps interpreting Babylonian gods in terms of their own pantheon. But whether Cyrus was a Zoroastrian or not, we can tell that Zoroastrianism did exist in the 6th century in the region generally known as Babylon. Darius and Cyrus were contemporaries, and Darius ruled in the early 6th century to the late 5th century. Even if the Jews were not influenced by Cyrus, they very likely would have been influenced by their neighbors. The Jewish religion was influenced by its neighbors for years; only during their years of captivity in Babylon did they start removing foreign influences.

We should look at Judaism in the 6th century for a moment. In a world dominated and influenced by Christianity, we tend to think the monotheism of the Jews made them unique from their Mesopotamian neighbors. This assertion has been thoroughly debunked.[21] According to Alberto Green, the name "Yahweh" is actually a verb, meaning "to be." If we consider the Biblical passage of Moses and the burning bush, we recall that Yahweh says, "I am who I am" or "I will be who I will be" (Exodus 3:14). When Yahweh becomes more than a verb, it is obvious that he functions as a creator—one who causes something "to be." Green notes that Yahweh has many features of the Canaanite god El, and in fact Yahweh is often referred to with the prefix "El" or sometimes as "El". For instance, in 2nd Isaiah 45, Yahweh says, "I am El, righteous and victorious; there is not another. Turn to me and be saved, all the ends of the earth! For I am El, and there is no other" (2 Isaiah 45:21-22).

Yahweh is also part of a council of gods, another carryover from neighboring religions. Psalm 82 is the most obvious example of this:

> God presides in the great assembly;
> he renders judgment among the "gods":
> "How long will you defend the unjust
> and show partiality to the wicked?

---

[21] For a study of the connection between Yahweh and the Canaanite gods El and Baal, see: Green, Alberto and Ravinell Whitney. *Storm god in the Ancient near East*. Winona Lake, IN, USA: Eisenbrauns, 2003.

Defend the weak and the fatherless;
uphold the cause of the poor and the oppressed.
Rescue the weak and the needy;
deliver them from the hand of the wicked.
"The 'gods' know nothing, they understand nothing.
They walk about in darkness;
all the foundations of the earth are shaken.
"I said, 'You are "gods";
you are all sons of the Most High.'
But you will die like mere mortals;
you will fall like every other ruler."
Rise up, O God, judge the earth,
for all the nations are your inheritance. ("Psalm")

This passage could account for the free reign that Yahweh gives Satan in the *Book of Job*; Satan is an adversarial role taken up by another divine being, though "Satan" often works in the service of Yahweh in the Old Testament, opposing those who attempt to go against his will. He is part of this "council" of "gods". But the Yahweh of *Job* is markedly different from the Yahweh of *Isaiah*. In *Job*, all the dead go to the same place: "I would be asleep and at rest with kings and rulers of the earth, who built for themselves places now lying in ruins, with princes who had gold, who filled their houses with silver" (3:14-15). Second Isaiah 45:17 says, "But Israel is saved by Yahweh with an eternal salvation; they shall not be ashamed or humiliated forever." We might assume this is a military or political "salvation," but this is not suggested by the word "eternal." There is no specific mention of going to "Heaven," but Yahweh is clearly involved in the fate of the soul in the latter verse.

Judaism is important as a forerunner to Christianity for the purposes of this study. Somehow they moved from a religion with a central tribal god (Yahweh), who was part of a heavenly court, to having only one God, who became capable of saving them from death, as implied by Second Isaiah 45:17, among other verses. It is not unreasonable to assume that the change came from outside influence, in spite of Deuteronomist efforts to purge foreign religious elements from Jewish practice. The difference in Babylon is that the now monotheistic Jews found religious ideas compatible with their own in Zoroastrianism.

What is the relationship of the Jews to the Greeks at this time? It is unclear exactly when Greeks and Jews came into contact with each other. Max Radin suggests that Jews were seen as Syrians by the Greeks, and that their first contact with the Greeks would have been military, as they served in the Persian armies (78). By 300 B.C.E., the Jews were "undeniably" known to the

Greeks; Herodotus referred to them as "the Syrians of Palestine" (80). An interesting quote is attributed to Theophrastus of Lesbos, the successor of Aristotle, by Porphyrius:

> As a matter of fact, if the Jews, those Syrians who still maintain the ancient form of animal sacrifice, were to urge us to adopt their method, we should probably find the practice repellent. Their system is the following: they do not eat of the sacrificial flesh, but burn all of it at night, after they have poured a great deal of honey and wine upon it. The sacrifice they seek to complete rather rapidly, so that the All-Seer may not become a witness of pollution. Throughout the entire time, inasmuch as they are philosophers by race, they discuss the nature of the Deity among themselves, and spend the night in observing the stars, looking up at them and invoking them as divine in their prayers. (Radin 82)

Radin scoffs at this interpretation of Jewish practice. However, the text presents two possibilities. First, Theophrastus may be confusing the Jews with their Babylonian neighbors, who certainly practiced astrology and observed the stars. The other possibility is that the Jews were doing just that—worshipping a celestial host. Deuteronomy 4:19 is a specific injunction against doing this exact thing:

> And lest thou lift up thine eyes unto heaven, and when thou seest the sun, and the moon, and the stars, even all the host of heaven, shouldst be driven to worship them, which the Lord thy God hath divided unto all nations under the whole heaven. ("Deuteronomy" 356)

At this time, there was upheaval in Jewish society; they venerated Cyrus II, but saw their lot as part of their disobedience to Yahweh. Simcha Paul Raphael indicates other archaic practices that survived among the Jews. The archaic Israelites kept and believed in something called *teraphim*, which roughly translates to household idols. Raphael writes:

There is certainly indication that the *teraphim* were actual images of the dead ancestors used as oracular devices when consulting the deceased. There is certainly indication that the *teraphim* were used for some sort of divinatory purposes. According to the medieval biblical commentator Nahmanides, the *teraphim* were used to gain knowledge of future events. This is inferred in both Judges 17:5 and Hosea 3:4, which mention the *teraphim* along with the ephod, a known ancient divinatory device ... While these activities and ritual objects were not sanctioned by the prophets, they persisted as cultic remnants of early Israelite religion. (50)

The role of kings among the Jews was also changing at this time. Peter Grey suggests that Deuteronomy 17:14-20 is not just an attack on foreign kings, but on the role of the kings of Judah:

> Their king is to be controlled by the priesthood. Along with this, many elements of temple practice are to be swept aside, from which they, as Levites, have been excluded. It was a definitive attack on the form of monarchy exemplified by Solomon and the royal cult of Jerusalem. When Deuteronomy 17:17 pronounces: neither shall he multiply wives to himself, that his heart turn not away, it can only have Solomon in mind. (Grey 61)

Crisis causes upheaval, and this is clear among the Jewish people. Their response to the anxiety of their situation was to blame it on insufficient worship of their main deity. It is notable that First and Second Isaiah were written about two hundred years apart; Second Isaiah is a direct product of the Babylonian captivity and the Deuteronomists, and would not have been written by the original prophet (Cogan 3508).

Reflections and Conclusions

Immortality and possibly salvation are common themes in both the religious and philosophical systems, but the relationship between these elements is not straightforward. We don't know when Zoroaster was alive, let alone if he was ever a real person. We don't know when Zoroastrianism began as a religion. From Hippolytus we get the idea that Zoroaster gave his teachings to Pythagoras, though this has been thoroughly debunked as folklore (Kingsley 245). The idea of an "Orphic" religion is controversial and difficult to define. We do know that Pythagoras influenced Plato, but everything attributed to Pythagoras is second-hand; we have no original writings. Persian influence on Greek and Jewish religion seems obvious, but our documentation raises more questions than answers.

If we look back at the early Archaic period, we recall a culture that does not believe in the immortality of the soul. The gods are neither good nor evil; the attitudes of the gods towards mortals are largely based on the mortals' actions. However, there is a prevailing faith in *dike*, divine justice. Odysseus avenges the wrongs done to him by killing all of his wife's suitors. The Greeks win the war with the Trojans, avenging the initial wrong done to Menelaus as explained in the *Iliad* and the various books of *Homerica*. Hesiod tells us in *Works and Days* that life is not fair, but there is an acceptance of life as it is, and a sense that humans ought to do their best to live in accordance with its vicissitudes (Hesiod 3-5).

Walter Burkert tells us "Injustice hurts; to punish makes happy" ("Plead-ing" 141). The Greeks may have accepted that life is short, but they also want-ed it to be fair. The *polis* offers more opportunities for its citizens; Maslow's hierarchy of needs tells us that when our basic needs are met, there is more time for what he calls self-actualization, true psychological human develop-ment (162). Society had certainly changed at the beginning of the Classical Greek period; cities were more diverse, and the benefits of the larger *polis* became more important than that of the tribal *oikos*. The larger the group, the more complicated the dynamics; while Greek citizens may have worried less about their neighbors stealing their land, there was more opportunity for greed and corruption to flourish. This did not go unnoticed by Greek philosophers and dramatists; not only was *dike* called into question, but the existence of the gods themselves:

Much more dangerous is the theory which derives religion from a con-scious and purposive lie. This was expounded in a drama attributed to either Euripides or Kritias. Once more the origin of culture forms the framework. In the beginning the life of man was unregulated and brutish; then men set up laws so that law should be a tyrant. Yet secret evil-doers remained un-punished. Then a clever man invented fear of the gods; he persuaded men that there was a *daimon* puffed up with imperishable life who hears and sees with his mind, and to whom nothing that anyone says, does, or thinks is unknown; as a dwelling place he allotted these gods the sphere from whence both terror and gain come to men, that is, the sky. (*Greek* 314-315)

The subject of atheism may have been broached by philosophers, but as we have seen, they largely considered themselves believers. The nature of the gods was called into question, but not their existence. Nonetheless, ques-tions were being asked for the first time in Greek literature that may or may not have been part of earlier Greek consciousness.

The 6th through 2nd centuries B.C.E. were times of major change and up-heaval for civilized Greece. Just as we have difficulty keeping up with tech-nological changes today, the rise of the ancient Greek *polis* would have ex-panded the rather narrow intellectual world of the *oikos* and the chieftain. While we see the development of Greek humanism and the celebration of human reason, we also see a rise in fear. It is not coincidental that ideas about death, the ultimate human unknown and therefore its greatest fear, would start to shift under such circumstances. When the beliefs a culture has taken for granted start to be questioned, and, perhaps, moved to the realm of su-perstition, they never entirely go away. There may also be a backlash against attempts to disenfranchise "traditional values." We must be careful, though, not to conflate our modern conflicts between secularism and fundamentalism with ancient Greek tradition; new ideas could gradually take hold because there was no dogmatic doctrine in Greek religious thinking. Much of the motivation for keeping new ideas out had more to do with cultural identity and political allegiance than with any kind of religious purity.

Why do some of these new ideas take hold and not others? On the subject of self-reflection and self-knowledge, Jung suggests someone who accesses the collective unconscious can exert great influence:

The effect on all individuals, which one would like to see realized, may not set in for hundreds of years, for the spiritual transformation of mankind follows the slow tread of the centuries and cannot be hurried or held up by any rational process or reflection, let alone brought to fruition in one generation. What does lie within our reach, however, is the change in individuals who have, or create for themselves, an opportunity to influence others of like mind. I do not mean by persuading or preaching—I am thinking, rather, of the well-known fact that anyone who has insight into his own actions, and has thus found access to the unconscious, involuntarily exercises an influence on his environment. (*Meaning* 303)

As mentioned earlier, one notable shift was towards *goetia*, the regular role of the necromancer in Greek life and affairs. Plato mentions them disparagingly in a dialogue about virtue and honesty (*Republic* 1: 132-135) and they are satirized in Aristophanes' play *The Frogs*. Many scholars treat the *goes* as a fringe element, but Johnston states that there is no reason to assume that their services were not welcome among the common people. The *goes* or *goete* is the magician who re-animates the dead or calls them to the gates of Hades in order to gain information about a current or future event. Herodotus mentions the Corinthian tyrant Periander, who sends henchmen to ask the *goete* where a certain object was located. The *goete* calls up the spirit of his dead wife Melissa, who refuses to tell him because she is "cold and naked"; the clothes buried with her were not burned properly. Periander responded by having all the women in Corinth come in their best clothes to the temple of Hera, where he ordered them to strip naked and burn their clothes to appease his dead wife. Only then would the dead woman tell him where to find the missing object. (Herodotus 3:112-113) Necromancy was accomplished in a number of ways, usually at some place designated as a gateway to the underworld. It is likely that the messages came to the *goete* in a sleep state after performing the required ritual.[22]

People turn to prophecy when there is anxiety about the future, just as they may turn to new prophets when their civilization and culture is in cri-

---

[22] For information about the necromantic rites of the Greeks and Romans, see: Ogden, Daniel. "Technology." *Greek and Roman Necromancy*. Princeton, NJ: Princeton UP, 2004. 161-216. Print.

sis. We do not know about the use of such practices in the Archaic period or before, but it is clear that they were popular in the Classical and Hellenistic eras and never really lost influence even when they were forced underground.

But on the other side of the equation are the philosophers; in spite of their opposition to what they considered superstitious magical practices, they were related to these Eastern ideas through the influence of Pythagorean, Orphic, and Zoroastrian thought. There was a tradition that claimed Pythagoras traveled to Media and was a student of Zoroaster, though there is no historical evidence for any such relationship. More than likely it was the Zoroastrian flavor of Pythagorean ideas that caused Greeks to connect the philosopher with the prophet.

Plato is said to have been influenced by both Zoroaster and Pythagoras, as well as some of the other early philosophers. Certain traditions also hold that Er in Plato's story from the *Republic* was actually Zoroaster (Beck). This is clearly folklore, but it demonstrates the similarity between the understanding of these ideas and Plato's ideas.

How do we begin to sort out this collection of influences and their meaning to our subject? There are two things we can say about Greek psychology at this time without controversy. First, we can see "foreign" influence on Greek religion, whether it comes from Persia, Egypt, or Thrace. Second, we see the rise of the *polis*, and the early formation of a city-state with a democratic governance structure. This was punctuated by frequent war, particularly by invaders from the East, leading to an ambivalent relationship with Eastern influence. The practice of necromancy appears in Greece during the late Archaic age, and Johnston notes that the Greeks "were particularly primed to accept such an idea because of various changes within their own culture" (115). This interest in communicating with the dead was part of a broader interest in life after death, including immortality and the idea of divine reward or punishment. The "bridge" figure here may be Dionysus. He is often portrayed as a foreign figure, but some of the earliest cult evidence for Dionysus comes from Athens (Guthrie and Chambers 46). So, he is both foreign and Greek. Dionysian rites in Greece are said to originate with Orpheus, who also has strong connections to Apollo. Pythagoras is also intimately connected to Apollo.

Nietzsche is instructive on the Apollo vs. Dionysus dynamic. On the subject of the "Apollonian" he says, "Apollo is at once the god of all plastic powers and the soothsaying god. He who is etymologically the 'lucent' one, the god of light, reigns also over the fair illusion of our inner world of fantasy" (21). He equates Apollo with the "perfecting" influence. As for Dionysus, he represents a "shattering of the *principium individuationis*," and the Dionysiac rapture's "closest analogy is furnished by physical intoxication. Dionysiac stirrings arise either through the influence of those narcotic potions of which all primitive races speak in their hymns, or through the powerful approach of spring, which penetrates with joy the whole frame of nature. So stirred, the individual forgets himself completely" (22).

What we see here is another metaphor for rational and irrational forces in the human psyche. The rational, Apollonian track that brings "light" to our lives represents the development of the individual. The Dionysian element brings us back to nature and to the collective. In this light, the Dionysus and Demeter mysteries come together—both represent a confronting of the collective.

Nietzsche continues his explanation of these opposite forces:

> What kept Greece safe was the proud, imposing image of Apollo, who in holding up the head of the Gorgon to those brutal and grotesque Dionysiac forces subdued them. Doric art has immortalized Apollo's majestic rejection of all license. But resistance became difficult, even impossible, as soon as similar urges began to break forth from the deepest substratum of Hellenism itself. Soon the function of the Delphic god developed into something quite different and much more limited: all he could hope to accomplish now was to wrest the destructive weapon, by a timely gesture of pacification, from his opponent's hand. (26)

The Gorgon image is interesting, as Medusa objectifies and turns to stone; it removes the dynamism and life from the Dionysiac impulse. Jungian psychology tells us that these influences do not go away; they simply recede from our consciousness, and hold more sway over us as an unconscious shadow force. "[R]ationalism and superstition are complementary. It is a psychological rule that the brighter the light, the blacker the shadow; in other words, the more rationalistic our conscious minds, the more alive becomes the spectral world of the unconscious" (Jung, *Foreword* 144).

So, the sixth century world is one in upheaval and leads to repression and rationalization as a means of dealing with major changes—the Dionysiac is transformed by the Apollonian in the "Orphic" way of thinking, and in the popular mystery rites influenced by this religious modification. The impulse towards magic and necromancy is another aspect of this; knowledge is power, and knowledge of the future and the unknown could provide a sense of security in the face of upheaval.

The notion of the immortal soul provides strength against the chthonic as well; we do not simply fade away helplessly when we die. This is another impulse of the rational, masculine mind, and it creates profound changes in the psyche:

What is most important is the transformation in the concept of the soul, *psyche*, which takes place in these circles. The doctrine of transmigration presupposes that in the living being, man as animal, there is an individual, constant something, an ego that preserves its identity by force of its own essence, independent of the body which passes away. Thus a new general concept of a living being is created, *empsychon*; 'a *psyche* within.' This *psyche* is obviously not the powerless, unconscious image of recollection in a gloomy Hades, as in Homer's Nekyia; it is not affected by death: the soul is immortal, *athanatos* ... The idea finally that the soul is some light, heavenly substance and that man's soul will therefore eventually ascend to heaven set the stage for a momentous synthesis of cosmology and salvation religion. (Burkert, *Greek* 300)

In this new view, human beings share in the divinity of the gods, and that is evidenced through human reason and consciousness. Bruce Lerro connects the changes in social structure to this change in thinking: "The lower castes 'do the doing.' The upper classes specialize in the consciousness phases of labor—they interpret needs, set goals about what will be produced, and then evaluate the process" (289). This is no doubt true in the early democratic societies as well, who divided themselves into citizens and slaves, and there were no doubt economic classes within this stratification.

In secondary magical practices of Bronze Age agricultural states, we begin to see a reorganization of the creation myths: not only do gods become more prominent than goddesses, but consciousness starts to become superior to and beyond matter. Just as the upper classes control society by thinking, so the deity is imagined to create and rule the world through consciousness without matter. (Lerro 289)

Is this the practical reason for the shift in thinking? It's possible, certainly as possible as other variables in the changing social structure of Western civilization. The important point is the separation of consciousness and matter. In Zoroastrianism the separation is clear; Ahura Mazda is a celestial god of light; Ahriman is a god of darkness and the depths. Orphism takes the foreign rites of Dionysus and makes them more "Apollonian" in nature, making them more orderly for the civilized Greek. The philosophers look at the gods ethically, and in their attempts at natural philosophy, exalt the celestial over the material. This way of thinking considers humans as individuals, and as separate from nature. Our inner immortal souls and our reason give us greater status.

Before we leave this chapter we should consider Jung once again, and the idea of the earth and the chthonic as feminine. Jung characterizes the libido as drive and desire, just as Freud did. The libido can move from rational masculine consciousness to the feminine unconscious:

When the libido leaves the bright upper world, whether from choice, or from inertia, or from fate, it sinks back into its own depths into the source from which it originally flowed, and returns to the point of cleavage, the navel, where it first entered the body. This point of cleavage is called the mother, because from her the current of life reached us. Whenever some great work is to be accomplished, before which a man recoils, doubtful of his strength, the libido streams back to the fountainhead—and that is the dangerous moment when the issue hangs between annihilation and new life. For if the libido gets stuck in the wonderland of this inner world, then for the upper world man is nothing but a shadow, he is already moribund or at least seriously ill. But if the libido manages to tear itself loose and force its way up again, something like a miracle happens: the journey to the underworld was a plunge into the fountain of youth, and the libido, apparently dead, wakes to renewed fruitfulness. (Jung, *Battle* 293)

We can equate this with the impulse towards mystery rituals and necromancy; there is a need to penetrate the unconscious, to make a heroic journey to arrive safely on the other side. We also saw such rituals in the first chapter, especially with the rites of passage of girls and boys, and men and women. The rationalization of the psyche and the gods is a different way of approaching the problem of the liminal. Rationality is the bridge to individuality; we learn to separate ourselves from our family and our surroundings to identify who we are and what we want to be in the world. It represents a necessary component of human psychological development. However, at some point the rational human needs to reintegrate the irrational material of his or her life into consciousness. The Greeks haven't entirely discounted these natural, chaotic and irrational forces, but we now see a value judgment in their negotiation. These changes in thinking about life after death among the Greeks and the Jews would set the stage for a further splitting of consciousness and devaluing of the feminine in the Roman Empire period.

Works Cited: Chapter 3

Afnán, Ruhi Muhsen. *Zoroaster's Influence on Greek Thought*. Philosophical Library, 1965.

Anchor Bible: Job. Translated by Marvin H. Pope. Doubleday, 1965.

Anchor Bible: Second Isaiah. Translated by John Mackenzie. Doubleday, 1968.

Aristophanes. *The Peace ; The Birds ; The Frogs*. Translated by Benjamin Bickley Rogers. Harvard UP, 1924.

Beck, Roger. "Zoroaster v. as Perceived by the Greeks." *Encyclopædia Iranica*. 20 July 2002.

Benardete, Seth. "The Persians." *The Complete Greek Tragedies: Aeschylus*. By Aeschylus. Edited by Richmond Alexander Lattimore and David Grene. U of Chicago, 1969, pp. 216-259.

Betegh, Gábor. *The Derveni Papyrus: Cosmology, Theology, and Interpretation*. Cambridge UP, 2004.

Bidez, Joseph, and Franz Cumont. *Les Mages Hellénisés Zoroastre, Ostanès Et Hystaspe D'après La Tradition Grecque*. Les Belles Lettres, 1973.

Boyce, Mary. "Achaemenid Religion." *Encyclopædia Iranica*. Columbia University Press, n.d. Web. 31 Jan. 2016.

Burkert, Walter. *Greek Religion*. Cambridge, MA: Harvard UP, 1985. Print.

Burkert, Walter. "Pleading for Hell: Postulates, Fantasies, and the Senselessness of Punishment." *Numen*, vol. 56, no. 2/3, 2009, pp. 141-60.

Burkert, Walter. *The Orientalizing Revolution: Near Eastern Influence on Greek Culture in the Early Archaic Age*. Harvard UP, 1992.

Bremmer, Jan N. *The Rise and Fall of the Afterlife*. Routledge, 2002.

Cogan, Mordechai. "Isaiah." *Encyclopedia of Ancient History*. Blackwell, 2013, pp. 3508.

Ctesias. *Ctesias' History of Persia: Tales of the Orient*. Translated by Lloyd Llewellyn-Jones and James Robson. Routledge, 2010.

De Jong, Albert. "Zoroastrianism." *Encyclopedia of Ancient History*. Blackwell, 2013, pp. 7183- 7185.

"Deuteronomy." *The Interpreter's Bible: The Holy Scriptures in the King James and Revised Standard Versions with General Articles and Introduction, Exegesis, Exposition for Each Book of the Bible*. Edited by George Arthur Buttrick. Vol. 2. Abingdon, 1955.

Diodorus Siculus. *Diodorus of Sicily: in 12 Volumes*. Translated by Charles M. Oldfather, vol. 1, London, Heinemann, 1968.

Edmonds, Radcliffe G. *Redefining Ancient Orphism: A Study in Greek Religion*. Cambridge UP, 2013.

Empedokles. "From Chapter V., Empedokles of Akragas." *John Burnet, Early Greek Philosophy*. Translated by John Burnet. Classic Persuasion, n.d..

Finkel, Irving, ed. *Cyrus Cylinder: The Great Persian Edict from Babylon*. I.B. Tauris, 2013, pp. 5-6.

Goodrick-Clarke, Nicholas. *The Western Esoteric Traditions: A Historical Introduction*. Oxford UP, 2008.

Graf, Fritz and Sarah Iles Johnston. *Ritual Texts for the Afterlife : Orpheus and the Bacchic Gold Tablets*. Routledge, 2007.

Green, Alberto and Ravinell Whitney. *Storm God in the Ancient Near East*. Eisenbrauns, 2003.

Grey, Peter. *Lucifer: Princeps*. Scarlet Imprint, 2015.

Guthrie, Kenneth Sylvan, and David R. Fideler, editors. *The Pythagorean Sourcebook and Library: An Anthology of Ancient Writings Which Relate to Pythagoras and Pythagorean Philosophy*. Phanes, 1987.

Guthrie, William, and Keith Chambers. *Orpheus and Greek Religion: A Study of the Orphic Movement*. Princeton UP, 1993.

Herodotus. *Herodotus*. Trans. A. D. Godley. Vol. 1 and Vol. 3. Harvard UP, 1971.

Hesiod, and Homer. *Hesiod, the Homeric Hymns, and Homerica*. Trans. Hugh G. EvelynWhite. Cambridge, MA: Harvard University Press, 1964. Print.

Horace. *The Odes of Horace*. Trans. W. E. Gladstone. C. Scribner's Sons, 1894.

Johnston, Sarah Iles. *Restless Dead: Encounters Between the Living and the Dead in Ancient Greece*. University of California, 1999.

Jung, C.G. *Analytical Psychology: Notes of the Seminar Given in 1925*. Princeton University Press, 1989.

Jung, Carl G. "The Archetypes and the Collective Unconscious." *Collected Works*. Translated by R. F. C. Hull. Vol. 9.1. Pantheon, 1959.

Jung, C. G. "Battle for Deliverance from the Mother." *Collected Works*. Translated by R. F.C. Hull. Vol. 5. Pantheon, 1956, pp. 274-305.

Jung, Carl G. "Foreword to Moser: 'Spuk: Irrglaube Oder Wahrglaube?'."Translated by R.F.C Hull. *Psychology and the Occult*. Princeton UP, 1977.

Jung, C. G. "Meaning of Self-knowledge." *Collected Works*. Translated by R. F.C. Hull. Vol. 10. Pantheon, 1964, pp. 302-05.

Jung, C.G. "Phenomenology of the Spirit in Fairytales." *Collected Works*. Translated by R. F. C. Hull. Vol. 9i. Pantheon, 1959.

Jung, C.G. "Psychological Types." *Collected Works*. Revision by R.F.C. Hull of the translation by H.G. Baynes. Vol. 6. Princeton University Press, 1971.

Kingsley, Peter. "The Greek Origin of the Sixth-Century Dating of Zoroaster." *Bulletin of the School of Oriental and African Studies* 53.02 (1990): 245-65. *JSTOR*. Web. 11 Jan. 2016.

Laertius, Diogenes. *Lives of the Eminent Philosophers.* Translated by Robert Drew Hicks. Vol. 2. Harvard UP, 1950.

Lerro, Bruce. *From Earth Spirits to Sky Gods: The Socioecological Origins of Monotheism, Individualism, and Hyperabstract Reasoning from the Stone Age to the Axial Iron Age.* Lexington, 2000.

Maslow, Abraham H. *Motivation and Personality.* Harper & Row, 1970.

"Matthew." *The Interpreter's Bible: The Holy Scriptures in the King James and Revised Standard Versions with General Articles and Introduction, Exegesis, Exposition for Each Book of the Bible.* Edited by George Arthur Buttrick. Vol. 7. Abingdon, 1951.

Nietzsche, Friedrich Wilhelm. *The Birth of Tragedy and the Genealogy of Morals.* Translated by Francis Golffing, Doubleday, 1956.

Nilsson, Martin P. *The Dionysiac Mysteries of the Hellenistic and Roman Age.* New York, Arno Press, 1975.

Ogden, Daniel. "Technology." *Greek and Roman Necromancy.* Princeton UP, 2004, pp. 161-216.

Plato. *Cratylus, Parmenides, Greater Hippias, Lesser Hippias.* Translated by Harold North Fowler. Harvard UP, 1939.

Plato. *The Dialogues of Plato: Translated into English with Analyses and Introductions.* Translated by Benjamin Jowett, Vol. 1, Clarendon Press, 1953.

Plato. *Phaedo.* Translated by R. Hackforth, Cambridge: UP, 1955.

Plato. *The Republic.* Translated by Paul Shorey, Vol. 1, William Heinemann, 1956.

Plato. *The Republic.* Translated by Paul Shorey, Vol. 2, William Heinemann, 1956.

Plutarch. "Solon." *Internet Classics Archive.* N.p., n.d. Web. 27 Jan. 2016.

"Psalm 82 New International Version." *Psalm 82 NIV.* Biblica, 2011. Web. 31 Jan. 2016.

Radin, Max. *The Jews among the Greeks and Romans.* Jewish Publication Society of America, 1915.

Raphael, Simcha Paull. *Jewish Views of the Afterlife.* 2nd ed. Rowman & Littlefield, 2009.

Russell, Jeffrey Burton. *The Devil: Perceptions of Evil from Antiquity to Primitive Christianity.* Cornell UP, 1977.

West, Martin L. *Early Greek Philosophy and the Orient*. Oxford University Press, 1971.

Xenophanes. "Xenophanes: Fragments and Commentary." *The Eleatic School*. Translated by Arthur Fairbanks, Hanover Historical Texts Project, n.d.

Xenophon. *Cyropaedia*. Translated by Walter Miller, Vol. 1, Harvard UP, 1914.

CHAPTER 4: THE MOVEMENT WEST: THE RISE OF ROME

Translatio studii is a term often used to describe the transfer of knowledge from East to West. Gem Wheeler defines it succinctly as "the art of rewriting" (Wheeler), which our most ancient Near Eastern epics from the Sumerians and Babylonians exemplify. In the early Iron Age, the Greeks provide us with poetry, drama and mythological stories. Farther to the West, Italy and its most powerful city, Rome, initiated and developed formal literature. Romans admired the Greeks for their drama and poetry and sought to emulate the best writers, so in the last century before the Common Era, Virgil wrote the *Aeneid*, an epic emulating Homer's *Iliad* and *Odyssey* in many ways. The local Roman gods became associated with the Greek myths, and Roman equivalents to the Olympian pantheon and other deities appear in the writings of Ovid, Apuleius, Apollonius of Rhodes, and many other Roman writers. Knowledge was indeed moving from East to West, but rewriting was occurring as well, as stories were adapted to Roman values and beliefs. Because the dominant civilizations and their rulers determine the norms of society, this chapter traces the beliefs of the Romans developed and merged with other Near Eastern cultures, further changing religious and philosophical ideas in the Western world.

Background

Some background on Roman history clarifies any discussion of Roman religion. There are no primary sources from the first four centuries of Roman history, since the oldest writings are from the 2nd century B.C.E. (Dumézil

10). Livy's *Annals* is the main source for historic tales and stories about the founding of Rome. Livy's account tells us that Rome was founded in 753 B.C.E. by Romulus, a son of the god Mars and a Vestal Virgin, and a descendant of Aeneas. The first Roman kingdom was said to be a co-rule with the Sabine king Titus Tatius and Romulus. In the legend, the Latin and Sabine tribes were at war, but the Sabine women sought an end to the conflict by intermarrying with the Latin tribes and encouraging their king to rule harmoniously with Romulus, thus beginning the era of monarchy in Rome, which lasted until 509 B.C.E.

In spite of the initial Latin/Sabine rule, most of the Roman kings came from Etruria in the North, and hence affirming the association between the Romans and the Etruscans. However, the power of the Etruscans waned, the last king, Tarquinius Superbus, was deposed by Lucius Junius Brutus, and a government by elected assembly was established. This heralded the beginning of the Roman Republic and enabled the beginning of Rome's influence in the world. By the third century, Rome, along with Carthage, was a major Mediterranean power. Initially allies, the Romans and Carthaginians became enemies after the First Punic War in 264 BCE. Rome had conquered the Greek territories of Southern Italy, and Carthage's recent occupations in Messana and Syracuse were too close for Roman comfort, so Rome then became involved with three Punic Wars, lasting until 146 BCE, when they finally destroyed Carthage and assumed dominance in the Western World.

While Rome was powerful outside its walls, it began to fall apart internally, and civil wars ravaged the Republic until Octavian was declared emperor in 27 B.C.E (Wells). Octavian was part of what was known as the Second Triumvirate ruling Rome, consisting of himself, Antony, and Lepidus. However, Lepidus stepped down in 31 B.C.E., and Octavian was at war with Antony, who ruled Egypt with Cleopatra. Octavian defeated Antony, Cleopatra committed suicide, and Egypt now became part of Rome. The establishment of Octavian as emperor with the title Caesar Augustus marked the end of civil war, but also the beginning of the Roman Empire. The Roman citizens, weary of war, were grateful for a unifying leader and the resulting peace that allowed Virgil to compose the *Aeneid*, an epic of the Trojan hero Aeneas as a forefather to Rome, with his mother Venus as a grandmother goddess to the city. Just as Greek forays into Persia and constant warfare led to changes in Greek thinking about life after death and the gods, the constant upheavals in the lives of Roman citizens and the introduction of new ideas from other lands led to a similar change in Roman thinking. What stands out is the very "masculine" nature of Roman thought and belief, and the corresponding attempts to find a "feminine" balance in foreign mystery cults and religions. But just as the Roman Republic fell apart through civil wars, an increasing separation between the "masculine" and "feminine" in Roman consciousness occurred during the pre-Empire period that would be more pronounced in the Common Era. We will look at these factors as they pertain to religious practices, beliefs, and the Latin language.

Roman Language

On the subject of "masculine" and "feminine," Anthony Corbeill noted a trend in the Latin language away from neuter words to deliberate distinctions between masculine and feminine, even going as far as "masculinizing" feminine words and vice versa, when the writer felt it was appropriate. This tendency does not appear in ancient Greek writing. Latin poets might feminize or masculinize a word incorrectly either to match the original Greek gender or to make the word match its mythic or folkloric association (71). The Latin term *uenus* (or *venus*, meaning grace or favor) was originally neuter, but the Romans changed it to a feminine, and it became the name of the mother goddess also associated with love and beauty. Livy (8.9.6) refers to *ueniam'fero* (I ask for a favor, or grace). Dumézil sees this as a "personifying" effort on the part of ancient Romans, a way of making the impersonal forces of nature into something relatable (91-92).

The ancient Roman grammarians referred to language as having gender (*sexus*), number and case (Varro 407), but the word *sexus* is later replaced by *genus* (category or type) as the default term for gender. Nonetheless, Corbeill tells us, "*sexus* does make its appearance in these philological texts when the writers choose to echo a preexistent tradition—one that seemingly dates back to Varro—in affirming that grammatical gender and biological sex are to be closely identified" (Corbeill 5).

Corbeill suggests that there are "cognitive reasons" for dividing words into gendered categories, and these persist to this day in most modern languages. What is the reason? Corbeill responds:

> I have no doubt that, by the classical period, Latin scholars and speakers both sensed and exploited a relationship between linguistic gender and physical sex. Perhaps seduced by the need to see a more-than-human logic at work in the creation of their language, they used grammatical gender to create a world that is divided, like language, into opposing categories of male (masculine) and female (feminine). (4).

Does this really have an effect on our thought processes? Language is symbolic and has associated ideas, just as images and myths do. Corbeill cites recent research on gender in language:

A recent survey of laboratory research on grammatical gender shows that the mere creation of categories causes human subjects to create meaningful similarities among the members of each category. For example, when learning that an unfamiliar word for "violin" was feminine, English speakers chose as descriptors of the word adjectives such as "beautiful," "curvy," and "elegant"; when told that the unfamiliar word was masculine, subjects described the object as "difficult," "impressive," and "noisy." Experiments such as this can show how the grammatical categories of "masculine" and "feminine" can help reinforce a normative dichotomy of "masculine" and "feminine" in society at large. (4-5)

This study examines masculine and feminine language constructs that are relevant to the underworld and the soul; therefore, *genius* is the word we think of that is closest to the idea of "soul" for the ancient Romans, though it was not until much later that the *genius* was thought to have any connection to survival after death. The term relates to the forehead, interestingly enough (Dumézil 359). While I don't know if this implies a connection between the soul and the head, it's an interesting observation in light of the legal/rational tone of Roman belief. *Genius* could represent an individual soul, but could be a collective term as well, as in *genis Urbis Romae* [soul of the city of Rome], or *genius populi Romani* [the soul of the Roman people] (Dumézil 362). The idea of the *genius* as the soul of a man had no importance until the time when Greek thought influenced Rome and the philosophers gained influence (Dumézil 362).

Later, the *genius* ended up with a female counterpart, the *juno*. Juno also became the name of Jupiter's wife, and a counterpart to Hera in Roman myth. This might imply Juno's origins as a kind of numinous feminine spirit or earth mother. The collective name for the dead, *di Manes*, was originally masculine, but later appeared in Latin literature as feminine (Corbeill 126). The word *Dis*, the term for the underworld and its ruler comparable to Hades, is masculine, though it also has connotations of general divinity, and as an adjective suggests wealth. Other terms associated with the underworld, including *Orcus* and *Infernus*, are also masculine. In these cases, we do not see examples of the terms being used in other genders. In any event, the terms for the underworld seem to mirror the Greek genders, with the later exceptions being feminized. In ancient Greece, the earth is feminine, but the underworld is named for a masculine deity. However, in mystery rites the focus tends to be on Persephone, the wife of Hades (Proserpina in the Roman). The masculine deity Hades/Pluto plays a passive role, which is unusual—we tend to associate passivity with the feminine. There is no definitive way to interpret these associations; however, given the liminal nature of the under-world, these role reversals may not be so strange.

In a discussion of voice, Varro puts the world into gendered categories:

> In his discussion of sky and earth, he observes that since the sky acts (*faciat*), it possesses a masculine force, whereas the acted-upon earth (*patiatur*) necessarily possesses feminine characteristics. According to Augustine, our source for this statement, Varro continues from this premise to conjecture that all male divinities arise from the sky and all female from the earth—as a result, the entire Roman pantheon divides into an active, male half and a passive, female half. (Corbeill 120)

We may remember at this point the quote from Jungian writer Erich Neumann, in his study of the myth of Amor and Psyche:

> In the history of the development of the conscious mind, for reasons which we cannot pursue here, the archetype of the Masculine Heaven is connected positively with the conscious mind, and the collective powers that threaten and devour the conscious mind both from without and within, are regarded as Feminine. (172)

This brings us back to the idea of Roman "practicality" and "rationality." The rational mind puts things into categories; it creates rules, it organizes, it sets boundaries. This tendency grew as Rome became a center of civilization, a trend we also noted in the ancient Greek kingdoms, in the movement from *oikos* to *polis*. Varro lived from 116-27 BCE, which is the late Republic period, and after the Punic Wars. Varro's etymologies are considered questionable by linguists (Dumézil 97), but at least they tell us the grammatical conceptions of his time. In our exploration of psychological influences, this need to split language into further gendered categories is at least an important observation with regard to changing thoughts about the gods, the soul, and death in the Roman world.

Religion

Ancient Roman religion was devoid of mythology. Like many tribal religions, there was the idea of *numen*, which is similar to the concept of *mana*. It is not the name of a god, but represents the "numinous" and terrifying power of the deity. *Numen*, a neuter word, literally means "to nod," and certain omens in the environment suggested the approval or disapproval of the gods (Dumézil 20). The reliance on divination through augury and haruspicy was shared by the Romans and the Etruscans, including Cacu and Umaeale, famous Etruscan diviners. Umaeale played the lyre, and on an Etruscan bronze mirror he is shown translating utterances from a severed head, which is an obvious connection to Orpheus. At the end of the period of Roman kings, Tarquinius Superbus purchased the Sybilline Books, a collection of oracles written in Greek that were said to vouchsafe the future of Rome. These books were handled by two patricians in the Roman government, and kept in a vault in the temple of Jupiter. Like the Greeks with the oracle of Apollo, the Romans tended to consult these books when there was a crisis or a bad omen. The books were burned in the 4th century C.E. by the Roman army general Stilicho, who felt the books were being used against him (De Grummond). The *Aeneid* is also replete with references to omens, dreams, and oracles; Aeneas is the son of Venus (Aphrodite), and has a distinctly "feminine" quality compared to warriors like the Telemonian Ajax in the *Iliad*. He is not all brute force; he is about receptivity, about community, and creating peace and stability. He relies heavily on his intuition and the utterances of the gods.

Roman gods were very much associated with place; divinities belonged to a particular well or grove or hill. In the *Aeneid*, the Arcadian king Evander tells Aeneas, "Some god ... it is not sure what god, lives in this grove, this hilltop thick with leaves" (Virgil 241). This is typical of the archaic worship of the *numen*. Gods were associated with rivers, springs, and wooded groves (Bailey 42-43). There were multiple "triads" of deities whose associations with each are not always clear. The original "Archaic Triad" was Jupiter, Mars, and Quirinus; later, the Capitoline Triad would be celebrated as Jupiter, Juno, and Minerva. Dumézil theorizes that these associations had to do with the functions of Roman life; Jupiter with physical power, Mars with bravery, and Quirinus with fertility and prosperity (160). He sees a relationship between this archaic Triad and the triads of other Indo-European myth systems, such as the Norse (Odin, Thor, Freya) and the Vedic (Mitra-Varuna, Indra, Nasatya).[23] How this translates into the more well-known Capitoline Triad may be debatable; Jupiter may retain his worldly power, Juno would take over Quirinus' role as guarantor of fertility and prosperity, and Minerva could replace Mars as representing bravery. The latter would make sense once Mars became associated with the Greek Ares, a god of brute force in warfare. Minerva's counterpart, Athena, was a better warrior, as she balanced strategy and force, which is essential for a successful military.

[23] For more information on the Indo-European link, see Dumézil, Georges. *Archaic Roman Religion with an Appendix on the Religion of the Etruscans*. Vol. 1. Chicago: U of Chicago, 1970. Print: 147-175.

Even before the arrival of the Greeks, Roman religion was very "masculine" in nature. It centered on the correct performance of rituals, which were more important that the devotion or piety of prayers. The gods served practical functions, and the sets of rules for the various *flaminis* (priests) of the gods were a forerunner to what we think of as the "legal" nature of Roman society and religion. This is an important tendency to note, as it is a likely influence on the development of Western religion once the Romans were in contact with the Greeks, the Egyptians, and various groups from Asia Minor, including the Persians.

Paradoxically, this very "masculine" society provided more freedom and opportunity for women than the republican society of ancient Athens. Livy's *Annals* place women and their role in the family in a crucial spot, reminiscent of the importance of *oikos* in early Greek tribal society. In the mythical founding of Rome, Romulus' new city might never have developed because there are few women, and no children are being born. Their Sabine neighbors take matters into their hands, and the Sabine women go to Rome to marry the men. The Sabine men think there has been foul play and wish to go to war with Rome; yet the women tell them they have gone of their own free will, and need both their Roman husbands and Sabine families. To quote Dio Cassius:

> Hersilia [a Sabine woman] and the rest of the women of her kin, on discovering them [Romans and Sabines] drawn up in opposing ranks, ran down from the Palatine with their children—for some children had already been born,—and rushing suddenly into the space between the armies said and did many things to arouse pity. Looking now at the one side and now at the other they cried: 'Why do you do this, fathers? Why do you do it, husbands? When will you cease fighting? When will you cease hating each other? Make peace with your sons-in-law! Make peace with your fathers-in-law! For Pan's sake spare your children! For Quirinus' sake spare your grandchildren!'" (19)

The women urge the men to kill the children "whom you hate," as these are the children of men on both sides of the war. The actions and words of the women caused the men to weep, and they "desisted from battle and came together" (19).

This brings about a truce, and a striking result: "What is particularly interesting about this story is the way in which it provides an etiology and rationalization for Roman imperial expansion by 'domesticating' it: by seizing and marrying the Sabine women, the Romans are able not only to ensure their city's continued survival into the next generation but also to incorporate the rest of their families into the Roman state" (Milnor 115-116). In this way, the conquered cities become part of the Roman *domus*, or collective "household." Roman domestic life was very much separate from political life; however, women frequently did get involved in dealing with politicians, and this was not frowned upon if the woman could do this and maintain her domestic duties. Women seemed to play prominent roles in times of crisis for the Republic. Cicero appealed to a certain woman called Caerellia for money, and spoke admiringly of Caecilia Metilla, "who assisted the poverty-stricken Sextus Roscius of Ameria with both her social contacts and money" (Milnor 120). There is also evidence that women worked as doctors, midwives, and tavern keepers, and owned cook shops and market stalls (Milnor 121). Whatever role they played, their status depended on the dignity of their dealings with men. Prostitutes were of course degraded and seen as an evil, as were women who served men in taverns or held other menial jobs. Money and adherence to normative sexual/gender roles was what determined the status of a woman. This influence of women extended to the early days of the Christian church. It is interesting that Rome kept foreign influences at bay for a long time, at least until the period of Empire. This "domestic" Rome was maintained without much outside influence for a while. As we saw with the Greeks, the more diverse their major cities became, the harder it became to maintain this "family" view of the community.

Ancient Roman religion was very much like the archaic Greek religion when it came to ideas about life after death. The Romans made reference to *di manes*, which translates to "kindly ones." It is a collective term for the spirits of the dead, who seemed to exist as a kind of shadowy cluster rather than having any individual identity. It is interesting to note that the Romans chose a term equivalent to the Greek *Eumenides*, the title of Aeschylus' last play in the *Oresteia*. *Eumenides* is a term used for the Furies, and it is a euphemistic term used by Athena to placate them when Orestes is judged innocent by the jury. Indeed, as Johnston tells us, the Furies became known as the *Semnai Theai* (good goddesses) after this mythical event.

Even if the Erinyes had a beneficent alter ego in a cult who was approached by worshippers under a title expressing that beneficence in the hope that she would display it, or else was approached under no name at all—anonymity is another way of avoiding the pronouncement of ill-favored names that are out of place where favors are sought from a divinity. (269)

Just as the term "kindly ones" is meant to placate the angry Furies, calling the dead "kindly ones" demonstrates a fear of the dead. There was another term for the dead, *larvae*, or "ghosts," which has a "hostile connotation" (Bailey 39). There were two festivals of the dead in ancient Rome, the *Parentalia* in February, and the *Lemuria* in May. The former celebration was an honoring of the dead at their tombs. The Romans believed that whatever remained of the spirit of their loved ones existed in the tomb, which led to a place under the earth. Like the ancient Greeks, they believed the dead required sustenance, so food and libations were brought to family tombs on this day. *Lemuria* is a very different kind of festival. Like Halloween, it was a day when the dead could communicate with the living, and they came up through a *mundus*, which was a trench in the earth. The *Lemuria* was considered highly inauspicious, but was observed as a *dies religiosi*. No one went out on that day, no temple sacrifices were made, no business was conducted, and certainly, no one was married on that day. There were folkloric charms and spells to keep the dead ancestors from coming into the house, as there was a fear that this could happen:

> The rite-remembering, ghost-abhorring son arises gently, and no shoes put on. Then points with his closed fingers and his thumb put in the midst, lest ghosts near him should come. Then in spring-water he his hands doth cleanse, and first doth roll about his mouth blue beans, then o'er his shoulder throws them down; says he 'These beans I throw my house and self to free.' Nine times 'tis said. The ghost doth trace his track and picks them up, if that he looks not back. Again he washes; then a basin beats; and so the spirits to leave his house entreats. Then nine times crying, 'Kindred ghosts, begone,' he looketh back, and all is purely done. (Ovid 125)

The *larvae* were unpleasant spirits who tormented the living. In spite of the machinations of the *Parentalia*, the Romans were not devotedly worshiping their ancestors; they were appeasing them to keep them away from the living. Funerals were rites of purification; the dead person was seen as a pollution, and the tending of the tombs was mainly a ruse to keep the dead from getting angry and tormenting their surviving relatives. None of this implied immortality of the soul, or even punishment after death. While death was not a pleasant state, the Romans were like the Greeks in viewing it as something inevitable.

There are ancient Etruscan tombs that have elaborate and horrific wall paintings detailing an underworld that is likely influenced by the Greeks. Archaeologists have uncovered many examples, particularly from Tarquinii, and the Tomb of the Cardinal is a striking example:

Death is the common theme; but we see it illustrated, or rather hinted at, in different ways. The demons of the Underworld are active everywhere to guide the dead on their last journey. Sometimes they stand quietly waiting, or take a menacing attitude. Sometimes they themselves lead the defunct away; occasionally they use violence, but they also kindly assist the aged and entice the infant. The journey is performed on foot, on horseback, or in carriage. The scenes are dexterously varied, and the entire frieze is divided into sections by gates, effective caesuras in the artist's long poem of death. It is the gate through which no mortals return. (Riis 115-116)

Death was portrayed as a scary, demonic looking creature called Charun, not to be confused with the Greek underworld ferryman Charon. He was accompanied by the Furies and other demons, and together they took the dead person on their journey to the underworld. (Dumézil 694) However, the underworld itself was not a horrific place; there are images of feasting and games in a place that bears some resemblance to the Elysian Fields. The only horrible part was the actual transition. The Etruscan belief demonstrates a variation of the archaic view of death: it was inevitable and scary, but like many transitions in life, things are better once the transition has occurred.

The Second Punic War and Outside Influence

The Etruscans may have been the original influence on Roman religion, but they were not the only ones. Rome grew in power and influence as their armies expanded farther into Italy, where they learned the customs and practices of other peoples, particularly the Greeks. The Greeks were allies of Rome in the First Macedonian War, which was partially contemporary with Rome's battle against Carthage. The result of all the warfare of this period was Roman domination of the former Macedonian Empire. The Romans were impressed by Greek culture, and initially they were appreciative of Greek poetry and drama. However, Greek religious ideas came into Rome and provided a mythology for existing figures. Dionysus of Halicarnassus says that "Romulus copied the best customs in use among the Greeks, but he knew how to limit his borrowing from them" (qtd. in Dumézil 49). During the Republican period in particular we see the government attempting to reign in foreign influence. It was not only Greek religious ideas, including Orphism, but the writings of the philosophers, and "Eastern" ideas including astrology and the first introduction to Judaism. There was a famous episode in 186 BCE when the Roman Senate banished philosophers, astrologers, and Jews from the country. We will discuss this in detail in a later section in this chapter. Nonetheless, Rome's old pastoral, localized religion was changing in reference to outside influences that are natural when a region expands its horizons through trade or conquest. We will now examine the factors that put Roman religious belief on a similar track to the changes that occurred in Greek society before Roman domination.

Philosophy

The previous chapter discusses the influence of Greek philosophy on Greek religious thought. Still, the Romans were not quick to accept outside influences into their culture, and there was a period when philosophy was viewed with suspicion, especially during the Republic period. Franz Cumont makes an important observation:

> In periods of skepticism, pious souls cling to old beliefs; the conservative crowd remains faithful to ancestral traditions. When religion is resuming its empire, rationalistic minds resist the contagion of faith. It is especially difficult to ascertain up to what point ideas adopted by intellectual circles succeeded in penetrating the deep masses of the people. (*After Life* 2)

Philosophy may have been part of the education of the elite but had little influence on the uneducated masses of Rome and its surrounding territories. Nonetheless, the skepticism of the Epicureans and Stoics was not entirely out of step with existing ideas about the afterlife.

The Epicureans suggested that the soul disintegrates with the body, so there is no future life or sensibility:

> Epicurus took up again the doctrine of Democritus, and taught that the soul, which was composed of atoms, was disintegrated at the moment of death, when it was no longer held together by its fleshly wrapping, and that its transitory unit was then destroyed forever. The vital breath, after being expelled, was, he said, buffeted by the winds and dissolved in the air like mist or smoke, even before the body decomposes. (Cumont, *After Life* 7)

With regard to the appearance of phantoms, Epicurus felt these were "no more than emanations of particles of an extreme tenuity, constantly issuing from bodies and keeping for some time their form and appearance" (Cumont, *After Life* 7). This was the opposite conclusion to Plato's:

> As Plato deduced the persistence of the soul after death from its supposed previous existence, so Epicurus drew an opposite conclusion from our ignorance of our earlier life; and according to him, the conviction that we perish wholly can alone ensure our tranquility of spirit by delivering us from the fear of eternal torment. (Cumont, *After Life* 7)

An example of an Epicurean epitaph found on a grave in Rome says, "I was not; I was; I am not; I do not care" (Cumont, *After Life* 9-10).

Indeed, the works of Lucretius, who lived near the end of the Roman Republican period, suggested that there was a freedom in not believing in the survival of the soul:

> Death therefore to us is nothing, concerns us not a jot, since the nature of the mind is proved to be mortal; and as in time gone by we felt no distress, when the Poeni from all sides came together to do battle, and all things shaken by war's troublous uproar shuddered and quaked beneath high heaven, and mortal men were in doubt which of the two peoples it should be to whose empire all must fall by sea and land alike, thus when we shall be no more, when there shall have been a separation of body and soul, out of both of which we are each formed into a single being, to us, you may be sure, who then shall be no more, nothing whatever can happen to excite sensation, not if earth shall be mingled with sea and sea with heaven. (Oates 131)

This is a vastly different view from that of the ancient Egyptians, who would consider the annihilation of the soul its worst possible punishment.

The Stoics were not quite as atheistic as the Epicureans; however, their beliefs about life after death were hardly uniform. They did believe in the gods and in *daimones* as forces of nature, and they marginally accepted the idea of life after death. The human being is seen as a fragment or microcosm of the divine, and this led to a marginal belief in reincarnation, though the soul is subject to the fate of the collective soul, and a "universal conflagration will cause them to return to the divine home whence all of them came forth" (Cumont *After Life* 13).

It is worth thinking about the role of the elements in beliefs about life after death. Air is connected to the soul as "breath" or "wind" in both Greek and Roman paganism. The word *psykhe* comes from *psykho*, meaning "to blow". The terms *anima* and *animus*, later terms for "soul," are related to the Greek word ἄνεμοι, meaning "wind" (Cumont *After Life* 59). Fire is also connected to the soul as part of purification and as the "divine spark" in humankind. To quote Umberto Eco:

> Seeing that our first experience of fire happens indirectly, through the light of the sun, and directly, through the untamable forces of lightning and uncontrollable fires, it was obvious that fire had to be associated from the very beginning with divinity, and in all the primitive religions we find some form of fire cult, from worship of the rising sun to keeping in the inner sanctum of the temple the sacred fire that must never burn out. (47)

Fire is associated with life, and so the spark of "life" within us, which moves like the wind or a breath, becomes the association for the soul. Bailey tells us that Stoicism is the origin of the later Christian doctrine of purgatory, in which "the soul is refined from contaminations of earth and made fit to rejoin the divine fire—a doctrine set out immortally by Virgil in the sixth *Aeneid*" (240). In these philosophical conceptions of the soul, earth is a hindrance and contaminating, while fire and air represent spirit and immortality. If we think about this in conjunction with the Roman notion of death as a pollutant, we might anticipate the change in thinking that makes the earth and everything associated with it suspect.

Book VI of the *Aeneid* is our most striking account of the underworld from the Roman period, but it was written much later than the archaic period. Virgil wrote the *Aeneid* during the early reign of Caesar Augustus, approximately between 29 and 19 B.C.E. The view of the underworld shown in Virgil demonstrates the influence of the Greek philosophers, particularly Plato. Aeneas goes to the Sibyl of Cumae, who lives in cave in the woods of "Diana of the Crossroads" (i.e., Hecate) (159). After giving them a prophecy about the forthcoming war with the Latins, Aeneas asks her to take him to the underworld to see his father. The Sibyl tells him that he must retrieve a golden bough to bring to Prosperina—he can do this easily if he is "called by fate" (164). He achieves this with the help of his mother, Venus. Virgil paints a grim picture of the gates of the underworld:

> About the doorway forms of monsters crowd—Centaurs, twiformed Scyllas, hundred-armed Briareus, and the Lernean hydra hissing horribly, and the Chimaera breathing dangerous flames, and Gorgons, Harpies, huge Geryon, triple-bodied ghost. Here, swooped by sudden fear, drawing his sword, Aeneas stood on guard with naked edge against them as they came. If his companion, knowing the truth, had not admonished him, how faint these lives were—empty images, hovering bodiless—he had attacked and cut his way through phantoms, empty air. (169-170)

It is curious to see all the monsters of Tartarus at the underworld gates; Virgil puts the horrors on display, but then treats them as the Greeks treated the *eidolon*; they are only empty shadows. Here we see the combination of Hesiod and Homer's traditional view with the contemporary philosophical view. Charon the ferryman, who is a late addition in the Greek, appears in this narrative. We see references to Charon around the same time we start seeing the god Hermes act as a psychopomp. The Sibyl points to Aeneas' golden bough, and Charon then agrees to ferry them over. We see Minos judges the dead, who are said to be imprisoned by the river Styx which "winds nine times around" (177). Rhadamanthus is the judge of the wicked dead and oversees their punishments, the dead in chains and whipped by the Furies

(179). The traditional inhabitants of the Greek underworld are also here, with Tityus, Ixion and Pirithous specifically mentioned, as well as the Titans. Even Theseus is still bound in a chair of forgetfulness, a strange inconsistency if we consider the festival of Hercules that occurs in Book VIII. Hercules rescues Theseus from the underworld when he comes to fetch the dog Cerberus in his final labor. Yet, he is still there in Virgil's underworld (180-181). After purifying himself, Aeneas then enters the "Blessed Groves," populated by "those who suffered wounds in battle for their country; those who in their lives were holy men and chaste or worthy of Phoebus in prophetic song; or those who bettered life by finding out new truths and skills; or those who to some folk by benefactions made themselves remembered" (183). Aeneas sees his father, and like Odysseus with his mother, his attempts to put his arms around him fail—Anchises is "weightless as wind and fugitive as dream" (184). His father tells him, "Souls for whom a second body is in store: their drink is water of Lethe, and it frees from care in long forgetfulness. For all this time I have so much desired to show you these and tell you of them face to face" (185). Anchises then proceeds to give Aeneas a cosmology, and talks about the cycle of the soul in a manner very similar to Plato's *Vision of Er*, which is the likely inspiration of this vision. In the early Empire we see that the ancient Greek vision had not entirely gone away, but Plato's idea of divine punishment, reward, and metempsychosis was now codified in the national Roman epic.

Another philosophical contribution of the Stoics was the emphasis on *fatum*, or Fate. The Greeks had the idea of the three *Moirae* who spun the destinies of humans as a length of thread; one goddess spun the thread, another measured it, and the last cut it at the time of death. Fate could not be averted, even by the gods. In the opening of the *Aclestis* play by Euripides, Apollo says, "I am a just god and recognize just men; Admetus, the son of Pheres, I then encountered him and I saved him from Death, deceiving the Three Fates who promised Admetus should not die if some one person would take his place instead and die for him" (Eurpides, *Alcestis* 7-8). Thus, we see that death can only be averted by having a substitute go to death for the living person.

The Romans had not previously believed in Fate; the actions of the gods were spontaneous, reflecting the unexpected nature of events in life (Dumézil 197). But with the Stoic addition of fatalistic determinism, there also came the belief in astrology, which again became more popular with the introduction of Oriental belief systems in Rome in the early Empire. We will take a closer look at astrology and its implications for our theme of celestial vs. chthonic religion later in this chapter.

By the 3rd century B.C.E., Pythagoreanism was also influential in Rome, though it had limits. The famous Roman king Numa was said to be a Pythagorean, and it was espoused by writers as influential as Cato and Cicero. According to Jerome Carcopino, "When the consciousness of an Italic nationality came into being, it turned to Pythagoreanism" (qtd. in Dumézil 523). The documents connecting Numa to Pythagoras turned out to be a forgery, but the association with the origins of Rome and Pythagoras were still cemented in folklore. The wise king was also a philosopher. But by the 180s BCE, even Pythagoreanism was suspect in Roman life:

> As long as Pythagoreanism suggests a way of life, or recommends such harmless practices as vegetarianism, or offers the consolations of another world with Rome, left to her own devices, cannot populate or give life to, it is welcome, and it is a matter of general satisfaction that Numa is a Pythagorean, or even that some bolder spirits make Pythagoras into a Roman citizen (Plut. Num. 8.11). But when it begins to produce writings like those of which the purge of 213 rid the city; when only a few years after the business of the Bacchanalia, it risks stirring up the religious emotions of the masses by means of a sensational discovery, then Numa must be put back in his proper place, in the Annales ... A century and a half later the Pythagoreans will perhaps form their own chapels. Those of this earlier era did not mix the genres of religion and philosophy, and their religious practice was not contaminated by their dreams of wisdom. (Dumézil 524-525)

As we can see, the 3rd century B.C.E. brought new influences to Rome, but by the 2nd century B.C.E., the government sought to curtail this influence. For example, the famously named Bacchanalia of 185 B.C.E. brought about this mass censorship, exile, and burning of books. It is not surprising that about fifty years later, Rome would descend into civil war. As Howard Bloom has observed:

> Human superorganisms show the same pattern. In times of trouble, they tend to shun the new. When the Turkish Empire was crumbling in the sixteenth century, Ottoman authorities were sure they could recapture former glories by returning to the traditions of the past. Europeans came up with improved methods for preventing plague, but the Turks refused to use them. Why? The foreign techniques departed from the customs that had once made Turkey great. Like hungry birds, the Ottomans sought their comfort in clinging to tradition. When plague did break out in the land, the Turks blamed it on the few foreign innovations they had failed to eradicate. (300)

Societies cling to tradition when they are threatened; foreign influence is seen as a negative threat. Whether outside influence is negative or not, its rejection suggests a crisis in the society rejecting it.

The Epicureans in particular managed to maintain influence in Rome for a long time, but their influence all but disappeared when Oriental mysticism and Neoplatonism triumphed in Rome (Cumont, *After Life* 9). These will be discussed in the next chapter.

Greek, Asian, and Egyptian Influences

Discussion of foreign cults begins with Bacchus and the Bacchanalia of 185 B.C.E. A previous section discusses the expulsion of the Bacchus cult from Rome, in the same period as the philosophers and the Jews. Livy tells of the coming of an "unknown Greek" whom he suspects of practicing magic and sorcery, as the one bringing these "immoral rites" to the Roman people (240-242). There is a story of a young man whose mother wanted him to be initiated into the Bacchic rites, but after carelessly mentioning this to a slave woman, he starts a chain of events that leads to an investigation of the rites by the Roman Senate. The terrified women called in as witnesses claim that:

> Ex quo in promiscuo sacra sint et permixti viri feminis, et noctis licentia accesserit, nihil ibi facinoris, nihil flagitii praetermissum. Plura virorum inter sese quam feminarum esse stupra. Si qui minus patients dedecoris sint et pigriores ad facinus, pro victimis immolari. Nihil nefas ducere, hanc summam inter eos religionem esse.[24] (Livy 254)

This alarmed the senators, who declared that there should not be gatherings "without reason," and they viewed this as a conspiracy to overturn the social order. Women are blamed as the main participants, as well as men who are guilty of "being effeminate." Those who had participated but did not kill anyone were rounded up and imprisoned; those who were said to have killed were summarily executed. The scapegoats for the incident were two plebians, Marcus and Gaius Atinius, said to be the priests of the whole affair. However, the number of adherents was so numerous they had to shut the courts down for a month to investigate (268-269). It is interesting that Livy mentions three types of culprits—a Greek magician, women and effeminate men, and plebians who were part of the lower classes. This dramatic account

---

[24] "At this [time] the rites were performed mixing men and women, and the freedom of darkness added, nothing there is wicked, nothing shameful overlooked. More men were violated among themselves than with women. If one was less inclined to endure shameful acts, for this they were to be sacrificed as victims. Nothing was esteemed against divine command, this being the highest form of devotion among them." – My translation and brackets.

is likely exaggerated, as two terrified women who were not proper witnesses to the initiations might say anything. Their moralistic sense causes them to complain to the Senate, and what was actually a secret initiation was suddenly interpreted as a conspiracy against the State. Bailey correctly notes that this is the bigger crime, not the religious practice; morals were also the domain of the government (179). As we noted earlier with Pythagoraeanism, as long as private religious practice did not interfere with the State or the State cult, it was allowed. After this, the Bacchic cult did not resurface in Rome until the time of Julius Caesar (Bailey 180). Bailey suggests that there was a craving for emotion in religion that was absent from the religious life of the average Roman, and he believes that this was the reason three other cults—those of the Magna Mater, the Cappadocian goddess Mâ , and the goddess Isis—became popular in Rome after the Punic Wars, flourishing particularly in the late Republic, through the first centuries of the Empire.

The Magna Mater (Great Mother, sometimes called Meter) cult came from Phrygia, and is clearly based on the cult of Cybele and Attis. This cult was formally introduced into Rome on the advice of the Sibylline Oracles. (Beard et al 62) In the Greek version of this story:

> Zeus, having tried in vain to marry Cybele, let some of his semen fall on a nearby rock. This begot the hermaphrodite Agdistis. Dionysus made Agdistis drunk and castrated him/her. From the blood grew a pomegranate tree. Nana became pregnant by inserting one of the fruits in her womb, and gave birth to Attis. At Sangarius' wish she abandoned him, but he was taken in by some passers-by and reared on honey and billy-goat's milk, hence his name (Attis = he goat (attagus) or beautiful in Phrygian). Attis grew very handsome, and King Midas of Pessinus determined he should marry one of his daughters, but during an argument between Agdistis and Cybele, Attis and his attendants became frenzied. Attis castrated himself beneath a pine tree and died. Cybele buried him, but violets grew around the pine tree from the blood which had fallen from his wounds. Cybele also buried Midas' daughter, who had killed herself in despair, and violets grew from her blood and an almond tree over her tomb. Zeus granted Agdistis that Attis' body should not decay, his hair should continue to grow, and his little finger should move. (Grimal 27-28)

Worship centered on a large black stone said to represent the goddess. It is hard not to wonder about a connection to the Kabba, the black stone in the temple of Mecca, a place venerated on the Islamic Hajj. Later, the worship of Mâ became conflated with the worship of Magna Mater, and also with the goddess Bellona (Bailey 190). The rites of these religions were just as chaotic

as the previous Bacchanals. In fact, Cumont points out the relationship between Dionysus worship and Cybele worship: "Thus Attis became one with
the Dionysus-Sabazius of the conquerors, or at least assumed some of his
characteristics. This Thracian Dionysus was a god of vegetation" (*Oriental*
48). As noted, the Phrygians were from the Thracian region, the same country of origin as Dionysus. The rites of this religion were violent:

> The religion of Phrygia was perhaps even more violent than that of
> Thrace. ... In the midst of their orgies, and after wild dances, some of
> the worshipers voluntarily wounded themselves and, becoming intox-
> icated with the view of the blood, with which they besprinkled their
> altars, they believed they were uniting themselves with their divinity.
> (Cumont, *Oriental* 50)

Once again, Rome took control in this case by incorporating the rituals
into the State religion. Like the similar Dionysus cult in Greece, the public
rituals were more watered down and consequently safer.

The gory nature of the Magna Mater cult may seem shocking, but Jung
suggests that this is characteristic of the Earth Mother:

> The Earth Mother is always chthonic and is occasionally related to
> the moon, either through the blood-sacrifice already mentioned, or
> through a child-sacrifice, or else because she is adorned with a sickle
> moon. In pictorial or plastic representations the Mother is dark deep-
> ening to black, or red (these being her principal colors), and with a
> primitive or animal expression of face; in form she not infrequently
> resembles the neolithic ideal of the "Venus" of Brassempouy or that of
> Willendorf, or again the sleeper of Hal Seflieni. Now and then I have
> come across multiple breasts, arranged like those of a sow. The Earth
> Mother plays an important part in the woman's unconscious, for all her
> manifestations are described as "powerful." This shows that in such
> cases the Earth Mother element in the conscious mind is abnormally
> weak and requires strengthening. (Jung, "Psychological" 185-186)

In Chapter 2 we noted the motif of virgin sacrifice, which Jung also connects with the Earth Mother. Blood is associated with the passage into womanhood. But we also see the Earth Mother as representing the unconscious
mind—Jung speaks of a woman's unconscious, but this is also true in a man.
We see two types of religious rites: one involves the performance of certain
sacred actions in a prescribed order. In the Roman world, these could be very
complex, as the Romans were fond of rules, order, and the careful observance
of restrictions and taboos. The other type is the orgiastic rite; there is a method to the madness, but it is about removing restrictions rather than observing them. The two types of ritual can keep the psyche in balance between

the conscious need for order and the irrational and sometimes savage nature of the unconscious. In modern religion we have deemed the former type true of religion, while the latter is considered depraved and evil, associated with Satanic cults. There is something "Satanic" in the sense of rebelling against the order in favor of the freedom of chaos and anarchy. But this is not a negative; it is part of what is in Shadow in our souls and needs some kind of safe expression. When religion becomes increasingly cerebral, the urge toward irrational practice increases. Chaotic outlets are necessary to psychological health. But in Rome we see the first concerns about the moral social order, and there is an attempt to either annihilate or assimilate the wayward religion into the existing community. As we noted with Dionysus, this has its advantages and disadvantages. The rites become safer, but they are also less psychologically effective.

Another mother goddess cult from Egypt gained prominence in the late Republic. The cult of Isis and Serapis (or Osiris) flourished until the time of Octavian, who banned the cult. Herodotus noted the influence of Egyptian thought on Orphism, discussed in Chapter 3. The Isis mysteries bore a striking resemblance to the story of the goddess Demeter told in the *Homerica*. Isis was searching for her murdered husband; Demeter was searching for her missing daughter. Both goddesses pose as nurses and enter royal households. While there, they attempt to make the son of the king and queen immortal by a similar process of holding them in the fire, and in both cases they are interrupted by the queen and reveal who they are. The children do not become immortal, but have other gifts bestowed upon them. In the end, Demeter is reunited temporarily with Persephone, and Isis makes love to her dead husband and produces the child Horus.[25]

We have previously discussed the Demeter and Persephone myth as a rite of passage story per Jung, but in comparison to the Isis story, and in connection with the Roman interest in mother goddesses, we see these myths as representing the life-giving dimension of the Feminine. Hence we see the connection with the great Mothers and the idea of immortality. Even if someone does not believe in life after death, the expansion of the family is

---

[25] For the full Hymn to Demeter and Plutarch's description of the Isis/Osiris cult see: Hesiod, and Homer. *Hesiod, theHomeric Hymns, and Homerica.* Trans. Hugh G. Evelyn White. Cambridge, MA: Harvard University Press,1964. 288-323.Print. Plutarch. "Of Isis and Osiris, or of the Ancient Religion and Philosophy of Egypt." *Plutarch's Essays and Miscellanies, Comprising All His Works Collected under the Title of "Morals,"* Boston: Little Brown, 1911. 65-139. Print.

a means of continuing life through the generations. Jung also suggests that the archetypal mother has more to do with inward individual development:

> The "mother" corresponds to the "virgin anima" who is not turned towards the outer world and is therefore not corrupted by it. She is turned rather towards the "inner sun," the archetype of transcendent wholeness—the self.("Dual" 323)

If we accept this, the Mother cults may have been an obvious compliment to solar cults that became popular as Rome moved into its early Empire period. Roman religion was lacking in mythology, and the highly rational, masculinized nature of society no doubt left its citizens looking for some kind of balance that would satisfy their deeper questions and make them feel some level of completion. This sudden influx of feminine deities from the East as a result of war fits in with the context of a society that is looking for a balance with domestic tranquility and peace. This is further evidenced by the expansion and endurance of these cults through the civil war period. When religion and public life follow a pre-determined script, the need to satisfy the Dionysiac/Trickster urge in the unconscious will undoubtedly find its way into the mix, either through rebellion or secret rites. The Roman government perceived no threat, as long as the private rites didn't violate the public space.

This tension between public and private religion is mirrored in Stoic philosophy, in the idea of the microcosm vs. the macrocosm. As a rational soul, and a being made from the elements, the individual human contains a universe within himself or herself that reflects the larger cosmos. From a secular perspective, the Roman citizen represents the city of Rome and its influence. Jung would call this human microcosm the Self archetype:

> It is a figure comparable to Hiranyagarbha, Purusha, Atman, and the mystic Buddha. For this reason I have elected to call it the "self," by which I understand a psychic totality and at the same time a centre, neither of which coincides with the ego but includes it, just as a larger circle encloses a smaller one. ("Study" 247)

The psychological journey is an inward one and usually takes place when we find ourselves dissatisfied or discontented with our outer lives. But as we explore our inner life, we break it apart; as we encounter archetypal content, we label it. We can't help ourselves; it's a condition of living in space and time, where everything is measured in relation to everything else. When we encounter something new to our experience, we have to find a way to integrate it into our existing experience or reject it outright. Philosophy and foreign religion would not have impacted the Romans if it did not touch some kind of archetypal nerve. It is not really surprising that the Romans took up Mother Goddess worship and the Bacchanalia with such fervor, and that the external State would find this internal power a threat. Thus, the tension between state and individual, public and private, becomes more defined in the beliefs of Roman citizens. The State demands that we focus on the outer world, but the reality is that our inner development is what makes us better citizens of the outer world. The individual who seeks to become whole by confronting his or her inner life comes through the ordeal of the dark unconscious with something to offer the rest of the world. This is the core of the myth of the hero.

Astrology and Magic

The last factor to consider for the Republican period of Roman history is the influence of astrology and magic. The origins of astrology are usually attributed to the Chaldeans, a group that came from the south part of Babylon. Their connection to Babylon might explain why Zoroastrian magi were often confused with astrologers; it is not unlikely that Hellenized Zoroastrian practice included astrology. Modern practitioners of Eastern religions often mix elements of Buddhism, Hinduism, and Christianity, so it would follow that the adoption of a foreign religion would include the blending of native elements.

If we are concerned about the movement of the afterlife and the destiny of the soul with respect to the earth and sky, then astrology's assertion that destiny lay in the stars is crucial. When Jake Stratton-Kent discussed the movement of the Underworld and its deities from the earth to the sky (177), he was literally referencing astrology and the movement of deities and mythical figures to the constellations. The constellations were not necessarily a new construct; the ancient Greek Titan Crius was associated with the zodiac and the movement of stars along the horizon in general, and the constellation Aries (the Ram) in particular. When the fate of the soul is read in the stars, there is an implied relationship between the two; many astrologers claimed that the human soul was in fact a star (Cumont, *Oriental* 177). Franz Cumont sees the Roman interest in astrology as a combination of factors:

> This alliance of the theorems of astrology with their old belief supplied the Chaldeans with answers to all the questions that men asked concerning the nature of heaven and earth, the nature of God, the existence of the world, and their own destiny. Astrology was really the first scientific theology. Hellenistic logic arranged the Oriental doctrines properly, combined them with the Stoic philosophy and built them up into a system of indisputable grandeur, an ideal reconstruc-

tion of the universe, the powerful assurance of which inspired Manilius to sublime language when he was not exhausted by his efforts to master an ill-adapted theme. The vague and irrational notion of "sympathy" is transformed into a deep sense of the relationship between the human soul, an igneous substance, and the divine stars, and this feeling is strengthened by thought. The contemplation of the sky has become a communion. (*Oriental* 178)

Thus, astrology becomes the map of our connection to the gods, who are in the sky in the constellations, and we were originally stars who will eventually return to the stars again:

In descending to the earth they travel through the spheres of the planets and receive some quality from each of these wandering stars, according to its positions. Contrariwise, when death releases them from their carnal prison, they return to their first habitation, providing they have led a pious life, and if as they pass through the doors of the superposed heavens they divest themselves of the passions and inclinations acquired during their first journey, to ascend finally, as pure essence to the radiant abode of the gods. (Cumont, *Oriental* 177-178)

It is not a stretch to think of our souls, made of fire and air, as ascending to the stars and somehow, being related to them. Plato in fact says in the *Timaeus*, "And into this body, subject to the flow of growth and decay, they [the divine agents of the creator] fastened the orbits of the immortal soul." (Beck "Religion" 182) This focus on ascension and the stars further devalues the earth as the place of passions and emotional behavior, which are to be discarded if we wish to ascend to the heights of the heavens. Astrology has a very Stoic bent, and the disavowal of earthly pleasure for higher truth and expression of our "divine" selves further develops the gap between the celestial and the chthonic.

Astrologers were often associated with magicians, whether they were necessarily connected or not, and this gave them a mixed reputation. Both magic and astrology grew as practices in the early part of the Common Era and have never entirely left our civilization. Like other new ideas, astrology was a mixed blessing. We can attribute interest in astrology at least partially to the need for answers to unknown questions, even ultimate questions about life after death. But the pre-deterministic nature of astrology led in some cases to a belief that no one had to take actions in their lives; everything would just "happen" according to their star chart:

The Chaldeans were the first to conceive the idea of an inflexible necessity ruling the universe, instead of gods acting in the world according to their passions, like men in society. They noticed that an immutable law regulated the movements of the celestial bodies, and, in the first enthusiasm of their discovery they extended its effects to all moral and social phenomena. The postulates of astrology imply an absolute determinism. Tyche, or deified fortune, became the irrepressible mistress of mortals and immortals alike, and was even worshiped exclusively by some under the empire. Our deliberate will never plays more than a very limited part in our happiness and success, but, among the pronunciamentos and in the anarchy of the third century, blind chance seemed to play with the life of every one according to its fancy, and it can easily be understood that the ephemeral rulers of that period, like the masses, saw in chance the sovereign disposer of their fates. (Cumont, *Oriental* 179)

There are two important things to note here. The first is the notion of the universe acting according to necessity rather than the whim of the gods. This is a psychological move from disorder to order; the universe and our role in it is not an accident. As we see with other changes in cosmic and religious perceptions, this has both advantages and disadvantages. Combined with the idea of fate, one might believe one is moving to a cosmic script, and can do nothing about the course of life. It is similar to modern dilemmas about neuropsychology, and whether a criminal is really responsible for actions, or "genetically" predisposed. The other item of note is the dating—Cumont is talking about the third century of the Common Era. We have not yet reached that point in our investigations; still, the influence of astrology, like many other foreign influences, finds its genesis in Rome during this Republican period. It will have an expanded role among the Mithraists and Neoplatonists in the ensuing years.

Cumont takes a very dim view of astrology, but the fault is really not with the astrologers. It is human to try to make order out of disorder, to find a reason for the course of our lives. Certainly modern science runs on the notion that there are natural/physical laws, or other rational/material explanations for everything that occurs in our experience. In fact, astrology and magic, with their desire to learn the inner workings of life and the universe, are an integral part of the history of science.

Reflections

There is a vast difference between the religious practices of the Roman monarchic era and the beginning of the Empire. The influx of Greek, Etruscan, and Oriental influences all made their mark on Roman religion, though it is argued that their importation of foreign religion largely comes from Greece. In addition to the cults and philosophies mentioned here, Mithraism became a popular religion in the early Empire, with its Roman origins in the Second Punic War as a religion mostly practiced by soldiers (Cumont, *Oriental* 149). We will discuss Mithraism and the influence of these cults in the next chapter on the early years of the Roman Empire. The Greeks and Romans both went from collective ideas about death and the soul to very specific ideas that glorified the divine spark in the individual. In Rome, this took a very special turn in light of the dogmatic and rational nature of their society. The influx of Oriental mother goddess cults and the Bacchus cult may have offered some level of balance to an increasingly rote mode of existence in public and private life. Both Greek and Roman expansion changed the culture of the major cities, though we see efforts to curtail new ideas for different reasons. The Athenians were independent people who did not want their culture taken over by Persian conquerors; the Romans were more concerned about the centrality of the State and regulating morality and order among the populace. We don't see this particularly moral concern in Greece. The Greeks were eventually conquered, but much of their civilization was copied by their conquerors. When the Romans dissolved into civil war, we see an occasion for the kind of anxiety present in Greece during the Achaemenid Empire. For a people that needed the emotional and intuitive outlet of mother goddess religions and mystery cults, there was the additional anxiety of craving the law and order that was a particular characteristic of the city's collective consciousness. Octavian, later known as Augustus, would provide this stability at the cost of the Republic. But changes in belief had already been put in motion, and the early Empire was anything but peaceful in this arena. Roman influence added its own legalistic element to the *translatio studii* of Near Eastern culture, which would further separate the celestial and chthonic into categories of "good" and "evil."

Works Cited: Chapter 4

Bailey, Cyril. *Phases in the Religion of Ancient Rome*. Berkeley, CA: U of California, 1932. Print.

Beard, Mary, et al. *Religions of Rome*. Vol. 1, Cambridge University Press, 1998.

Bloom, Howard K. *The Lucifer Principle: A Scientific Expedition into the Forces of History*. New York: Atlantic Monthly, 1995. Print.

Corbeill, Anthony. *Sexing the World: Grammatical Gender and Biological Sex in Ancient Rome*. Princeton: Princeton UP, 2015. Print.

Cumont, Franz. *After Life in Roman Paganism*; Lectures Delivered at Yale University on the Silliman Foundation. New York: Dover Publications, 1959. Print.

Cumont, Franz. *The Oriental Religions in Roman Paganism*. New York: Dover Publications, 1956. Print.

De Grummond, Nancy T. "Religion, Etruscan." - *The Encyclopedia of Ancient History*. Wiley, 26 Oct. 2012. Web. 03 Apr. 2016.

Dumézil, Georges. *Archaic Roman Religion, with an Appendix on the Religion of the Etruscans*. Vol. 1 and Vol. 2. Chicago: U of Chicago, 1970. Print.

Eco, Umberto. "The Beauty of the Flame." *Inventing the Enemy*. Trans. Richard Dixon. Boston: Houghton Mifflin, 2012. 44-66. Print.

Euripides. "Alcestis." *Euripides, 3*. Ed. David R. Slavitt and Smith Palmer Bovie. Philadelphia: U of Pennsylvania, 1998. 3-59. Print.

Grimal, Pierre. "Agdistis." *The Penguin Dictionary of Classical Mythology*. Ed. Stephen Kershaw. London, England: Penguin, 1991. 27-28. Print.

Johnston, Sarah Iles. *Restless Dead: Encounters between the Living and the Dead in Ancient Greece*. Berkeley: University of California, 1999. Print.

Jung, C. G. "The Dual Mother." *Symbols of Transformation*. Trans. R.F.C. Hull. New York: Pantheon, 1959. 306-395. Print.

Jung, C. G. "The Psychological Aspects of the Kore." *Collected Works*. Trans. R.F.C. Hull. Vol. 9.1. New York, NY: Pantheon, 1959. 182-203. Print.

Jung, C. G. "Study in the Process of Individuation." *Collected Works*. Trans. R.F.C. Hull. Vol. 9.1. New York, NY: Pantheon, 1959. 290-354. Print.

Livy. *Livy: With an English Translation in Fourteen Volumes*. Trans. Evan Taylor Sage. Vol. 11. Cambridge (Mass.): Harvard UP, 1965. Print.

Milnor, Kristina. "Public and Private." *A Cultural History of Women in Antiquity*. Ed. Janet H. Tulloch. Vol.1. London: Bloomsbury, 2013. 105-24. Print.

Neumann, Erich. *The Fear of the Feminine and Other Essays on Feminine Psychology*. Princeton, NJ: Princeton UP, 1994. Print.

Oates, Whitney J., ed. *The Stoic and Epicurean Philosophers; the Complete Extant Writings of Epicurus, Epictetus, Lucretius Marcus Aurelius*. New York: Random House, 1940. Print.

Ovid. *Selected Works*. Ed. J. C. Thornton and M. J. Thornton. London: J.M. Dent & Sons, 1948. Print.

Plutarch. "Of Isis and Osiris, or of the Ancient Religion and Philosophy of Egypt." *Plutarch's Essays and Miscellanies, Comprising All His Works Collected under the Title of "Morals,"* Boston: Little Brown, 1911. 65-139. Print.

Riis, P. J. *An Introduction to Etruscan Art*. Copenhagen: Ejnar Munksgaard, 1953. Print.

Stratton-Kent, Jake. *Geosophia: The Argo of Magic: From the Greeks to the Grimoires.* Vol. 1. Dover: Scarlet Imprint/Bibliothèque Rouge, 2010. Print.

Varro, Marcus Terentius. *Varro on the Latin Language: In Two Volumes.* Trans. Roland G. Kent. Vol. 2. London: Heinemann, 1958. Print.

Virgil. *The Aeneid.* Trans. Robert Fitzgerald. New York: Vintage, 1983. Print.

Wells, Scott C. "Roman Empire." *Berkshire Encyclopedia of World History, Second Edition.* Ed. William McNeill. Great Barrington: Berkshire Publishing Group, 2011. *Credo Reference.* Web. 3 Apr. 2016.

Wheeler, Gem. "'Bastard Normans! Norman Bastards!'." *New Histories.* Ed. Rose Colville. University of Sheffield, 19 Jan. 2010. Web. 03 Apr. 2016.

Chapter 5: Splits and Reversals

The *Aeneid* commemorates the peace brought by Octavian, who became the first Roman Emperor, Caesar Augustus. After years of civil war, the Romans were anxious to settle down and enjoy their expanded influence and prosperity. This interlude was not destined to last. Even though the first two centuries of the Empire were known as the *Pax Romana*, there were brutality, corruption, assassinations, civil wars, and foreign invasions. The Empire continued to expand until the reign of the Emperor Trajan (98-117 C.E.), and as it expanded, the shifts in moral and religious thinking that the Roman Republican Senate fought to avoid became inevitable.

If Rome and its territories were in upheaval politically and socially, there was an even greater upheaval in the collective psychology and beliefs of the society. While some of the changes in thought occurred over time, there was a perfect psychological storm that permanently shifted thinking about the idea of god, and reversing the associations of deities and other spiritual beings. Underworld gods became celestial, good gods became bad, and what was thought of as the "atheism" of the Jews held the seeds of the new religion of the Empire. In the previous chapters we discussed Orphism, Zoroastrianism, the mystery cults, and philosophical influences. In the early Empire after the death of Caesar Augustus, we see a return of the Isis religion and the rise of another Zoroastrian-influenced mystery cult known as Mithraism. But the most significant change in thought came from apocalyptic Judaism. After the Babylonian exile, the Jews became part of the Graeco-Roman world, and their "Hellenization" led many Jews with strong ties to their Jewish identity to fear that the promise of a "nation of Israel" from their god Yahweh had failed. While Yahweh was always the central deity of the Jews, and later their only deity, he was increasingly identified with "one" universal god as the Jews became more monotheistic. The rise of monotheism created a new religious problem that had its roots in rational philosophy: theodicy.

Theodicy is a term that comes from the Greek *theos dike*, "the justice of god" (Kempf), and is used in religious studies scholarship to denote "the problem of evil." Monotheism requires one God, and that God is "good" by definition. The "good" becomes equated with the "just." But if God is good, then why is there evil in the world? This is most famously expressed in what is called the Epicurean paradox: God either wishes to take away evils and cannot; or, God is able, and is unwilling; or God is neither willing nor able, or God is both willing and able (Tooley). The result is that if God is able to take away evil, but is unwilling, then he is not all good. If he is willing but unable, then he is not all-powerful. This paradox is part of a frequent argument by atheists against the existence of God.

This brings us full-circle; as we noted in Chapter 2, the chief attribute of Zeus as king of the gods was *dike*. It was this belief in *dike* that led Socrates to state that if there is justice in this world, there must be justice in the other world. The question of "evil" was first explained by the capriciousness of the gods; humans were subject to their whims, and they were unpredictable. Then we see the idea of *moira*, or fate. There is much in Greek mythology and drama addressing the problem of free will vs. determinism; Oedipus can't avoid his fate, neither can Orestes. The Erinyes were the keepers of *dike*; Heraclitus states that if the sun tried to go out of its bounds by even an inch, the Erinyes would drive it back.[26] The Erinyes drive Orestes to avenge his father's death, and then they torment him for killing his mother. Human behavior is not orderly and rational, and what is "just" is not always "good." The myths expressed the paradoxes of evil, but there was no attempt to explain them away. It is true that dike appears as a female winged daemon in sculpture reliefs of the Bacchic mysteries, and most notably on a fresco in Pompeii, and here she seems to represent post-mortem judgment. But there is little evidence for this in the Dionysian mysteries before the late Hellenistic and early Classical era. (Nilsson 123-124)

With the advent of apocalyptic Judaism, ideas about justice and evil cause a greater split between the heavens and the earth. It was a return to Platonic thought combined with eschatological thinking. Many post-exilic Jewish groups believed Israel's fall was short-lived, and Yahweh would send a Messiah to raise Israel to greatness once again. They attribute the fall not to Yahweh, but to a malevolent spirit roaming the world. This is quite a rationalization, in light of the fact that Yahweh commits many atrocities in the

---

[26] See Chapter 2

Old Testament that make the Assyrian and Babylonian gods appear docile. But if Yahweh embodies the Platonic idea of the "good," then the evils befalling Israel must come from somewhere else. In this line of thinking, we see forming the idea of an ultimate evil comparable to the Zoroastrian Ahriman. However, if Yahweh is all-powerful, then evil must be under his rule as well. This leads to a monotheistic worldview with a dualism problem, which it attempts to solve in the figure of Satan or the Devil. One of the notable developments of this formulation of an evil deity is its identification with the feminine. While Satan is not female, he and his demons become associated with women in the apocalyptic literature, with major consequences.

We will begin our exploration in this chapter with a summary of the religious and spiritual influences of the early Empire. There are two distinct elements that stand out in these researches: syncretism and eschatology. The first element relates to the overlap of Greek, Roman, Egyptian, Persian and Jewish in the religious writings of the early Common Era. The second element is introduced in Jewish thought, with the belief that the coming of a Messiah or the end of the world was imminent. This had a tremendous impact on ideas about the soul and life after death. The "split" between Heaven/Earth and good/evil turns into a full-fledged conflict. While pagan Greek and Roman beliefs could easily withstand opposites, the introduction of monotheism into the mix made the relationship impossible. The syncretistic writers struggled with the varieties of religious belief, trying to come up with solutions that neatly explained the contradictions. There is an ironic metaphor in the process, as the "civil war" within religious belief was settled by the Emperor choosing one belief and one way, just as Roman civil war was ended by Octavian's becoming the first Emperor. However, when it comes to human consciousness, picking one side at the expense of the other is problematic on both the personal and societal levels, as we will see.

Foreign cults and Mithraism

In our previous chapter we looked at the cults of Isis and Serapis/Osiris, as well as the Magna Mater cults that included worship of Mâ and Cybele, two mother goddess deities from the Near East. We can add Mithraism to this list during the time period we are now exploring. Originally Mithraism came to Rome during the Second Punic War, and was a religion popular among the Roman soldiers. As Rome moved into its Empire period, Mithraism became very popular among the people (Cumont, *Oriental* 144).

In the Zoroastrian religion, Mithras is seen as the mediator in the "middle zone between Heaven and Hell" (Cumont, *Mysteries* 127) and is treated as one of the *yazatas*, which were lesser deities or *genii* that served as protectors and battled against *devas* (demons) (Cumont, *Mysteries* 5). Cumont theorizes a link between Mithras and the Vedic deity Mitra, as the two gods have "so many traits of resemblance that it is impossible to entertain any doubt concerning their common origin" (Cumont, *Mysteries* 1). We only have fragmentary knowledge of Mitra as a deity, and Mithras is mentioned in the *Avestas*, but only briefly. Here he is treated as a deity of celestial light, which fits in with his later role as a protector in the Zoroastrian religion.

As a side note, the crossover between Far Eastern Vedic deities and Zoroastrian ones is curious. There is a clear connection, though we can't definitively establish the origins of the Zoroastrian deities in the Vedic. What is of greater interest for our study is the use of the term *deva* for demon in the Persian religion, and the term *asura* for benevolent spirit. In the Vedic world these terms are reversed. Why did the Zoroastrians adopt these terms and reverse their meanings? This is a very early example of a reversal of function for a spirit or deity that will become prevalent in the much later Roman Empire.

As popular as Mithraism was in Rome, we know little about the cult or its practices. It appears to be a syncretism between the Greek version of Zoroastrianism and Middle Platonism, which we will discuss in the next section. Mary Beard et al doubt a direct connection to Zoroastrianism: "Mithras was an ancient Persian deity, known to the Greeks from at least the 5th century B.C.; and his cult may indeed have become better known in Asia Minor from the first centuries B.C. and A.D. through Persian settlements there. However, the form of the cult most familiar to us, the initiatory cult, does not seem to derive from Persia at all." (279) If the Greek adoption of Zoroastrian ideas was complex, the diluting of any original Persian concepts was even more so in ancient Rome.

What is of interest to this work is Mithras' role as an afterlife intermediary, and also as an embodiment of the sun god. His title in the Roman mysteries was *Deus Sol Invictus Mithras*, which not only likens him to Apollo the sun god, but the term *invictus* offers implications of a redeemer. He is undefeatable in the war of good and evil (Beck "Mithraism"). It is worth noting that the title *Sol Invictus* became attached to the Roman Emperor cult, particularly in the time of Aurelian (Davis). This is a continued exalting of the masculine, celestial divinity in the form of the sun. The central image associated with Mithraism, the tauroctony, shows Mithras slaying a bull, in an image that includes a raven, a dog, a snake, and a scorpion. The figures have celestial correspondences. Mithras represents the unconquerable Sun, the bull represents the Moon, and the other figures represent the constellations

Corvis, Canis Minor, Hydra, and Scorpius respectively (Beck Religion 114). Mithras' slaying of the bull represents the triumph of the sun over the moon (199). Beck suggests that this has to do with the new moon, when the moon is barely visible, if at all. From a purely symbolic perspective per our study, this would include the triumph of the masculine over the feminine, and perhaps the celestial over the underworld, if the moon was now considered its location. Whatever else this event may have meant to worshippers, these associations exist nonetheless.

There are no surviving scriptures from this group, save one writing in the PGM (*Papyri Magicae Graeciae*) called "The Mithras Liturgy" (Betz *Greek* 148-154). It is so different in principle from the Zoroastrian Mithras that scholars like Franz Cumont believed it had no real connection to Mithraism at all (Betz "Magic" 252). Hans Betz disagrees with this assertion:

> Since the Mithras mysteries developed differently in different countries, there is really no reason to exclude the possibility of an Egyptian version. Whether the Mithras Liturgy is the product of just one magician's efforts or whether there were connections with a Mithraic cult community cannot be determined on the basis of this one text alone; but even if the former holds true, the author of the Mithras Liturgy may still be a serious devotee of the god. ("Magic" 252)

The liturgy certainly brings us back to the idea of syncretism discussed in our chapter introduction. The liturgy is a spell, appealing to Providence and Psyche to reveal the secrets of immortality through the archangel of "Helios Mithras" (Betz, *Greek* 48). Here we see the use of Greek deities (Psyche, Helios), and the Jewish idea of an archangel, as well as "Providence," which may refer to a more general Platonic idea of a cosmological god who is universally good. It also applies the Greek name of the sun god, rather than the Roman Sol.

Besides Mithras, the Greek goddess Hekate assumed a central role in the second and third centuries C.E. as an intermediary in the astrological *Chaldean Oracles*. The *Oracles* as they were read and interpreted assumed a Platonic idea of the heavens, with the underworld in a space between the earth and the moon. The earth was related to the body, and the sun to the mind and universal consciousness. Other planets and stars were part of the zodiac, divided up into "decans," or one-tenth of the cosmos. The "sublunary" sphere between the earth and the moon was the location of the underworld, now moved to the sky. In the Chaldean system, Hekate was regarded as the "cosmological soul."[27] As we saw in Chapter 2, Hekate began as a Titan glo-

---

[27] For evidence of Hekate as cosmological soul, see Appendix 1 of Johnston, Sarah Iles. *Hekate Soteira: A Study of Hekate's Roles in the Chaldean Oracles and Related Literature*. Atlanta,

rified by Zeus, and was later noted for her role in helping Demeter locate her daughter in the underworld. As an "underworld Artemis," she ran with her pack of hounds, and was associated with crossroads and boundaries, making her a liminal figure. Sarah Iles Johnston suggests that "she was elected to play them [cosmological roles] because of her earlier importance in traditional Graeco-Roman religion as a goddess associated with liminal points (e.g. crossroads, doorways)" (Hekate 12). Hekate becomes identified with Plato's Cosmic World Soul (Hekate 13). If the underworld exists in the sublunary region, then Hekate helps the soul cross into the higher realms. Like Artemis, she is associated with the moon, and the moon stands between the underworld and the celestial heights of the sun in this cosmology. The notion of an "intermediary" between the three worlds (Sun/Stars, Moon/Sublunary, Earth/Waters) was popular at this time; I cannot help but wonder if this was part of the interest in Mithras as well, who served as an intermediary deity in Zoroastrian religion. Hekate is also a goddess of witchcraft and magic, and this role may have also caused her to assume this cosmological role. Magic requires knowledge of nature and an ability to negotiate forces from the "other world." A goddess of crossroads and boundaries would be considered ideal for this. She carries a torch, and therefore lights the way in the darkness. There is some syncretism here, as Hekate and other goddesses like Persephone had interchangeable roles in this celestial afterlife.

Sarah Iles Johnston notes Hekate's earlier role as a protector and goddess of witchcraft, which gave her some fearful guises in Greek literature. In some portrayals she is like Medusa, with snakes for hair and running with her baying hounds, which were associated with falsehoods and deceptive spirits (Hekate 140). How did the philosophers, with their striving for what was "Good" and "True," reconcile this aspect of Hekate? The answer is: they didn't. The idea of an opposing, irrational Cosmic Soul developed, called Physis. Iles Johnston quotes the Proclus: "Boundless Physis is suspended from the back of the goddess." (138) Scholars agree that the goddess is Hekate, and Physis takes on the chthonic aspects of Hekate. Physis is a feminine noun, and is assumed to be the goddess who rules over the "daemon-dogs," which Iles Johnston describes as "soul-devouring." (140). This is reminiscent of the Egyptian idea of eternal punishment as annihilation of the soul, and may represent a syncretic belief. Indeed, the whole concept is syncretic, combining elements of philosophy and religion, and taking from the Egyptian and the Persian as well as the Greek. What is of interest here is how Hekate, a chthonic deity with both positive and negative characteristics, is split into

GA: Scholars, 1990. Print.

two deities, with her new celestial characteristics seen as positive, and her chthonic aspects as negative.

Middle Platonism

We have already discussed the role of philosophy in developing ideas of the "good" in relationship to the intellect and the celestial idea of a soul. In the previous section we looked at Hekate's changing role in Greek and Roman cosmogony, and this is owed to extensions of Platonic thinking known as Middle Platonism and Neoplatonism. For our purposes we will stick to discussing the Middle Platonists, as the Neoplatonist time frame pushes the chronological boundaries of our inquiry, though we will discuss their relationship to the early Church Fathers in a later section.

Middle Platonism covers the period from about 90 B.C.E. until the 3rd century C.E. Neoplatonism can only be understood with reference to this period, and a number of important esoteric works came from this school, including the writings of Hermes Trismegistus and the previously mentioned *Chaldean Oracles*. Plutarch is one of the most well-known Middle Platonists. Plutarch's interpretation of Plato, which was meshed with other schools of thought, "cherished a pure idea of God that was more in accordance with Plato. Nevertheless he had to avail himself of a second principle in order to explain the constitution of the phenomenal world. This principle he sought, however, not in any indeterminate matter but in the evil world-soul which has from the beginning been bound up with matter, but in the creation was filled with reason and arranged by it." (Zeller 285-286) This association of matter with what is evil was taken up by other Middle Platonists, including Maximus of Tyre and Celsus, the latter branching out into Christian Gnosticism, believing God could not have influenced matter and that there was a separate world-creator or Demiurge. (288) We will look at Gnosticism later in this chapter. Here we see a clear connection between the demonizing of the world and moralistic religious thinking. Plato held up reason and intelligence as divine, and associated with the "good." His later followers would attribute such moral concepts as "good" and "evil" to the heavens and the earth respectively. Both Middle Platonic and Neoplatonic writings often served as attacks against Christianity. While the Christian view ultimately won out, the influence of this philosophical position did not disappear in the theology and doctrine of the Church. Matter was not considered evil, but the split between the "heavenly" and "earthly" remained, with the former associated with spiritual progress.

Role Reversals of Deities

If the Mithras and Hekate discussions illustrate anything, it is how a deity that originally had one association can end up interpreted in a dramatically different and sometimes opposite way. In the last chapter we discussed the rising influence of astrology in the metaphysical thinking of the new Roman Empire. As the idea of the immortal soul became standard through the philosophers and Near Eastern cults, astrology firmly created an association between the sky and the immortal soul. Concurrent with this was the movement of the underworld to the sky. Jake Stratton-Kent quotes Plutarch on this subject:

> Every soul, whether without mind, or joined to mind, on departing from the body, is ordained to wander the region lying between the moon and earth for a term, not equal in all cases; but the wicked and incontinent pay a penalty for their sins; whereas the virtuous, in order, as it were, to purify themselves and to recover breath, after the body, as being the source of sinful pollution, must pass a certain fixed time in the mildest region of air, which they call the Meadow of Hades. (qtd. in Stratton-Kent 170)

Plutarch's ideas are typical of the astrological movement of the underworld to the sky in this era. (Stratton-Kent 170) Stratton-Kent further explains:

> So too from the 3rd century B.C.E. Hellenistic astrological thought made the interconnectedness of the planetary worlds and human fate an increasingly familiar idea. As in Plato the personification of these forces was a powerful factor, where he gives us Ananke and the Fates, the Judges and the Sirens, so to in astrological thought the decans, the planets, the Arabic Parts, degrees and so on were all understood as personified mythological intelligences. So too astrology itself was held to be literally a divine science, in which the revelations of destiny were comprehended as if in a vision. This is also seen in Jewish apocalyptic literature, the *Book of Enoch* contains references to visionary journeys revealing calendrical and astrological secrets. (171)

We will examine Jewish apocalyptic literature in the next section of this chapter. But this demonstrates the far-reaching influence of the connection between the soul, the underworld, and the sky at this point. Stratton-Kent mentions the association at this time of Persephone with the Moon, and sometimes her husband, Hades or Dis Pater, as associated with the sun. Heraclides of Pontus' work on the underworld, which only survives in fragments, speaks of the gates to the world of the gods in the sky, with the Gate of Heracles being the most notable. Plato also spoke of celestial gates in the "Vision of Er," which he referred to as the Gate of the Gods and the Gate of Men. The Milky Way became the path of souls en route to Hades. These gates were located in certain signs of the zodiac, which corresponded with certain deities (Stratton-Kent 175). Plato's gates are in the constellations of Capricorn and Cancer. This leads to Stratton-Kent's further question:

> As has been seen, the Sun and Moon were equated with the Isles of the Blessed and also with rulers of the Underworld in the Sky. This meant particularly Persephone in the case of the Moon, but also Dis Pater in the case of the Sun. This much is fairly straightforward, even if the idea of these deities ruling the luminaries seems counter-intuitive from a conventional view of myth. On the other hand, what are we to make of the Gates in Cancer and Capricorn? (Stratton-Kent 176)

He goes on to note that the Olympian god associated with Cancer is Hermes, the guide of souls. But Capricorn is associated with Hestia in Orphic tradition. This doesn't make much sense, until we recall that Hestia stepped down from Mount Olympus to give her place to Dionysus. In addition to Dionysus' connection to the Orphic mysteries as a savior-figure, the non-Orphic myths of Dionysus have him going to the underworld to lead out his mother Semele, bringing her to Mount Olympus. So, you have two "psychopomps" at the gates. (Stratton-Kent 176) Hermes has always been an Olympian, but Dionysus was a deity of the earth who gained Olympian status, possibly through the crossing of "Dionysus the foreigner" with the Orphic Dionysus.

I quote Stratton-Kent at length here because he clearly demonstrates what I am calling the reversal: what was chthonic has now become celestial. Persephone (or Proserpina) and Hades (or Dis Pater/Pluto) live in a kingdom between the sun and moon, not under the earth. Another example of a reversal is seen in the Egyptian system with the god Seth. Seth was the Egyptian god of storms, and was referred to as the god "Great of Strength" that fought against the forces of chaos (Cruz-Uribe 6175). Once the Romans conquered Egypt and Graeco-Roman influence spread in the region, Seth was seen as an evil god for killing his brother Osiris; he was identified in the Greek religious system with the monster Typhon. Seth may have been identified with Typhon because of his battle for kingship with Osiris; there may be some conflation with the Greek Gigantomachy, in which Zeus battles Typhon, though the circumstances of the opposition couldn't be more different. More likely is the association with storms, as the monstrous Titans under the earth were often associated with natural catastrophes. The text of the PGM retains the better aspects of Seth, who is referred to as Typhon. In a magical spell to produce "holy power," the supplicant appeals to Typhon:

I'm he who searched with you the whole world and
Found great Osiris, whom I brought you chained.
I'm he who joined you in war with the gods (or 'gainst the gods)
I'm he who closed heavn's double gates and put
To sleep the serpent which must not be seen,
Who stopped the seas, the streams, the river currents
Where'er you rule this realm. And as your soldier
I have been conquered by the gods, I have

Been thrown face down because of empty wrath. (Betz *Greek* 40-41)

The reference here is to Seth's role in the sun's night journey. The "serpent which must not be seen" is Apep, who is defeated daily by Seth in order for the sun to rise and the universe to move in its ordered fashion. He protects the barque of the Sun as it makes its journey through the underworld at night. Later he is "cast down" because of "empty wrath" (Cruz-Uribe 6176). Does this refer to the Osiris/Horus story in which Seth battles them for supremacy? If it does, then it suggests a different ending; "Seth was neither vilified nor punished" (6175). The PGM is a syncretistic work, so it is likely that different mythologies have been combined in the text. But it is certainly true that Seth later became associated with evil, as ethical and moral considerations were attached to his acts. The god who battled chaos became associated with chaos. Not only is Seth an example of a reversal; he is also a deity later associated with the Christian Satan.

We will further explore these reversals in the realm of other religious systems; the early Christian Gnostics did this, as did apocalyptic Jews with their idea of "fallen angels."

Apocalyptic Judaism: Introduction

I would like to introduce this topic with a story from Lon Milo DuQuette, a scholar, musician, and occultist who has written on the "demonic" and why anyone in the modern world would have interest in evoking these kinds of spirits. Lon has a chapter in his book *Low Magick* entitled "The Rabbi's Dilemma" in which he tells the story of an Orthodox Jewish rabbi he calls Ezriel (not his real name). After entreating Lon to keep his information and request confidential, he told Lon he would pay all his expenses if he would come to the East Coast from California for "black magick work" (DuQuette 135).

Lon did some research on this rabbi's credentials and found him to be legitimate. He asked the rabbi about his specific problem. He learned that the rabbi's son had been married for two years but still was not a father. It was critical that his son have a male child, and he wanted Lon to summon a demon of the Goetia[28] to make his daughter-in-law pregnant. He responded to the rabbi by saying "even if I were willing and able to raise a fertility demon, and Sarah (the daughter-in-law) did become pregnant and give birth to a baby boy, there would be serious and unavoidable psychological consequences for both the child and his family." The rabbi responded, "I am willing to take such a curse upon myself" (DuQuette 136-137).

I tell this story as an illustration of the Orthodox or Chasidic view of the demonic, a view that comes straight from the Jewish apocrypha as well as the Talumdic writings of the first five centuries C.E. In particular, the pseudepigraphic text called the *Testament of Solomon* deals with the building of the First Temple in Jerusalem by King Solomon. Solomon accomplishes this task with the help of seventy-two demons, after the archangel Michael gives him a signet ring that he uses to imprint the demons and make them obey his commands. He calls both male and female demons; here is an example of a female demon, as her associations will be common among later female demonic archetypes:

> I then asked of the demon if there were females among them. And when he told me that there were, I said that I desired to see them. So Beelzeboul went off at high speed, and brought unto me Onoskelis, that had a very pretty shape, and the skin of a fair-hued woman; and she tossed her head. And when she was come, I said to her: "Tell me who art thou?" But she said to me: "I am called Onoskelis, a spirit wrought ...[?shabtai/Saturn?], lurking upon the earth. There is a golden cave where I lie. But I have a place that ever shifts. At one time I strangle men with a noose; at another, I creep up from the nature to the arms [in marg: "worms"]. But my most frequent dwelling-places are the precipices, caves, ravines. Oftentimes, however, do I consort with men in the semblance of a woman, and above all with those of a dark skin. For they share my star with me; since they it is who privily or openly worship my star, without knowing that they harm themselves, and but whet my appetite for further mischief. For they wish to provide money by means of memory (commemoration?), but I supply a little to those who worship me fairly." And I Solomon questioned her about her birth, and she replied: "I was born of a voice untimely, the so-called echo of a man's ordure dropped in a wood." And I said to her: "Under what star dost thou pass?" And she answered me: "Under the star of the full moon, for the reason that the moon travels over most things." Then I said to her: "And what angel is it that frustrates thee?"

---

[28] The Goetia often refers to a grimoire giving the names of legions of demons for purposes of magical evocation. It is sometimes referred to as *The Lesser Key of Solomon*. The practice of "goetia" has an older origin.

And she said to me: "He that in thee [or "through thee"] is reigning." And I thought that she mocked me, and bade a soldier strike her. But she cried aloud, and said: "I am [subjected] to thee, O king, by the wisdom of God given to thee, and by the angel Joel." So I commanded her to spin the hemp for the ropes used in the building of the house of God; and accordingly, when I had sealed and bound her, she was so overcome and brought to naught as to stand night and day spinning the hemp. ("Testament")

There is disagreement among scholars about the syncretism of this text, as its source may not entirely be Jewish. However, if Lon's story is any indication, the notion of demons acting as servants for Yahweh and his chosen people is accepted by at least some Orthodox Jews even today. It is worth noting the relationship of these demonic fallen angels to the Titans in the Orphic story of Dionysus. The Titans were chaotic forces that tore apart the divine child Dionysus; Zeus then reduced them to ashes and made mortals. The demons in the Solomon story are also chaotic forces, thrown to the earth to roam among mortals for their transgressions against Yahweh, and can be made to serve mortals. While there is a difference, both the Titans and the demons represent forces of the Earth. They are embodiments of the trickster archetype; Jung explains why these trickster figures are important:

These mythological features extend even to the highest regions of man's spiritual development. If we consider, for example, the daemonic features exhibited by Yahweh in the Old Testament, we shall find in them not a few reminders of the unpredictable behavior of the trickster, of his senseless orgies of destruction and his self-imposed sufferings, together with the same gradual development into a savior and his simultaneous humanization. It is just this transformation of the meaningless into the meaningful that reveals the trickster's compensatory relationship to the saint. ("On" 256)

The Bacchanals and wild rituals of Dionysus were one version of channeling these chaotic forces; the commanding of Biblical demons is another possible one, though this is more dangerous. Just as the gods are archetypes, so are demons, and "possession" by an archetype, meant literally or figuratively, is tantamount to psychosis. However, confronting these demons in ourselves leads to our transformation into individuated human beings. There is no growth without suffering. This reminds us of the dangers of the "liminal."

Where did the idea of "demons" originate? The word comes from the Greek *daimon*, which referred to a kind of *genius* or guiding spirit that aided men. As we noted earlier, Socrates credited his wisdom to a *daimon*. Hesiod suggests they are souls of the dead that enforce justice. Plato, believing that men and gods do not mix, saw *daimones* as messengers between gods and men. Plutarch believed that souls ascending to the moon became *daimones*. As we can see, this associates the demonic with the dead, but not with evil; they are closer to angelic beings in this belief. The philosophers and early Roman writers saw demons as spirits of the air, related in this way to the *psykhe* and *anima* (Smith). The underworld belief of this period placed *daimones* in the space between the earth and the moon; as we noted, this is the celestial location of the underworld. So, the connection between these air spirits and the underworld is not hard to see. But in another reversal, the helpful spirit becomes a deceiver who seeks to ruin the soul, not to raise it up. It is very likely that *daimones* gained their unsavory status as syncretism brought together Jewish apocryphal beliefs about "fallen angels" who roam the earth with this older conception. The Jews also saw foreign gods as evil, so the fallen angels and foreign gods became part of the same group of dangerous spirits. But this idea is not entirely Biblical; as noted earlier, Middle Platonic and Neoplatonic philosophy attempted to split daimones into good and evil categories. The former helped the soul to its celestial ascent from earthly life, and led them down the path of truth and purity; the latter were deceptive, and tried to make the soul believe that evil things were good. (Hekate 139) We concurrently see a split in ideas about magical practice, as theurgy becomes a means for the philosopher/magician to achieve salvation. Iles Johnston cites Porphyry, who "approved of theurgy as a means of improving or purifying a lower level of the soul, although he understood contemplation and virtue to be necessary for salvation of the higher level; he also apparently recognized a level of theurgy concerned not at all with spiritual salvation but with more worldly, immediate goals." (Hekate 79) While all magical practice was rejected as negative in Christianity, church doctrine retained vestiges of the idea of the "lower" and "higher" souls. The inyx-wheel made sounds like heavy breathing when it was spun like a top, which gave it a connection to love spells and magic. But the theurgist used the sounds of the wheel as a kind of sympathetic magic, harmonized with the music of the spheres, to draw the messenger Hekate to them and receive divine wisdom. But, according to Iles Johnston, "iynges" also described "daemon-like entities in the Chaldean Oracles. (91) The Oracles suggest there are both positive and negative daimons, with celestial Hekate ruling the former and chthonic Physis ruling the latter. Some theurgists argue for the usefulness of "practical" theurgy; Iamblichus states in *De Mysteriis*, "We should not be afraid to say this thing as well; that we frequently need to perform rituals on account of pressing bodily needs, to the gods and good daemones of the body." (qtd.

in Iles Johnston, Hekate, 78) Still, this "practical" theurgy was distinct from *goeteia*, with the latter still associated with disreputable practices.

The *Testament of Solomon*, as well as other similarly written Biblical pseudepigraphic writings like the *Testament of St. Cyprian the Mage29* are meant to serve as a warning against involvement with demons. But what is noteworthy about the *Testament of Solomon* is that Solomon's crime is not summoning demons; Solomon is guilty of falling in love with a foreign woman called Shunammite who tricks him into worshipping Moloch:

> And when I answered that I would on no account worship strange gods, they told the maiden not to sleep with me until I complied and sacrificed to the gods. I then was moved, but crafty Eros brought and laid by her for me five grasshoppers, saying: "Take these grasshoppers, and crush them together in the name of the god Moloch; and then will I sleep with you." And this I actually did. And at once the Spirit of God departed from me, and I became weak as well as foolish in my words. And after that I was obliged by her to build a temple of idols to Baal, and to Rapha, and to Moloch, and to the other idols. ("Testament")

The same text treats the Queen of Sheba as a witch ("Testament"), and there is an implied connection between Solomon's involvement with foreign women and evil. As we will see in other examples later in this chapter, women are the ones who lead to the downfall of the righteous. It is also not a coincidence that these wicked spirits "roam the earth" with Yahweh's permission and are bound to the earth, and eventually in the Biblical *Book of Revelation* they are imprisoned under the earth. Women, forbidden knowledge, and the earth and places under the earth are associated in apocalyptic Judaism, and were probably connected as early as the 6th century B.C.E., during the reign of Cyrus the Great. What is different now is the way these beliefs affected the Graeco-Roman world and our Western civilization.

Apocalyptic Judaism: Historical Background

The origins of apocalyptic Judaism are found in the apocryphal *Book of Maccabees*. The Jews were always pressured to assimilate to the foreign dynasties that ruled them. At this time, they were part of the Seleucid Dynasty established by Alexander the Great. In 168 BCE, the Syrian king Antiochus Epiphanes outlawed the "barbaric" Jewish religion and rededicated the Jewish Temple to Zeus. The king's troops descended on the village of Modein to force the Jews to bow to foreign gods. The Jewish priest Matthias killed

---

[29] Text and commentary can be found in: Stratton-Kent, Jake. *The Testament of Cyprian the Mage: Comprehending the Book of Saint Cyprian & His Magical Elements and an Elucidation of the Testament of Solomon.* Dover: Scarlet Imprint/Bibliothèque Rouge, 2014. Print.

a Jew who was going to obey the king, and then killed the king's commissioner. He fled with his sons to the hills, and this was the beginning of the revolt led by Judas Maccabeus (Pagels, *Origin* 45). The ancient historian Josephus tells us that Judas took the unusual step of allying himself with Rome, and this as much as any other factor helped the Jews eventually win their independence (Josephus 28). The *Book of Macabees* starts the narrative with Alexander the Great, who divided up his empire on his deathbed, and the kings who ruled "wrought much evil on the earth." Antiochus is described as a "sinful shoot" from these kings (Charles 1:68).

However, this was not a simple battle between the Jews and their foreign oppressors. Many within the Jewish community wanted to assimilate and gain the benefits of Greek citizenship. This meant coining their own money and self-governance to a degree. They are not described favorably in *Maccabees*:

> In those days there came forth out of Israel lawless men, and persuaded many, saying 'Let us go and make a covenant with the nations that are round about us ; for since we separated ourselves from them many evils have come upon us.' And the saying appeared good in their eyes; and as certain of the people were eager (to carry this out), they went to the king, and he gave them the authority to introduce the customs of the Gentiles. They also submitted themselves to uncircumcision, and repudiated the holy covenant; yea, they jointed themselves to the Gentiles, and sold themselves to do evil. (Charles 1:68)

The Jews ultimately fought against Antiochus and won. They rededicated their Temple, an event commemorated by the holiday of Hanukkah (Pagels *Origin* 46). After driving out the Seleucids, the Jews were torn between the secular and the religious, but the theocratic state won out. A later fight between the Hasmoneans (the dynasty founded by Judas Maccabee's son Simon) and the Pharisees (separatists who opposed Hellenization) took place. The Hasmoneans gained the high priesthood, but abandoned Israel's ancestral ways. The Pharisees were joined in opposing the Hasmoneans and Hellenization by other radical groups, including the Essenes and early followers of Jesus of Nazareth (Pagels *Origin* 47).

The Pharisees sought to remove foreign influence from Jewish religion, as they saw this as the great evil that led to the downfall of Israel. This is similar to what happened with the Deuteronomists during the Babylonian exile. The difference was invoking the term *satan* to define those Jews who had violated the covenant. They believed those secular Jews were seduced by the powers of evil, and from this came stories about the fall of angels "swollen with lust or arrogance" (Pagels *Origin* 47). To quote the *Book of Enoch*:

And it came to pass when the children of men had multiplied in those days were born unto them beautiful and comely daughters. And the angels, children of the heaven, saw and lusted after them, and said to one another: 'Come, let us choose wives from among the children of men and beget us children.' (Charles 2:191)

Enoch tells us two-hundred angels swore an oath to do this together, as their leader Semjâza (identified with Satan) complained, "I fear ye will not indeed agree to do this deed, and I alone shall have to pay the penalty of a great sin" (Charles 2:191). The angels taught the women "charms and enchantments"; the angel Azazel taught the men to make armor, and how to use the metals of the earth (Charles 2:192).

I highlight these passages, because they offer some background to later beliefs about "wise women," magic and witchcraft. While *Enoch* is part of the Jewish pseudepigrapha and not part of the official canon of the Bible except in Ethiopia, it develops the story in *Genesis* 6 about the Nephilim, the race of giants created by angels mating with human women. These angels are known in this apocryphal literature as "Watchers." It is also part of the tradition later adopted by Christianity when the Catholic Church created its own doctrine on Satan, his demons, and Hell. We see that women learned "wortcunning," the use of herbs and plants for medicine and perhaps other purposes. This is presented as forbidden knowledge, and forms part of the archetypal idea of the witch or wise woman. We also see that it was the beauty of the women that drew the angels into the sin of lust. It is worth noting that metallurgy and smithcraft were also viewed as "magical" operations by the ancients. There is guilt among men and women, but the women are seen as the cause of the transgression. The *Book of Jubilees* tells us that Enoch "testified to the Watchers, who had sinned with the daughters of men" (Charles 2:19). The angels are responsible, but on the human side, women are responsible.

Jung and Theodicy in Judaism

Carl Jung was very much concerned with the question of theodicy, particularly as it manifested in the Biblical *Book of Job*. We often see Job as one who patiently bears the torments and tests of God. But there is nothing just about these tests; Yahweh allows Satan to torment Job on a bet. When Job finally asks God what he has done to deserve this, Yahweh silences him by arrogantly proclaiming his might: "Will you even put me in the wrong? Will you condemn me, that you may be justified? Have you an arm like God, and can you thunder with a voice like his?" (*Revised Standard Version*, Job 40:8-9) It is clear from Revelation and many other apocryphal works that Yahweh also lets evil loose in the world for no apparent reason. They blame the behavior of man, but if demons roam the earth causing evil, this could be solved by removing them. Giving Satan permission to rule on the earth for one thousand years is strikingly reminiscent of the contract negotiated by Mithras between Ahura Mazda and Ahriman in the Zoroastrian religion. But God and Satan are not equal cosmological forces; Satan is the servant of God, even though rebellious. With regard to Yahweh, Jung says "But a relationship of trust seems completely out of the question to our modern way of thinking. Nor can moral satisfaction be expected from an unconscious nature god of this kind" (*Answer* 23).

Jung resolves this conflict by suggesting Satan is the archetypal Shadow of God. Yahweh reveals to Job that he is an antinomy:

> Formerly he [Job] was naïve, dreaming perhaps of a 'good' God, or of a benevolent ruler and just judge. He had imagined that a 'covenant' was a legal matter and that anyone who was party to a contract could insist on his rights as agreed; that God would be faithful and true or at least just, and, as one could assume from the Ten Commandments, would have some recognition of ethical values or at least feel committed to his own legal standpoint. But, to his horror, he has discovered that Yahweh is not human but, in certain respects, less than human, that is just what Yahweh himself says of Leviathan (the crocodile). (*Answer* 21)

In Jung's view Yahweh has an animalistic unconscious, just as humans do. This might remind us of the capriciousness of the Olympian gods, who could do good or harm to mortals on a whim. But there is a difference:

> That was the essential difference between Yahweh and the all-ruling Father Zeus, who in a benevolent and somewhat detached manner allowed the economy of the universe to roll along on its accustomed courses and punished only those who were disorderly. He did not moralize but ruled purely instinctively. He did not demand anything more from human beings than the sacrifices due to him; he did not want to do anything with human beings because he had no plans for them. Father Zeus is certainly a figure, but not a personality. Yahweh, on the other hand, was interested in man. Human beings were a matter of first-rate importance to him. He needed them as they needed him, urgently and personally. (*Answer* 8)

This nicely sums up the difference between ancient Greek ideas about "god" and the monotheistic conception. Zeus' justice is not about morality; it is only about maintaining order. Humans are not to transgress the boundaries set by the divine and Fate through acts of hubris. But Yahweh has a personal interest, because man is made in his image. This follows from the mysteries of Dionysus, in which the mortals created from the Titan ashes also contain a bit of the divine because the Titans ate Dionysus. It is the idea of the "divine" that makes us more than irrelevant specks in the universe. When humans gain some level of divinity and immortality, the amoral caprices of the gods no longer suffice. Why should we believe that we are worthy of the label "divine" or "in God's image?" Yahweh sets Adam over the beasts of the field, and philosophy assumes it is our reason and intelligence that make us the best overlords. Our ability to be conscious and make rational decisions is a "divine" power. But we forget that there is also an unconscious and irrational side to our minds, and this is what dominates rather than reason. If we are a reflection of Yahweh, it is not surprising that Yahweh can act consciously (and therefore be just) but can also behave very unconsciously, under the influence of the "Trickster" Satan. "He is both subhuman and superhuman, a bestial and divine being, whose chief and most alarming characteristic is his unconsciousness" (Jung "On" 263).

The Feminine and Evil in Judaism: Foreignness and Impurity

Elaine Pagels believes that the story of the Watchers in *Enoch* and *Jubilees* is a form of sociopolitical satire, though scholars disagree about whether the fallen angels represent their arrogant Hellenistic rulers, or if they represent the secular rulers within Judaism itself. "David Suter suggests that the story aims instead at certain priests who, like the 'sons of God' in the story, violate their divinely given status and responsibility by allowing lust to draw them into impurity—especially marriages with outsiders, Gentile women" (*Origin* 50-51). In Proverbs 7 is the allegory of Folly, portrayed as the "loose woman" who decks out her bed with fine Egyptian linen. There is the implication of sensuality and worldliness in the description. Folly is described as a woman "Dressed as a harlot, wily of heart. She is loud and wayward, her feet do not stay at home; now in the street, now in the market, and at every corner she lies in wait" (7:10-12). The young man is warned, "Her house is the way to Sheol, going down to the chambers of death" (7:27). In another passage, we read "For the lips of a loose woman drip honey, and her speech is smoother than oil; but in the end she is bitter as wormwood, sharp as a two-edged sword. Her feet go down to death; her steps follow the path to Sheol" (5:3-5). It is worth noting in the *Interpreter's Bible* translation of the Greek *Septuagint* translates "loose" in this passage as "strange" (5:3). Is there a possible implication in the language that strange or foreign women are loose?

Let us digress for a moment from women to the specific idea of "foreign-ers" and evil. The non-Orphic mythology of Dionysus shows a "foreign" de-ity from Thrace who leads the people of the Greek cities into disorder and drunkenness. Both Pentheus and Lycurgus are kings who try to stop Diony-sus and his followers, and both meet terrible ends. We see how the Romans react to the Bacchanals, also dedicated to Dionysus as Bacchus or sometimes Liber, because of the "liberating" effect of alcohol.

I am reminded of a Protestant's dream account published by Carl Jung. The dreamer entered a room like the Hagia Sophia, and the inscription on the door stated it was the "universal Catholic Church." Those present were drinking wine, and the priest in the dream explained to the dreamer: "These somewhat trivial amusements are officially approved and permitted. We must adapt a little to American methods. With a large crowd such as we have here this is inevitable. But we differ in principle from the American churches by our decidedly anti-ascetic tendency" ("Individual" 133). The dream images demonstrate the "anti-ascetic" roots of Christianity. Drinking and reveling are treated as evils, because they free us from the bounds of civilized order and we descend into chaos. This can have positive or negative effects, but chaos cannot be eradicated in favor of order, any more than "evil" can be eradicated and only "good" remain. At least one moral of the Dionysus mythology is that we can't get rid of irrationality and chaos. We may live moderate lives, but at some point repressed instincts will come to the fore, and we must deal with them. Those who insist on rigid control may descend into madness. The consequences of repression are important to keep in mind when we start discussing Satan as a separate being of evil. Matthew Arnold refers to the "Hebraic" origins of the split and its problems for the Victorian era: "The governing idea of Hellenism is spontaneity of consciousness; that of Hebraism, strictness of conscience" (478). A system that demands obedience to the "good" will always put us in conflict with our realities.

Russell equates the image of Satan with Pan, a reveling satyr from Greek mythology (126), but there are also comparisons of Satan and Dionysus. This is ironic, because as we've already noted, in Orphic mythology we see a pro-totype for resurrection and salvation in the Dionysus birth and rebirth myth. In the Orphic system, Dionysus is closer to Christ than to Satan, but in an-other later reversal his trickster nature will identify him with the latter.

When we speak about eradicating evil, we refer to divine justice, and par-ticularly to "righteousness" and "purity." Whether it is the Jews admonishing those who do not conform to Yahweh's laws, or heavenly angels mixing with mortal women (or implied "Gentile" women), there becomes an implicit as-sociation between the idea of the "pure" and the "righteous." Plato may have focused on truth as the foundation of justice, but here it is about keeping the Law, and the Jews have this in common with Roman religious sentiments. It is not surprising that these concepts became conflated in the early Empire, as the correct performance of ritual and tradition was something Romans could identify with if they were raised in the state religion, though we also see this in the state rituals of ancient Greece. As we discussed in the last chapter, this legalistic tendency in religion is decidedly masculine. Jung takes this a step further: "God's marriage with Israel was therefore an essentially masculine affair, something like the founding of the Greek *polis*, which occurred about the same time" (*Answer* 33). The Jews were Yahweh's people, and his covenant is often described in terms of a marriage, with Israel as the bride. This metaphor would later be applied to the Catholic Church, and we will see in our discussion of the Jewish "feminine" that it was also used for *Sophia* and the *Shekinah*. But this does not feminize the arrangement: "At the bottom of Yahweh's marriage with Israel is a perfectionist intention which excludes that kind of relatedness known as 'Eros'. The lack of Eros, of relationship to values, is painfully apparent in the *Book of Job*: the paragon of all creation is not a man, but a monster!" (*Answer* 33). Note that Jung also applies this to the Greek *polis*; as we discussed earlier, the movement from *oikos* to *polis* was a move from the family unit to the city, from the private to the public. If Jung is correct, it also shifts focus from the feminine, or at least from a place of respect for the feminine as life giver, to the masculine. "The inferiority of women was a settled fact. Woman was regarded as less perfect than man, as Eve's weakness for the blandishments of the serpent amply proved" (*Answer* 33). This also would have been true for the authors of the apocryphal books; angels lusted after human women, and then all Hell broke loose on the earth.

This brings us to the concept of purity. We spoke about purity with respect to Roman death rituals; death was pollution, and funerals were attempts to rid the family of the pollution. This was similar to the Jewish focus on purity and strict obedience to the law, and avoiding pollution from "foreign" ways, as this also brought death. In the apocryphal literature, we see this idea of purity extending to women; certainly there is an exhortation against involvement with Gentile women, but woman herself brought death into the world, so she is responsible for this pollution. A woman who is not a virgin is also considered to be "impure." Even today we see evidence that women and girls are valued based on their state of chastity. Sexual education programs related to abstinence have referred to young girls who are not virgins as "used pieces of gum" (Hess). The "pure" woman is the one who follows this masculine religion of ritual perfection and sexual obedience. With this in mind, let us look at examples of the feminine in Jewish scripture, rabbinical literature, and folklore, which are instructive in how women became associated with the demons who roamed the earth.

Eve

Why does the woman walk in front of the corpse at a funeral, and why was the precept of menstruation given to her? Because she shed the blood of Adam (by bringing death to man). And why was the precept of the dough (*hallah*) given to her? Because she corrupted Adam, who was the dough of the world. And why was the precept of the Sabbath lights given to her? Because she extinguished the soul of Adam. (qtd. in Aschkenasy 3)

The story of Adam and Eve in *Genesis* 1-3 is well known to almost anyone raised in the Western or Near Eastern world. We see Yahweh creating the heavens and the earth out of the void and populating the world with plants and animals. He makes Adam, the first man, and takes a rib from him to make Eve, the first woman. They reside in the Garden of Eden with Yahweh and may eat of any fruit in the garden except from a tree in the middle. The serpent appears and convinces Eve to eat the fruit. She then shares the fruit with Adam, and at this moment they become aware of their nakedness and cover themselves (*Revised Standard Version*, Gen. 3:7). When Yahweh realizes what they have done, he curses and banishes them. Joseph Campbell has pointed out that this is the real beginning of life, because the Garden of Eden is outside the field of time (47). In the field of time there is the perception of separation and difference; everything exists in relationship to everything else. In this sense, it makes perfect sense for Eve to eat the fruit, as woman is the generator of life. Life is a paradox that involves death, and to remain forever with Yahweh in the garden would not allow for human life; humans would be more like divinities or angels.

This is obviously not the mainstream view of this myth. Eve is guilty of disobedience and is seen as weak for giving in to the serpent. The serpent itself is a trickster figure that would later become identified with the devil, or with a fallen angel. The apocryphal text *Vita Adae et Evae* (*Life of Adam and Eve*, or *Books of Adam and Eve*) goes into greater detail than *Genesis* about the fall of the Devil and Eve's corruption of the human race. The devil tells Adam that his condition is Adam's fault: "Adam, what dost thou tell me? It is for thy sake that I have been hurled from that place. When thou wast formed, I was hurled out of the presence of God and banished from the company of angels" (Charles 2:137). God asked the angels to worship Adam, who was made in his image, but the devil refused: "I will not worship an inferior and younger being (than I)" (Charles 2:137). Adam is portrayed as innocent in the whole process; the devil wants revenge because of his own pride. But Eve is considered guilty. After the devil takes possession of the serpent, and convinces Eve to eat the forbidden fruit, he then tells her, "I have changed my mind and will not give thee to eat until thou swear to me to give also to thy husband" (Charles 2:146). So Eve swears and then eats the fruit: "And when he had received the oath from me, he went and poured upon the fruit the poison of his wickedness, which is lust, the root and beginning of every sin, and he bent the branch on the earth and I took of the fruit and I ate" (Charles 2:146).

Here we see a minor plot twist—it is when Eve eats the fruit that she gains the root of every sin, which is lust. Perhaps this is not too different from the Buddhist assertion that desire is the root of suffering. But there is a definite sense of blame of the woman for allowing the devil to bring lust into the world. Eve regrets her decision but has sworn an oath and must convince Adam to eat the fruit as well, which she does. At this point the Archangel Michael blows his horn, and Yahweh comes and ejects them from the garden with curses. As Adam is dying she prays to Yahweh and says, "I have sinned before Thee and all sin hath begun through my doing in the creation" (Charles 2:149). The apocryphal writers blamed Eve for evil in the world, and it is clear from the Talmudic quote at the beginning of this section that the rabbis also interpreted the story in this manner. "Her story is thus seen as a parable of the moral weakness and strong proclivity for evil that characterizes the female of the human species" (Aschkenasy 39).

Lilith

If Eve was weak and defiant, she pales in comparison to the later folkloric figure of Lilith. In Jewish folklore Lilith becomes a symbol for the demonic female who refuses to submit to her husband. The name is first used in Isaiah 34:14 in connection with night demons and monsters, with *lilit* translated as "night hag" (*Revised Standard Version*). There is an interesting piece of physiology attached to the "night hag": the experience of sleep paralysis. In some cultures, "nightmares" are equated with what is called the "Old Hag" tradition. David Hufford defines this experience in the traditions of Newfoundland in the words of a twenty-year old student interviewed for his study: "You are dreaming and you feel as if someone is holding you down. You can do nothing only cry out. People believe that you will die if you are not awakened." (Hufford 2). There are different varieties of this experience and different rationalizations for it, but many include the actual appearance of an old woman or hag, or a shadowy figure. The connection between this type of sleep paralysis and the "Old Hag" is not limited to Newfoundland. One wonders how this terrifying feminine archetype, certainly connected with Lilith (though not proven as the origin of this idea), has become connected to a surprisingly common physiological phenomenon. (Hufford 245)

Lilith also appears in folklore as Adam's first wife. It is believed that Lilith was probably a carryover from Mesopotamian or Sumerian demonology, but we don't know anything about these original demonic figures or how they were viewed. A later story claims that Lilith left Adam and coupled with the archangel Samael, another name used for Satan. In the Talmud's story of Lilith, Samael is driven from Heaven as the Devil was in the *Book of Adam and Eve*. He then creates Lilith as a helpmate for Adam:

> Other Rabbis say that Adam looked out over the many animals on earth and noticed that they were all male or female, yet he had no female. So God first created a woman named Lillith out of dust. But Lillith set herself over Adam and balked at the way he wished to make love, with the man on top. 'Why?' She scowled. Who are you to lord over me? We are both made of dust! In her arrogance she recited the sacred, unspeakable name of God and disappeared from sight. After this miserable creature went to live among the demons, God felt sorry for Adam and decided to make him a good woman, Eve. Adam ruled over all the plants and male animals in the east and north of the Garden of Eden, while Eve ruled the female animals in the south and west. Adam and Eve went about naked, except for a band over their shoulders that was inscribed with the sacred name of God. And Adam and Eve lived in perfect innocence at this time. But Samael and Lillith were busy plotting how to confound these good people. (Bierlein 78)

The quote is J.F. Bierlein's retelling of several stories in the Talmudic literature. In this condensed re-telling, we observe a number of points of interest. Lilith and Adam are made out of the same substance, dust. Eve is taken out of Adam, so she is viewed as "part" of him; Lilith really is his equal. It is in the sex act that Lilith wishes to assert her dominance. We see here how sexual dominance for a woman is viewed as something wicked. She recites the forbidden name of God, something that would associate her with magic and witchcraft; magicians are the ones who learn and speak forbidden names. And she is associated with Samael, the Devil who will later cause Adam and Eve's fall from innocence.

Carl Jung states that Satan is Yahweh's "Shadow." If so, then Lilith is Eve's "Shadow." Eve comes across as weak and easily deceived, which is the reason for her disobedience. Lilith is strong and in charge of herself. If the idealized woman is passive and obedient, and this is the persona she must display, then Lilith represents the less developed side of the Feminine. She is the "Eve" of the underworld and knows secret things, which would associate her with the chthonic. Mircea Eliade speaks of the chthonian Great Mother, who "shows herself pre-eminently as the Goddess of Death and Mistresses of the Dead; that is, she displays threatening and aggressive aspects" (62). He also refers to the *vagina dentata*, which is the mouth of the Mother Earth: "In initiatory myths and sagas, the Hero's passage through a giantess' belly and his emergence through her mouth are equivalent to a new birth. But the passage is infinitely danger-ous" (63). Lilith's connection to the Devil and the "Fall" of humans, as well as her creation from dust, make her an Earth Mother.

We spoke earlier of the bloody and violent rites of the Magna Mater or Great Mother, and also of the initiatory functions of many of the Greek goddesses. In this sense, the Mother is associated with danger of death or being devoured. This is symbolized in many ways in mythology, including fighting dragons or monsters, being swallowed up, or descending into the underworld. We looked at several examples of liminal rituals related to this dangerous female aspect in Chapter 2. Erich Neumann calls this aspect of the Feminine archetype "The Terrible Mother," described vividly as follows:

> This Terrible Mother is the hungry earth, which devours its own chil-
> dren and fattens on their corpses; it is the tiger and the vulture, the
> vulture and the coffin, the flesh-eating sarcophagus voraciously lick-
> ing up the blood seed of men and beasts and, once fecundated and sat-
> ed, casting it out again in new birth, hurling it to death, and over and
> over again to death. (*Great* 149-150)

In Jungian thought, the dangerous descent into the collective uncon-scious usually takes place because of an event. The hero's journey begins with a call to adventure that threatens or significantly changes the idyllic life he led as a child. The hero is swallowed by the monster or battles it to achieve transformation. We are called out of our "Edens" to live our lives.

Sophia and Shekinah

If Eve and Lilith are mythic manifestations of the darker qualities of hu-man women, Sophia and Shekinah represent the divine Feminine present in Judaism. Many people are surprised to discover a positive female presence in what is considered a patriarchal religion. We see Sophia prominently in *Proverbs* 8, which might be seen as a third creation story in the *Bible*. Sophia means Wisdom, and it is Divine Wisdom who speaks in *Proverbs*:

> Ages ago I was set up,
> At the first, before the beginning of the earth.

When there were no depths I was brought forth,
When there were no springs abounding with water,
Before the mountains had been shaped,
Before the hills, I was brought forth;
Before he had made the earth with its fields
Or the first of the dust of the world.
When he established the heavens, I was there
When he drew a circle on the face of the deep,
When he made firm the skies above,
When he established the fountains of the deep
When he assigned to the sea its limit
So that the waters might not transgress his command
When he marked out the foundations of the earth,
Then I was beside him, like a master workman;
And I was daily his delight, rejoicing before him always
Rejoicing in his inhabited world and delighting in the sons of men.
(*Interpreter's Bible*, Prov. 8:23-31)

Jung also highlights a passage from the apocryphal book of *Sirach* regarding Sophia:

I came out of the mouth of the Most High
And covered the earth as a cloud.
I dwelt in high places,
And my throne is in a cloudy pillar,
I alone encompassed the circuit of Heaven,
And walked in the bottom of the deep,
I had power over the waves of the sea, and over all the earth
And over every people and nation.
He created me from the beginning before the world
And I shall never fail.
In the holy tabernacle I served before him;
And so was I established in Sion.
Likewise in the beloved city he gave me rest
And in Jerusalem was my power. (qtd, in *Answer* 25)

Sophia was a co-creator with Yahweh, and Carl Jung has suggested that his marriage to Sophia was later replaced by his marriage to Israel. Sophia "corresponds in almost every feature to the Logos of St. John" (Jung, *Answer* 26). We will talk about Gnostic Christian interpretations of Sophia in the section on Gnosticism and the problem of evil in this chapter; however, it is worth noting here that *logos* is a masculine word and assumed to be a masculine concept by Christian doctrine. Here we see it applied to the feminine. Sophia's symbol is the dove, which is akin to such ancient goddesses as Ishtar, and will later be used to symbolize the *Paraclete* (Holy Spirit) in Christianity. *Paraclete* is a neuter term, so neither of Sophia's later associations in mainstream Christianity are female. Nehama Aschkenasy views Sophia as an allegorical figure, set up in Proverbs against another feminine figure, Folly (175), which we discussed in an earlier section.

If we look at Sophia psychologically, she represents inward thought and reflection. Wisdom comes from experience over time. When Yahweh torments Job through Satan for no good reason, he is acting unconsciously. "Self-reflection becomes an imperative necessity, and for this Wisdom is needed" (Jung, *Answer* 29). The archetypal significance of Sophia is evident in later Judaism, specifically in Kabbalah, the system of Jewish mysticism that developed around the 11th century C.E. (Goetschel).

Another Kabbalistic feminine being is the Shekinah. Shekinah means "Divine Presence" in Hebrew, and is described as the presence of God that is present in the Holy of Holies in the Temple. She is the divine presence of Yahweh in the material world. In this view Shekinah rather than Sophia is the intimate partner of Yahweh, though Jewish theology treats Shekinah as part of Yahweh (Aschkenasy 16). However, the Jews did not view Shekinah as a feminine deity, or even as a female part of God, even though the word is feminine.

There are two considerations here. When we speak of Kabbalah, we are talking about a later development in Jewish thinking, so even though both Shekinah and Sophia appear in the *Bible* and other scriptures, these developed ideas of them as feminine deity or bride were not necessarily part of Jewish thinking of the first three centuries of the Common Era. Even if these ideas did exist in this earlier period, they do not represent any religious idea of a feminine deity in Judaism. However, as they are frequently pointed to as examples of the feminine embedded within Judaism, I mention them here for completeness.

In spite of these positive assertions of the Feminine, the negative ones are ingrained in our culture. Erich Neumann makes the point:

> The earthly side has to be sacrificed for the sake of Heaven, because "human" Earth is from the beginning fallen and corrupted Earth. And Earth, the Earth Serpent, Woman and the instinctual world, as represented by sexuality, are evil, seductive and accursed, and Man, who in virtue of his essential nature, really belongs to Heaven, is the one who is seduced and deceived. (*Fear* 170)

Judaism and the Graeco-Roman World

As we mentioned earlier, the Jews did not really come into contact with the Greeks until the conquest of Alexander the Great, and when they were discussed by Greek writers, they were mentioned as philosophers or astrologers. The Greeks and citizens of the Hellenistic world were interested in learning truth through rationality and philosophy; the Jews were more interested in obedience to ritual purity and their Law. The Middle Platonic Jewish philosopher Philo tried to bridge Judaism and Stoicism, but the pantheistic conception of God did not fit in with the Old Testament view (Harnack 110). Jewish theology had more in common with Roman thinking, and at the time the apocryphal works were written, the Jews were the subjects of Rome. The Romans regarded the Jews as atheists, because they did not participate in the State religion (Leitzmann 84). But just as other foreign cults influenced the beliefs of Romans at this time, Judaism became strongly influential, possibly because of the common affinity for ritual correctness and purity. The Jews did proselytize despite Roman disapproval. (83). The Jews were given special dispensation to practice their own religion, but the Romans did not want Judaism to spread. When the Jews pushed back at Rome in the same way they pushed back at the Greeks, they were definitely put down by the destruction of the Second Temple in 66 C.E. At that point the Jews were still torn by civil war, so the presence of the Romans was met with relief by many citizens of Jerusalem. Vespasian was now Emperor and had sent the general Titus in to put down the insurrection in Jerusalem. Josephus tells us the Romans burned the outer walls of the Temple, but were undecided about the inner Temple and sanctuary. But after a clash with Jewish forces stationed in the inner Temple, the hatred of the Roman forces was stoked:

> Then one of the soldiers, without waiting for orders and without a qualm for the terrible consequences of his action but urged on by some unseen force, snatched up a blazing piece of wood and climbing on another soldier's back hurled the brand through a golden aperture giving access to the chambers built round the Sanctuary. As the flames shot into the air the Jews sent up a cry that matched the calamity and dashed to the rescue, with no thought now of saving their lives or husbanding their strength; for that which hitherto they had guarded so devotedly was disappearing before their eyes. (Josephus 323)

The destruction of the second Temple is a traumatic event that echoes in the psychology of Western civilization. It is likely the event that spurred the writing of the Book of Revelation, the final book of the Bible by John of Patmos, an observant Jew who believed Jesus of Nazareth was the Messiah who had come to save the Jews. The timing of the Temple's destruction coincides with another monumental event in our collective mythical psychology: the rise of Christianity.

Early Christianity

The Jewish group closest in spirit to the early Christians was the Essenes. As a result of the Maccabean revolt and the trouble between secular and observant Jews, the Essenes formed their own community in the desert. They were considered devout by the Pharisees and Sadducees because of their attention to ritual purity; however, they went a step farther by separating national from moral identity. Like the Zoroastrians, the Essenes saw the battle between Yahweh and Satan as cosmological. Whether one was born a Jew or not, everyone had to enter into the new covenant to be saved (Pagels *Origin* 60).

Jesus of Nazareth allegedly lived until the age of thirty-three, when he was crucified by the Romans. Whether or not the Romans were really responsible for this, or whether they did it at the behest of the Jewish Sanhedrin who hated Jesus because of his ritual impurity, depends on which of the synoptic accounts is accurate. Regardless, Christianity started as an outgrowth of Judaism, and the problems of the early Empire Jews mirrored those of the early Christians. What we now think of as Roman Catholicism originally represented the "Orthodox" beliefs of writers like Irenaeus, and the established canon that we call the Bible came out of the Council of Nicaea, which met in 325 C.E. at the command of the Emperor Constantine. However, the early days of Christianity were tumultuous.

The earliest writings we have after the accepted death of Jesus are letters from Paul of Tarsus. Christianity was considered a sect of Judaism at that time, and both the Jewish authorities and the Roman government sought to eradicate its influence. Paul was originally sent to arrest Christians, but instead had a vision of Jesus that made him a zealous missionary of the new belief. He originally met James, the brother of Jesus, who had taken over Jesus' mission at his death, and also the apostle Peter. Paul was like the Essenes in believing in the idea of a new covenant, and persuaded Peter and James to allow him to preach to Gentiles. However, they later retracted their permission, and this started a conflict between Paul and Jesus' original disciples. Just as the Pharisees fought internally with Hellenized or Romanized Jews, so the followers of Jesus who wanted strict adherence to Jewish tradition came into conflict with Gentiles who believed in Jesus but did not want to follow tradition.[30]

Peter, Paul and James were all executed by the Roman government, and the destruction of the Second Temple was not long after this event. It was in light of these events that the books of Revelation were written. Elaine Pagels mentions at least twenty known "books of revelation" (*Revelations* 74), but the one that made it into the *Bible* was the Revelation of John of Patmos. John's sentiments were decidedly on the side of Jesus' apostles, and there are subtle references to "deceivers" that may point toward Paul and his Gentile followers. (*Revelations* 54). The books of Revelation, like a lot of apocryphal literature, were eschatological in nature—they referred to the end of times, when evil would have free reign over the earth, and Jesus would return as the conquering savior. The difference between all the other "Books of Revelation" and the Revelation of John is worth noting: "Many of them speak less about a Judgment Day at the end of the world than about finding the divine in it now" (*Revelations* 3). The other books stress the divine within the individual, which was the focus of Gnostic Christians. These other Revelations also speak of a divine Feminine: "While John of Patmos acknowledges no feminine power within the divine, many of the 'revelations' found at Nag Hammadi, from the *Secret Revelation of John* to Allogenes and *Thunder, Perfect Mind*, give voice to feminine manifestations of God" (*Revelations* 99).

These teachings do not fit into what became Christian Orthodoxy, which still retains inspiration from Apocalyptic Judaism. The true believers in Christ will be saved, and all others condemned. During the establishment of the Biblical canon, Athanasius began to define the "beast" and "whore" of John's Revelation with unorthodox Christians, which not only condemned pagans and Jews, but paved the way for the later Inquisition. (*Revelations* 173)

The Early Church Fathers on Death and the Soul

Most of us raised in the Western world have a concept of death and its connection to reward and punishment from Christianity. But what did the early Church writers actually say?

The Synoptic Gospels: The words of Jesus are the obvious place to start when talking about life after death. Jesus certainly talks of hell fire, and takes the worldly to task. Casey observes that Jesus' call for repentance in Matt. 3:2, 4:17, Mark 1:4, 15 and Luke 3:3 mirrors that of John the Baptist, an Essene. (103) In Matt. 19:16-22 he tells a rich man "If thou wilt be perfect, go and sell

---

[30] For more on this see Leitzmann, Hans. *The Beginnings of the Christian Church*. Trans. Bertram Lee Woolf. Vol. 1. NY: Meridian, 1953. Print: 104-130.

all though hast, and give to the poor, and though shalt have treasure I heaven: and come and follow me." But the young man has many possessions and goes away sorrowful, prompting Jesus to say that it is easier for a camel to pass through the eye of a needle than for a rich man to enter heaven. (Matt. 19:24) (qtd. from Casey 104-105) In Mark 9 and Matthew 25, Jesus suggests that there is eternal punishment for the wicked, and Casey suggests that the uncharitable are a particular target, because refusing benevolence to another human being is close to blasphemy, as the person is made in God's image. (108)

Earlier we mentioned the tendency of certain apocalyptic sects like the Essenes to treat the tension between Yahweh and Satan as something cosmological, similar in spirit to Zoroastrian dualism. The description of John the Baptist in Matthew 3 suggests that he lives in the wilderness, and this may be what connects him to the Essenes. Whether an Essene or not, it is clear that he embraces an ascetic purity that would have pleased the Pharisees, but also has apocalyptic notions: he speaks of one who will come after him who will "baptize with the Holy Spirit and fire." (Matthew 3:12) If this is the tradition taken up by Jesus, it is not difficult to see why he would take such a strict moral view. For our purposes, it is the demonizing of material wealth that is of interest. Certainly it takes a compassionate view of the poor and suffering that is admirable and worthy of emulation. But there is a demonizing of the material in favor of the spiritual.

Paul of Tarsus: Christian doctrine is what it is because of Paul. I recall a conversation with some Protestant ministers who felt "Christianity" was a misnomer; "Paulism" would be a better fit. In his first letter to the Corinthians, he implies that sinners will receive God's mercy, but that "the unrighteous shall not inherit the kingdom of God." (1 Cor. 6: 9-10). He suggests that humans are "sown a natural body" and "raised a spiritual body." (1 Cor. 15:42). As John Casey observes, he seems to suggest that salvation is a sort of "natural force," which hardly makes sense if one only achieves salvation by putting off "the old Adam" and "reborn only through the sufferings of Christ." (110-111) That is hardly "natural." Paul adds that "The first man is of the earth, earthy: the second man is the Lord from heaven." (1 Cor. 15:47) Whether intended or not, there is something very Platonic about Paul's conception of salvation—it is dualistic. "On the one hand, Christ's reversal of the consequences of the sin of Adam is seen as a natural fulfillment, even a necessity. On the other, there is the sharpest possible distinction between sinners and saved, the works of the flesh and the works of the spirit." (Casey 111) Faith in Christ is the essential criterion for salvation. But Paul "neither preached eternal damnation, nor had any clear notion of hell." (Casey 109)

Like the ancient Egpytians, Paul believed that wicked souls would cease to exist.

The Passion of Saint Perpetua, Saint Felicitas and Their Companions: This is an early Christian text that claims to include the diary of Perpetua, a young woman martyred on 7 March 203 (Bremmer 57). In her diary, she had a vision of Paradise, which she described as "a great open space, which looked like a park, with roses as high as trees and all kinds of flowers." (Bremmer 58) She climed a ladder to Heaven and saw "an immensely large garden, and in it a white-haired man sat in shepherd's garb, tall and milking sheep." (58) She knew some of those who were present in this place, and recognized them as other martyrs and Christians ("our brethren"). This white-haired shepherd is a likely influence for later images of God, and the garden suggests a return to Eden. Tertullian makes use of Perpetua's vision in his work, *On the Soul,* and claims that she saw only her fellow martyrs in this paradisical vision. Bremmer believes this is Tertullian promoting his own views of Heaven, as no such passage exists in the original work. (59) But it is a starting point for other theories put forth by the early Church Fathers. Tertullian's view resembles the Vision of Er, with the dead "detained in a subterranean abode pending the Resurrection and the thousand-year reign of Christ preceding the definitive Last Judgment" (Bremmer 59). Other related beliefs of the time are similar, but mention the grave as the "sleeping place" before Judgment. As we will see, Augustine took up this idea of resurrecting body and soul as a matter of faith.

Clement of Alexandria: Clement was a Christian convert who presided over the Catechetical School in Alexandria, which tended to combine Christian scripture with Greek philosophy and Gnostic thought. He claimed there were two grades of Christians: the "lower" grade had to rely on faith, but the "higher" grade could attain a higher state through discipline and study (Moore 85). "Thus Clement, in his turn, put himself in accord with the whole range of philosophic thought from the time of Plato and Aristotle to his own day, for his two lives are essentially the active and the contemplative lives that for more than five centuries had been distinguished by philosophers." (Moore 85) This idea has not entirely left Catholicism or Orthodoxy, as those living a monastic life are believed to gain a more profound understanding of God than "laymen". Clement conceived of Christ as the Logos, and believed that the true Gnostic knows God through His Son. (Moore 86)

Origen: Origen was Clement's pupil, and devoted his theological efforts to a philosophical system (Moore 86). Though Origen's works were later rejected, they were still very influential. He believed that men had two souls, a lower animal soul and a higher spiritual soul. "This latter soul is a fallen spirit, which in falling has become a human soul; but it may develop into a spirit once more and thus regain its spiritual endowments. God in the beginning had granted freedom to men who fell by evil choice, so that all are born into a sinful condition. Man's duty is to overcome his inherent sin by his own will aided by God's grace." (Moore 87) Christ is not needed as a redeemer in this model, but "he does bring into his scheme of salvation the historic revelation of the Logos and the death of Christ which he regarded as the first blow in the struggle against the Devil." (Moore 87-88) His belief about three levels of Christian life agreed with the views of Clement. His view of the afterlife was not a "future state of sensuous joys or sufferings" (89), but felt that the "righteous souls would enter directly into Paradise, while the wicked would begin to suffer their punishment at once." (89) This is reminiscent of Plato's "Vision of Er," minus any notions of reincarnation. He did not believe in eternal punishment; Christ would purify and restore everyone. (90) The Church later condemned this view as heretical, probably for the same reason they selected John of Patmos's *Revelation* over others. It goes back to our quote from Walter Burkert in Chapter 2: "Injustice hurts: to punish makes happy." (Burkert "Pleading" 141) All of the beliefs we have studied thus far eventually come to this moralistic view of salvation, and of the notion of divine justice that extends beyond life in the world.

Augustine: Saint Augustine of Hippo is one of Christianity's most famous converts, as he was born into the Manichean religion. Manichaeism was founded in the late third century C.E. by Mani, a Persian who mixed elements of Zoroastrianism, Babylonian folklore, Buddhist teaching, and some Christian ideas into a late syncretistic religion. The key theme is that of dualism, following the thread of other religions postulating a battle between good and evil.[31] In this sense it is similar to Platonic schools of thought at the time.

Augustine's writings reflect both Manichean and Neoplatonic influence, though he did not separate body and soul; both were essential to salvation. He also felt that souls were individual entities, and not part of the Platonic "universal soul." (Moore 119) Given that body and soul were both required, both were eligible for immortality and salvation. (120) We see this reflected in the notion of resurrection, which was not a new idea, but became part of the doctrine that required bodies to be buried rather than cremated in the Catholic Church's eschatological tradition. Augustine had no formal reasons for this view; he relied on his faith, though his arguments on immortality tended toward the Platonic. The Platonic idea suggests that the soul exists before the body, and thus it must be eternal (120); Augustine felt that the

---

[31] Catholic Encyclopedia, "Manichaeism," http://www.newadvent.org/cathen/09591a.htm

souls of men were descended from "the soul of the first man even as bodies descend through the parents by generation." (121). He also believes that the soul animates the body, so the body can die, but the soul cannot. The ability of humans to have reason and know truth, which are immortal, means the soul is likewise immortal. (122) Marrying these Platonic views with matters of Christian doctrine led to many questions and contradictions, and Augustine was never entirely satisfied with his rational arguments. Ultimately he fell back on Christian faith and tradition, and the philosophical question would later be taken up by Thomas Aquinas.

It is interesting to note that "salvation" and "the second coming of the Messiah" mean two different things in Judaism and Christianity. "But whereas the Jewish idea that this scene of judgment will be the occasion when the nation of Israel is justified against her enemies and persecutors, here Christ's words will be addressed to individuals." (Casey 115) Once again, the focus on the individual makes the terms of salvation about moralistic behavior, choosing "good" over "evil."

The Consequences of Salvation

Those who are "saved" are saved from death in the Christian view. The belief is that at his death, Christ bodily ascended into Heaven in the resurrection. In this way he triumphs over death, and the righteous will triumph with him at the end of time. Satan and his demons go under the earth at the last judgment, and the eternally damned go with them. We now have a perception of death and the underworld affected by what James Hillman calls "Christianism":

> Let us compare: Orpheus and Dionysos went down to redeem close personal loves: Orpheus, Eurydice; Dionysos, his mother Semele. Hercules has tasks to fulfill. Aeneas and Ulysses made their descents to learn: there they gained counsel from the 'father,' Anchises and Tiresias. Dionysos, in Aristophanes' Frogs, went down another time in search of poetry to save the city. But Christ's mission to the underworld was to annul it through his resurrected victory over death. Because of his mission, Christians were forever exempted from the descent. Lazarus becomes the paradigm for all humankind. We shall all rise. The eternal life is not in the underworld, but its destruction. (85)

As Hillman explains, there are consequences for this view of death and the underworld:

> The ascension requires that we leave not only our blood behind, like the *thymos* which did not belong in the underworld and whose desires

cost soul. Paul goes Heraclitus one better—or worse, because the Christian ascensional mystery exchanges *psyche* for *pneuma*. We pay for spirit with our souls. Christianism's defeat of the underworld is also the loss of soul. (87)

What does Hillman mean by "loss of soul"? According to Jung, the soul corresponds to the *anima* in particular, the "female" archetype representing the soul of a man. He did not identify the male *animus* with the soul in women; he believed the *animus* represented the judgments and opinions of women. The *anima* is more sensual in nature; it is the source of a man's creativity and represents his desires. When he falls madly in love with a woman, he is falling in love with a projection of his *anima*, seeing its qualities in an otherwise ordinary woman. We see how Judaism viewed women who were independent in their sexuality, and it is not a stretch to see the association between the archetypal *anima* and the dangerous Feminine that leads men into sin. Christianity inherited this idea from Judaism, devaluing both the *anima* and earth for the righteous Christian. The result is the individual who represses and denies all of his or her own natural instincts, and lives a life torn between what they "should" do and what they want to do.

Gnosticism and the problem of evil

Christian history separates early Christians into two main groups, the Orthodox and the Gnostics. This is a bit of a reduction. The groups lumped into the category of "gnostic" show a wide disparity of beliefs about Jesus, the scriptures, and eschatology. We can see Gnostic influence in the writings of the early Church Fathers from our earlier discussion. The gnostic Justin wrote a book called *Baruch* that manages to merge the mythology of Heracles with the story of Adam and Eve in Eden (Leitzmann 272-274). Pagan syncretism was frequently interwoven with Jewish scriptures. Other texts attempted to interpret the gospels, most notably Basilides' *Exegetica*. We know about this book from the writings of Clement of Alexandria and Iraneus (280). He promoted the idea that God is all good, and suffering only occurs because of sin. Even apparently "good" and pious people were sinful, and if they were suffering it was evidence that they had done wrong. Basilides also incorporated the Platonic idea of metempsychosis; if someone hadn't done wrong in this lifetime, they may have done wrong in a previous one. But suffering also belonged to the earth; the soul could be redeemed by finding the will of God acceptable and being re-absorbed into the "All," which is similar to the Platonic idea of *Nous* (281-282).

The basic ideas that all Gnostic thinking have in common include the notion that the human soul is of heavenly origin, and that the creator God is actually a spirit of lower rank. He keeps humans from knowing their own divinity, and it is through the intervention of Christ that people learn of their own divine connection again (285). The Gnostic Valentine had the most sophisticated and influential version of this myth:

> Above the universe, on invisible and ineffable heights, dwells the prime Father who is also called Bythos and Chaos. He is invisible, incomprehensible, superior to time, unbegotten, and dwells in eternal peace. At his side is his Ennoea, also called Sigē or Charis, i.e., God's thought, silence and grace. Personification of divine properties is by now quite familiar to us: it is a new thing, however, that the prime God should have a consort. This belongs to the nature of the system, for according to Valentine all the divine emanations proceed forth in duality; the mystery of marriage (Eph. 5:32) is predominant even in the world of the gods. (Leitzmann 288)

These "pairings" of gods are sometimes referred to as "aeons," and Valentine mentions thirty of them. However, one of the aeons, Sophia, does not follow the pattern:

> Only the last of the thirty aeons, Sophia, lets her desires grow into an unbridled passion, and tries to grasp the nature of the Father. But she would have been overcome by the sweet rapture of her feelings, and have dissolved into the All, had not Horos, the guardian of the borders of the plemora, held her back, supported her, and brought her back to her senses. ... But now at the command of the prime Father, Monogenes brings forth a new pair, Christ and the Holy Spirit, in order that the latter might restore order to the plemora which had been disturbed by Sophia's action. (289)

The "yearning" of Sophia becomes personified as well, into a female spirit called Achamoth. She experiences yearning and suffering similar to her mother, and her tears, laughter and sorrow form the elements of the material world (290). There are other versions of this Gnostic cosmology, some making Yahweh himself into an evil god created by Sophia on her own. But we see the world created in this way by a female spirit who does not follow the convention of "marriage," and once again "passion" is the sin. The world is therefore an unnatural place of suffering, and humans must strive toward the spiritual heights and the message of Christ to be "redeemed" to their properly divine places. This mystical version of Christianity represented a full rejection of the earth and the material world in favor of the spirit, going even farther than Paul. We see Sophia, the representation of Wisdom, acting in a

way that is treated as unwise, as she does not use discrimination but is over-
taken by her passions. She wants to learn the mysteries of the divine Father
on her own—it is an independent act. While the Gnostic beliefs are often
seen as an alternative view that exalts the human soul as divine, we can see
that it does nothing for the Feminine in principle, even if it includes it. The
culmination of Gnostic belief in the Church came in the Middle Ages with
the Cathars, who believed all matter was evil. The Third Lateran Council
of 1179 put down this group as heretical (Brenon). If the Cathars had their
way, no Christians could ever procreate, as bringing a soul into the world
was interpreted as an evil act. However, the idea of matter as evil did not go
away in consciousness, as the superiority of spirit over matter had already
been asserted for centuries. Women are the ones who bring humans into the
world of matter, and their connection with the "Fall" of humans made them
the embodiment of wickedness and weakness.

Christianity and the Feminine

The Virgin Mary inevitably enters discussions of the Christian Feminine.
Jung feels that the presence of Mary in Catholic theology gives it a psychological edge over Protestantism: "The feminine, like the masculine, demands
an equally personal representation" (*Answer* 103). The lack of a Feminine image in Protestantism means that:

> It [Protestantism] is obviously out of touch with the tremendous ar-
> chetypal happenings in the psyche of the individual and the masses,
> and with the symbols which are intended to compensate the truly
> apocalyptic world situation today. It seems to have succumbed to a
> species of rationalistic historicism and to have lost any understanding
> of the Holy Ghost who works in the hidden places of the soul. (*Answer*
> 101)

Jung acknowledges the need for the Christian Feminine, but Mary is
hardly a compensation for the chthonic element of the Great Mother. She
is allegedly born without sin, and Jesus is born without her "knowing man."
She represents a cleanliness and chastity that leaves her dangerous sexuality
untouched. She, like Satan, is a servant of Yahweh, not a being of possible
equal stature like Sophia. Jesus, as the product of a virgin birth, fits in with
the archetype of the Divine Child, who is more often than not the product of
a virgin birth in all mythologies: "Where there are heroes there are stories of
the miraculous birth" (Leeming 39). In this way she manages to be a Mother
without the pollution of desire or sexuality. This has reinforced the idea that

chastity and abstinence until proper marriage are the highest values for a woman in collective consciousness.

The *Book of Revelation* supports this value system with the characters of the Great Beast and the Whore of Babylon. Babylon is "drunk on the blood of the saints" (Rev. 17:6), and represents earthly desire and lust. Yet at the same time, Jung points out the vision of the Lamb on Mount Zion:

> ...where the hundred and forty-four thousand elect and the redeemed are gathered round the Lamb. They are the παρθένοι [*parthenoi*], the male virgins, 'which were not defiled with women.' They are the ones who, following in the footsteps of the young dying god, have never become complete human beings, but have voluntarily renounced their share in the human lot and have said no to the continuance of life on earth. (83)

Jung includes a very important footnote to this, pointing out that this virginal elect "really belong to the cult of the Great Mother, since they correspond to the emasculated Galli [i.e., eunuch priests of the goddess Cybele]" (*Answer* 83). He mentions the quote from Matthew 19:12 about men who have "made themselves eunuchs for the Kingdom of Heaven," a reference to devotees of the goddess Cybele who castrated themselves in honor of her son Attis (83). The fact that John included this in his *Revelation* is one of the things that make it paradoxical. The "elect" of *Revelation* are identified with the devotees of the Great Mother. Just as the Epicurean paradox makes the "goodness" of Yahweh unclear, these attitudes toward sexuality and the feminine suggest ambivalence. If humans are to follow the command to "be fruitful and multiply," then sexual relations and procreation are necessary. This is ultimately why the Cathar heresy was put down. I am not sure that we can reconcile these differing views on the Feminine and desire for the Christian. The best I can say is that sexual relations are allowable under very controlled circumstances. But this is a repression and denial of natural psychological processes.

The Edict of Milan and the Constantinian Shift

The Edict of Milan was issued by the Emperor Constantine in 313 C.E., and after a particularly harsh persecution of Christians by the Emperor Diocletian, Christianity was now legal. It existed side by side with other religions from 313 C.E. until 391 C.E. In 380 CE, the Emperor Theodosius I made Christianity, as defined in the Council of Nicea (325 C.E.), the official religion of the Roman Empire ("Theodosius"). It was not long after this that the pagan religions were abolished, as well as schools of philosophy. In 529

C.E., the Emperor Justinian I made philosophy illegal, and most philosophical scholars fled to Persia. The Dark Ages of the Roman Empire in the West began at this point, and classical learning and knowledge was only retained in the East. The place where the West originally learned ideas of immortality and the soul was now the place where the knowledge of the philosophers returned.

When Christianity became accepted, the sanctuaries of the older gods and goddesses were destroyed. In 375 C.E., the man who became Saint Ambrose convinced the Emperor Gratian to suppress the pagans, which he did by confiscating their property, destroying the temples, and removing the statue of the goddess of Victory from the Roman Senate ("Gratian"). Formal priestesses and sibyls of the ancient temples were exiled. The eradication of the old religion also meant eradication of female divinity. The newer models of the virginal, obedient feminine would dominate, with other models treated as demonic.

This is the logical consequence of the split between male and female, heaven and earth. In an essay on paganism, the *Catholic Encyclopedia* suggests that pagan religions like Mithraism failed because "nature worship ruined its hopes of perpetuity" ("Paganism"). The movement away from the earth toward the world of Spirit was seen as a progression. Even Jung himself is not immune from this split; Ann Ulanov discusses his typology of women, which makes feeling their primary modality:

To associate the feminine exclusively with eros (relatedness and value reached through feeling) and to associate the masculine exclusively with logos (spirit and truth reached through objectivity) is to introduce a split in the sensibilities of women. (337)

It is not only a split in women, but in all humans. The Feminine in our society is underdeveloped because we have been taught that desire is bad, and the mythical view we have inherited is behind this worldview. We have not learned to separate the archetypal Feminine from the biological woman, and society has projected all of the archetypal qualities of the Feminine onto women, though they can just as easily apply to men.

Now that we have examined the changes in thought about the Feminine with regard to the afterlife and death, we need to wrap up our exploration and see what we can conclude.

Works Cited: Chapter 5

Arnold, Matthew. "Hebraism and Hellenism." *Prose of the Victorian Period.* Edited by William Earl Buckler. Houghton Mifflin, 1958, pp. 476-85.

Aschkenasy, Nehama. *Eve's Journey: Feminine Images in Hebraic Literary Tradition.* U of Pennsylvania, 1986.

Baudrillard, Jean. *Symbolic Exchange and Death.* Translated by Iain Hamilton Grant, SAGE Publications, 1993.

Beck, Roger. "Mithraism." Encyclopædia Iranica. *Encyclopædia Iranica,* 20 July 2002. Web. 30 Apr. 2016.

Beck, Roger. *The Religion of the Mithras Cult in the Roman Empire: Mysteries of the Unconquered Sun.* Oxford University Press, 2010.

Betz, Hans Dieter. *The Greek Magical Papyri in Translation, including the Demotic Spells.* 2nd ed. U of Chicago, 1992.

Betz, Hans Dieter. "Magic and Mystery in the Greek Magical Papyri." *Magika Hiera: Ancient Greek Magic and Religion.* Ed. Christopher A. Faraone and Dirk Obbink. Oxford UP, 1991, pp. 244-259.

Bierlein, J. F. *Parallel Myths.* Ballantine, 1994.

Brenon, Anne. "Cathars, Albigensians." *Encyclopedia of the Middle Ages.* Oxford Reference, 2013. Web. 02 May 2016.

Campbell, Joseph, and Bill D. Moyers. *The Power of Myth.* Edited by Betty Sue Flowers. Doubleday, 1988.

Charles, R. H., ed. *The Apocrypha and Pseudepigrapha of the Old Testament in English: With Introductions and Critical and Explanatory Notes to the Several Books.* Vol. 1,Clarendon, 1913.

Charles, R. H., ed. *The Apocrypha and Pseudepigrapha of the Old Testament in English: With Introductions and Critical and Explanatory Notes to the Several Books.* Vol. 2,Clarendon, 1913.

Cruz-Uribe, Eugene. "Seth." *The Encyclopedia of Ancient History.* Blackwell Publishing, 2013. Print: 6174–6176.

Cumont, Franz. *The Mysteries of Mithra.* Dover Publications, 1956.

Cumont, Franz. *The Oriental Religions in Roman Paganism.* Dover Publications, 1956.

Davis, Raymond. "Aurelian (Lucius Domitius Aurelianus Augustus)." *The Encyclopedia of Ancient History.* Blackwell Publishing, 2013. Web. 30 Apr. 2016.

DuQuette, Lon Milo. *Low Magick: It's All in Your Head, You Just Have No Idea How Big Your Head Is.* Llewellyn Publications, 2010.

Eliade, Mircea. *Rites and Symbols of Initiation: The Mysteries of Birth and Rebirth.* Translated by Willard R. Trask. Harper & Row, 1965.

Goetschel, Roland. "Kabbala." *Encyclopedia of the Middle Ages.* Oxford Reference, 2013. Web. 28 Apr. 2016.

"Gratian." *Catholic Encyclopedia*. Catholic Online, n.d. Web. 30 Apr. 2016.

Harnack, Adolf Von. *History of Dogma*. Vol. 1, Dover Publications, 1961.

Hess, Amanda. "Elizabeth Smart Says Pro-Abstinence Sex Ed Harms Victims of Rape." *Slate Magazine*. Slate, 06 May 2013. Web. 30 Apr. 2016.

Hillman, James. *The Dream and the Underworld*. Harper & Row, 1979.

Hufford, David. *The Terror That Comes in the Night: an Experience-Centered Study of Supernatural Assault Traditions*. Philadelphia, University of Pennsylvania Press, 1992.

Holy Bible. Revised Standard Version Containing the Old and New Testaments. T. Nelson, 1952.

Johnston, Sarah Iles. *Hekate Soteira: A Study of Hekate's Roles in the Chaldean Oracles and Related Literature*. Scholars, 1990.

Josephus, Flavius. *The Jewish War*. Translated by Geoffrey Arthur. Williamson. Penguin, 1959.

Jung, C. G. *Answer to Job*. Translated by R. F. C. Hull. Princeton UP, 1973.

Jung, C. G. "Individual Dream Symbolism in Relation to Alchemy." *Collected Works*. Translated by R. F. C. Hull. Vol. 12, Pantheon, 1953, pp. 39-207.

Jung, C. G. "On the Psychology of the Trickster Figure." *The Archetypes and the Collective Unconscious*. Translated by R.F.C. Hull. Pantheon, 1959, pp. 255-272.

Jung, C. G. "Syzygy: Anima and Animus." Translated R. F. C. Hull. *Aion: Researches into the Phenomenology of the Self*. Princeton UP, 1959, pp. 11-22.

Kempf, Constantine. "Theodicy." *The Catholic Encyclopedia*. Vol. 14. New York: Robert Appleton Company, 1912. 30 Apr. 2016

Lake, Kirsopp, translator. *The Apostolic Fathers*. Vol. 1, Cambridge , Harvard Univ. Press, 1952.

Leeming, David Adams. *Mythology: The Voyage of the Hero*. Oxford UP, 1998.

Leitzmann, Hans. *The Beginnings of the Christian Church*. Translated by Bertram Lee Woolf. Vol. 1, Meridian, 1953.

Neumann, Erich. *The Fear of the Feminine and Other Essays on Feminine Psychology*. Princeton, NJ: Princeton UP, 1994. Print.

Neumann, Erich. *The Great Mother: An Analysis of the Archetype*. Translated by Ralph Manheim, Pantheon, 1955.

"Paganism." *Catholic Encyclopedia*. Catholic Online, n.d. Web. 30 Apr. 2016.

Pagels, Elaine H. *The Origin of Satan*. Random House, 1995.

Pagels, Elaine H. *Revelations: Visions, Prophecy, and Politics in the Book of Revelation.* Viking, 2012.

"Proverbs." *Interpreter's Bible: The Holy Scriptures in the King James and Revised Standard Versions.* Vol. 4, Abingdon, 1955, pp. 779-957.

Russell, Jeffrey Burton. *The Devil: Perceptions of Evil from Antiquity to Primitive Christianity.* Cornell UP, 1977.

Smith, Gregory A. "Demons, Greek and Roman." *The Encyclopedia of Ancient History.* Blackwell Publishing, 2013. Web. 30 Apr. 2016.

"Testament of Solomon." *Esoteric Archives.* Trans. F. C. Conybeare. Joseph H. Peterson, 1997. Web. 27 Apr. 2016.

"Theodosius I." *Catholic Encyclopedia.* Catholic Online, n.d. Web. 30 Apr. 2016.

Tooley, Michael. "The Problem of Evil." *Stanford Encyclopedia of Philosophy.* Stanford University, 16 Sept. 2002. Web. 30 Apr. 2016.

Ulanov, Ann Belford. *The Feminine in Jungian Psychology and in Christian Theology.* Northwestern UP, 1971.

Zeller, Eduard. *Outlines of the History of Greek Philosophy.* Humanities Press, 1951.

FINAL REFLECTIONS AND CONCLUSION

We have investigated approximately 1100 years of Western cultural thought on the afterlife and the archetypal Feminine. Our goal was to explore meaningful connections between beliefs about both of these categories. How does a society with a very egalitarian view of death differ in its treatment of the Feminine from a society that believes in the immortal soul and judgment after death? The topic seems odd at first glance, but I think the research demonstrates that we have much to think about.

The nostalgic longing for a "Golden Age" is part of the fear of change, and dramatic life change is associated with death. The life passage rituals of the ancient Greeks were designed to give divine aid to those making dangerous life changes, or to appease gods that might hinder the process. The same is true for the dead person in ancient Egyptian ritual. We see the idea of death as "pollution"; the ancient Greek and Roman funerary rites and festivals were designed to keep the dead away. Heraclitus took this view to the limit with his Zoroastrian view that called for exposure of the body to the elements, rather than polluting earth or fire with burial or cremation. Zeus as king of the gods was expected to maintain boundaries against the "Other." The fearsome Erinyes also maintained these boundaries and protected mothers and children, giving them the appellation *Semnai Theai*. Fear of the Other causes contraction; we do not expand and explore, we want to do what is safe. Dogmatic monotheistic religions like Christianity are ideal for those who fear the Other; one has a defined set of rules to follow to ensure one's safety throughout life and in death. Rules offer a clear path and a sense of order, even if this is truly an illusory barrier against the unknown. Magical formulae and elaborate rituals served a similar purpose.

The idea of justice or *dike* is another theme connected to our anxiety about life and death. From the Egyptian belief that the dead had to show they were committed to "truth" (Ma'at) to Socrates' belief that if there was justice in life, there also had to be in death, the idea of judgment after death grew when the underworld assumed a moralistic character. We do not like to think that the wicked escape punishment through death. On a broader scale, *dike* is concerned with maintaining social order. There need to be consequences for bringing about disorder.

Humans have many defenses against unknowns like death; one of these defenses is to seek information or to rationalize the situation. In the Greek *polis*, we see the rise of philosophy and some of the original recorded rationalizations about the human soul. As cities and empires grew, the focus on the individual soul was more pronounced. As we noted in Chapter 5, Jung pointed to the "masculine" nature of the development of the *polis*. We might think that such large communities would rely on the "feminine" instinct of relationship-building. Instead, there is the focus on the independent individual and the rise of humanism, which develops into ideas about the immortal soul and salvation.

Social values related to the individual vs. the community have a direct relationship to beliefs about death, and consequently the values and ethics of the society. The more a society focuses on the individual, the greater the "split," as one's accomplishments and failings are scrutinized. Paradoxically, the movement from smaller tribal communities to the city-state moved social consciousness from the collective to the individual. Perhaps this is because the family structure is more personal while the state is less so. In the modern world, the "state" is often viewed as a machine, and we fight for authenticity and uniqueness in a society where we are threatened with only being a "number." Whether or not life truly has a purpose, humans need to feel that there is a reason for living.

This study focuses on ancient Western civilization; however this pattern of social behavior continues into the Medieval Era. Philippe Ariès explains in his work on Western attitudes toward death that the early Christian Church was against the practice of burying the dead within the city walls, never mind the church walls. But the practice may have begun in the sixth century C.E., when St. Vaast, according to legend, became too heavy to carry outside the city walls. The priest interpreted this as a sign that he should be buried within the church itself, and the body immediately became light. Ariès notes: "In order for the clergy to circumvent the traditional interdict and to make provision within the cathedral for the tombs of the saints and the sepulchers which the holy tomb would attract, the old revulsion would already have had to become much weakened" (17). Once the dead were allowed within church walls, the churchyard became the standard burial spot, though not initially with individual graves. Bodies would be piled in a mass grave, and when that filled up, earth would be placed over the bodies and previous mass graves would be dug up and the bones placed in charnel houses. (20) The churchyard itself became a community gathering place, like the old Roman forum. (23) Additionally, the bedchamber of the dying person was a commu-nity place—friends and loved ones crowded around the bed of the dying per-son. (33) Death was a community phenomenon, and post-mortem judgment was not emphasized. It was believed that demons and angels fought over the soul as it was dying, and this was a kind of final test for the dying individual. If they passed the test, they went to heaven regardless of their conduct in life. (36) But death once again became an individual affair in the fourteenth and fifteenth centuries C.E., strengthening the role of the dying man. (38) It should not be surprising that individual coffin burial in a single grave be-came fashionable at this time as well. While this represents a later period in history, it demonstrates the relationship between individual judgment and social ideas about death also evident among the ancient Greeks and Romans. In our modern era, Jean Baudrillard points to the isolated nature of death: "The majority no longer have the opportunity to see somebody die. In any other type of society, this is something unthinkable. The hospital and med-icine take charge of you; the technical Extreme Unction has replaced every other sacrament. Man disappears from his nearest and dearest before being dead. He dies somewhere else." (182) We have returned to death as an indi-vidual event, and this reflects our cultural anxiety. We cannot face death; it is seen as unnatural. While we have this in common with the Egyptians, we have also lost our mythologies. Death has become a true void, and we do our best to fight it off or pretend it won't happen. Certainly the religious still have rituals, and the buffer this provides against death anxiety is at least part of the concept of religion as Terror Management (Kastenbaum 137-139).

Throughout this study we can observe the associations with ideas of "feminine" and "masculine" with the "collective" and "individual" respective-ly. While Joseph Campbell's "monomyth" is a controversial concept,[32] there is at least some validity to the idea that folklore and myth surrounding the "hero" represents a cultural norm in psychological development. As noted in the introduction, object relations theory suggests a movement from the collective (mother/family, idyllic childhood) to maturity as an individual through life experiences, including tests and trials with accomplishments

---

[32] For a full account of the "monomyth" (i.e., myth of the hero) see: Campbell, Joseph. *The Hero with a Thousand Faces*. Pantheon, 1961.

and failings, and the individual generally has a contribution that reconnects them to the community once again. This matches Jung's idea of individuation: the initial movement away from the "Mother" to development as an individual encountering the "Anima," who may be helpful or harmful. Marriage or a similar kind of relationship helps the individual recognize their "opposite," reconciling the masculine and feminine in themselves. Of course, the whole notion of discovering the Anima represents a male narrative, and Jung's comparable narrative for women is very much lacking, as it requires marriage and children for psychological fulfillment. But it is the narrative of our culture, which values rationality and individuality above other qualities.

The Western symbol for this rise of masculine rationalization is the sun. The sun and moon may play different mythological roles around the world, with Egypt being an example of an exception, but the masculine sun and feminine moon were definitely attributes of Graeco-Roman culture. Moon goddesses included Artemis, Hecate, and the Titan Selene, as well as the Roman Diana. The sun plays a curious role in the development of soul and afterlife beliefs. The Orphic mysteries take the earthy and chaotic Dionysus and make him Apollonian in nature; later, Dionysus would become an Olympian. Apollo is a god of enlightenment, and later Mithras would take on this role in his mysteries as *Sol Invictus*, a term used by the Emperor cult in the early years of the Common Era. *Sol Invictus* adds an element of triumph and conquest; the sun is "undefeatable." As a unified idea of a single or central Sun god took hold in the Roman Empire, it was not a huge step from this to a single belief in the "Son" of God, Jesus Christ, as the universally true religion.

Dionysus is a pivotal figure in this drama. On the one hand he is associated with the direct, individual experience of god through ecstasy from drinking wine. The religion of Dionysus is mystical, and inward-looking, but we also have Nietzsche's view that Dionysus represents the collective forces of nature. This is not as contradictory as it appears; turning to the collective involves "turning inward" rather than acting unconsciously. Dionysus was a balancing figure, and similar attempts at balancing the masculine nature of society and religion came in the cults of the Magna Mater.

However, the chthonic Feminine divine disappears in the Christian era. We are left with the Virgin Mary, who lives up to monotheistic standards of purity and obedience, the highest values for women in that system. The Earth Mother becomes associated with the demonic, from demons roaming the earth attempting to ruin souls to the eternal punishments of a Hell under the earth. In monotheism the Feminine is decisively connected to the root of sin, lust. The "worldly harlot" also becomes associated with what is foreign, and therefore evil. The "foreign" becomes another term for the fear of the "Other." Those who know too much about the Other become associated with another negative Feminine archetype—the Hag or the Witch. We have seen examples of powerful women associated with magic. In Greek and Roman times, these women served as oracles or were regarded as goddesses or the offspring of divinities. In the Christian era, women with "secret" knowledge were treated as associates of the Devil.

The obsession with purity starts with Orpheus, who encourages followers to purge themselves of their "Titan" tendencies. Purity is not a priority in Greek religion, but the idea of an evil body and a good soul grew in Hellenistic times via the philosophers. When this merges with Eastern dualistic ideas, and the complex dualism of monotheism, we definitely see the separation of heaven and earth, and the demonization of the latter. Women, as the ones who brought the sin of lust to the world, are associated with material vices, and are anti-spiritual. And as I noted in Chapter 5, James Hillman demonstrates how Paul of Tarsus cut us off from the underworld with the assertion that Christ conquered death.

I have demonstrated the connection between the earth, the Feminine, and death. We can see how the movement from *oikos* to *polis* was transformed by a focus on individuality and rationality. The movement toward a masculine, rational society was more firmly entrenched with Roman and Jewish tendencies toward law and dogmatism. The combining of these elements with Eastern dualistic beliefs and Jewish eschatology has tipped the scales in favor of an overly-masculinized religion. Dogmatic religion does not have to be "negative"; it is, however, out of balance. We will feel perpetually torn until we examine our relationship to our instincts that are in "Shadow" by learning to listen to our own voices and promoting empathy and compassion as values. It also involves looking at our inner "darkness"—the thoughts, desires, and impulses that are unacceptable in our cultural normative worldview.

We tend to think of monotheism and salvation as a "progression" from the chaotic beliefs of the pagans. But a religion that strictly divides good and evil creates an unnatural psychological situation. Life events and conflicts are rarely "black and white" scenarios. Our unconscious associations with the term "evil," as well as our tendency to ignore our instincts in favor of rationality can lead to psychological states of repression and neurosis, and at the worst, psychosis. In a way, our whole society is afflicted with a psychosis, because our worldview is struggling to get beyond this psychological split. Science's exclusive emphasis on the rational and the denial of anything "teleological" as truth only adds to the anxiety. The only way out of the conundrum is to explore and integrate those "demons" that have been avoided. In a world connected by technology through the Internet, future mythologies must gravitate toward the Feminine aspect if we don't want to tear ourselves apart completely. There needs to be a focus on community and empathy rather than an emphasis on difference and overpowering or eliminating the Other.

Works Cited: Final Reflections and Conclusion

Ariès, Philippe. *Western Attitudes toward Death From the Middle Ages to the Present.* Translated by Patricia Ranum. Johns Hopkins UP, 1974.

Baudrillard, Jean. *Symbolic Exchange and Death.* Translated by Iain Hamilton Grant. SAGE Publications, 1993.

Campbell, Joseph. *The Hero with a Thousand Faces.* Pantheon, 1961.

"Jung on Life After Death." *Atlantic Monthly.* Dec. 1962. 39-44.

Bibliography

Aeschylus. "The Persians." *The Complete Greek Tragedies: Aeschylus*, edited by Richmond Lattimore and David Grene, University of Chicago Press, 1969, pp. 216–59.

Afnán, Ruhi Mhusen. *Zoroaster's Influence on Greek Thought*. Philosophical Library, 1965.

Albinus, Lars. House of Hades: Studies in Ancient Greek Eschatology. Aarhus University Press, 2000.

Apollodorus. *The Library*. Translated by James George Frazer, Vol. 1, W. Heinemann, 1965.

Apuleius. *The Golden Ass*. Translated by Jack Lindsay, Indiana University Press, 1962.

Ariès, Philippe. *Western Attitudes toward Death From the Middle Ages to the Present*. Translated by Patricia Ranum, Johns Hopkins University Press, 1974.

Aristophanes. *The Peace ; The Birds ; The Frogs*. Translated by Benjamin Bickley Rogers, Harvard University Press, 1924.

Aristotle. *Aristotle's De Anima in the Version of William of Moerbeke and the Commentary of St. Thomas Aquinas*. Translated by Kenelm Foster and Silvester Humphries, Yale University Press, 1959.

Arnold, Matthew. "Hebraism and Hellenism." *Prose of the Victorian Period*, edited by William Earl Buckler, Houghton Mifflin, 1958, pp. 476–85.

Aschkenasy, Nehama. *Eve's Journey: Feminine Images in Hebraic Literary Tradition*. University of Pennsylvania Press, 1986.

Assmann, Jan. *Death and Salvation in Ancient Egypt.* Translated by David Lorton, Cornell University Press, 2001.

Bailey, Cyril. *Phases in the Religion of Ancient Rome.* University of California Press, 1932.

Baudrillard, Jean. *Symbolic Exchange and Death.* Translated by Iain Hamilton Grant, SAGE Publications, 1993.

Beard, Mary, et al. *Religions of Rome.* Vol. 1, Cambridge University Press, 1998.

Beck, Roger. *The Religion of the Mithras Cult in the Roman Empire: Mysteries of the Unconquered Sun.* Oxford University Press, 2010.

Betegh, Gábor. *The Derveni Papyrus: Cosmology, Theology, and Interpretation.* Cambridge University Press, 2004.

Betz, Hans Dieter. "Magic and Mystery in the Greek Magical Papyri." *Magika Hiera: Ancient Greek Magic and Religion,* edited by Christopher Faraone and Dirk Obbink, Oxford University Press, 1991, pp. 244–59.

———. *The Greek Magical Papyri in Translation, Including the Demotic Spells.* 2nd ed., University of Chicago Press, 1992.

Bidez, Joseph, and Franz Cumont. *Les Mages Hellénisés Zoroastre, Ostanès Et Hystaspe D'après La Tradition Grecque.* Les Belles Lettres, 1973.

Bierlein, J. F. *Parallel Myths.* Ballantine, 1994.

Bloom, Howard. *The Lucifer Principle: A Scientific Expedition into the Forces of History.* Atlantic Monthly Press, 1995.

Bly, Robert, and William Booth. *A Little Book on the Human Shadow.* Harper & Row, 1988.

Boroditsky, Lera. "Sex, Syntax, and Semantics." *Language in Mind: Advances in the Study of Language and Thought,* edited by Dedre Gentner and Susan Goldin-Meadow, MIT Press, 2003, pp. 61–79.

Bremmer, Jan. *The Rise and Fall of the Afterlife.* Routledge, 2002.

Budge, E. A. Wallis. *Osiris : The Egyptian Religion of Resurrection.* University Books, 1961.

———. *The Book of the Opening of the Mouth : The Egyptian Texts with English Translations.* Benjamin Blom, 1972.

———. *The Egyptian Heaven and Hell: The Contents of the Books of the Other World.* Open Court, 1905.

———. *The Gods of the Egyptians, or Studies in Egyptian Mythology.* Vol. 1, Dover Publications, 1969.

Burkert, Walter. *Greek Religion.* Harvard University Press, 1985.

————. "Pleading for Hell: Postulates, Fantasies, and the Senselessness of Punishment." *Numen*, vol. 56, no. 2/3, 2009, pp. 141–60.

————. *Structure and History in Greek Mythology and Ritual*. University of California Press, 1979.

————. *The Orientalizing Revolution: Near Eastern Influence on Greek Culture in the Early Archaic Age*. Harvard University Press, 1992.

Buttrick, George Arthur, editor. *Interpreter's Bible: The Holy Scriptures in the King James and Revised Standard Versions with General Articles and Introduction, Exegesis, Exposition for Each Book of the Bible*. Vol. 1–5, 11 & 12, Abingdon, 1955.

Campbell, Joseph. *The Hero With a Thousand Faces*. Pantheon, 1961.

Campbell, Joseph, and Bill Moyers. *The Power of Myth*. Edited by Betty Sue Flowers, Doubleday, 1988.

Carspecken, J. F. "Apollonius Rhodius and the Homeric Epic." *Yale Classical Studies*, vol. 13, 1952, p. 101.

Casey, John. *After Lives: A Guide to Heaven, Hell & Purgatory*. Oxford University Press, 2009.

Charles, R. H., editor. *The Apocrypha and Pseudepigrapha of the Old Testament in English: With Introductions and Critical and Explanatory Notes to the Several Books*. Clarendon, 1913.

Combs, Allan, and Mark Holland. *Synchronicity: Science, Myth, and the Trickster*. Paragon House, 1990.

Conybeare, F. C., translator. "Testament of Solomon." *Esoteric Archives*, Joseph H. Peterson, 1997, www.esotericarchives.com/solomon/testamen.htm.

Corbeill, Anthony. *Sexing the World: Grammatical Gender and Biological Sex in Ancient Rome*. Princeton University Press, 2015.

Ctesias. *Ctesias' History of Persia: Tales of the Orient*. Translated by Lloyd Llewellyn-Jones and James Robson, Routledge, 2010.

Cumont, Franz. *After Life in Roman Paganism; Lectures Delivered at Yale University on the Silliman Foundation*. Dover Publications, 1959.

————. *The Mysteries of Mithra*. Dover Publications, 1956.

————. *The Oriental Religions of Roman Paganism*. Dover Publications, 1956.

Desborough, V. R. D'A. *The Greek Dark Ages*. St. Martin's Press, 1972.

Dodd, E. R. *The Greeks and the Irrational*. University of California Press, 1959.

Dumézil, Georges. Archaic Roman Religion, with an Appendix on the Religion of the Etruscans. Vol. 1 & 2, University of Chicago Press, 1970.

Edmonds, Radcliffe. *Redefining Ancient Orphism: A Study in Greek Religion.* Cambridge University Press, 2013.

Edwards, I. E. S., editor. *Cambridge Ancient History.* Vol. 1, Cambridge University Press, 1970.

Eliade, Mircea. *Rites and Symbols of Initiation: The Mysteries of Birth and Rebirth.* Translated by Willard Trask, Harper Torchbooks, 1958.

Eller, Cynthia. *The Myth of Matriarchal Prehistory: Why an Invented Past Won't Give Women a Future.* Beacon Press, 2000.

Erikson, Erik. *Childhood and Society.* W.W. Norton, 1993.

Euripides. "Alcestis." *Euripides,* edited by David Slavitt and Smith Palmer Bovie, vol. 3, University of Pennsylvania Press, 1998, pp. 3–59.

———. *Electra and Other Plays.* Translated by R.B. Rutherford, Penguin, 1998.

Evelyn-White, Hugh, et al. *Hesiod, the Homeric Hymns, and Homerica.* 1964.

Finkel, Irving, editor. *Cyrus Cylinder: The Great Persian Edict from Babylon.* IB Tauris, 2013.

Gilligan, Carol. *In a Different Voice: Women's Conception of the Self and of Mortality.* Harvard University Press, 1977.

Graf, Fritz, and Sarah Iles Johnston. *Ritual Texts for the Afterlife : Orpheus and the Bacchic Gold Tablets.* Routledge, 2007.

Green, Alberto, and Ravinell Whitney. *Storm God in the Ancient near East.* Eisenbrauns, 2003.

Grey, Peter. *Lucifer: Princeps.* Scarlet Imprint, 2015.

Guthrie, Kenneth Sylvan, and David Fideler, editors. *The Pythagorean Sourcebook and Library: An Anthology of Ancient Writings Which Relate to Pythagoras and Pythagorean Philosophy.* Phanes, 1987.

Guthrie, William, and Keith Chambers. *Orpheus and Greek Religion: A Study of the Orphic Movement.* Princeton University Press, 1993.

Herodotus. *Herodotus.* Translated by A.D. Godley, Vol. 1 & 3, Harvard University Press, 1971.

Hesiod. *Works and Days; and Theogony.* Translated by Stanley Lombardo, Hackett Publishing, 1993.

Hillman, James. *The Dream and the Underworld.* Harper & Row, 1979.

Homer. *The Iliad.* Translated by Robert Fagles, Penguin, 1998.

———. *The Odyssey.* Translated by Robert Fagles, Penguin, 1996.

Hornung, Erik. *Conceptions of God in Ancient Egypt: The One and the Many.* Translated by John Baines, Cornell University Press, 1982.

Hufford, David. *The Terror That Comes in the Night: An Experience-Centered Study of Supernatural Assault Traditions*. University of Pennsylvania Press, 1992.

Idel, Moshe. *Golem: Jewish Magical and Mystical Traditions on the Artificial Anthropoid*. State University of New York Press, 1990.

Iles Johnston, Sarah. *Hekate Soteira: A Study of Hekate's Roles in the Chaldean Oracles and Related Literature*. Scholars Press, 1990.

―――. *Restless Dead: Encounters between the Living and the Dead in Ancient Greece*. University of California Press, 1999.

Josephus, Flavius. *The Jewish War*. Translated by Geoffrey Arthur Williamson, Penguin, 1959.

Jung, Carl G. *Analytical Psychology: Notes of the Seminar Given in 1925*. Edited by William McGuire, Princeton University Press, 1989.

―――. *Answer to Job*. Translated by R.F.C. Hull, Princeton University Press, 1973.

―――. "Battle for Deliverance from the Mother." *Collected Works*, translated by R.F.C. Hull, vol. 5, Pantheon, 1956, pp. 274–305.

―――. "Dream Symbolism in Relation to Alchemy." *Collected Works*, 2nd ed., vol. 12, Routledge & Kegan Paul, 1952, pp. 41–213.

―――. "Dual Mother." *Collected Works*, translated by R.F.C. Hull, vol. 5, Pantheon, 1959, pp. 306–95.

―――. "Foreword to Moser: 'Spuk: Irrglaube Oder Wahrglaube?'" *Psychology and the Occult*, translated by R.F.C. Hull, Princeton University Press, 1977.

―――. "Individual Dream Symbolism in Relation to Alchemy." *Collected Works*, translated by R.F.C. Hull, vol. 12, Pantheon, 1953, pp. 39–207.

―――. "Marriage as a Psychological Relationship." *Collected Works*, translated by R.F.C. Hull, vol. 17, Pantheon, 1954, pp. 189–201.

―――. "Meaning of Self-Knowledge." *Collected Works*, translated by R.F.C. Hull, vol. 10, Pantheon, 1964, pp. 302–05.

―――. *Mysterium Coniunctionis : An Inquiry into the Separation and Synthesis of Psychic Opposites in Alchemy*. Translated by R.F.C. Hull, 2nd ed., Princeton University Press, 1989.

―――. "On the Psychology of the Trickster Figure." *Collected Works*, translated by R.F.C. Hull, vol. 9.1, Pantheon, 1959, pp. 255–72.

―――. "Phenomenology of the Spirit in Fairytales." *Collected Works*, translated by R.F.C. Hull, vol. 9.1, Pantheon, 1959, pp. 207–54.

―――. "Psychological Types." *Collected Works*, translated by R.F.C. Hull, Vol. 6, Princeton University Press, 1971.

———. "Study in the Process of Individuation." *Collected Works*, translated by R.F.C. Hull, vol. 9.1, Pantheon, 1959, pp. 290–354.

———. "The Archetypes of the Collective Unconscious." *Collected Works*, translated by R.F.C. Hull, vol. 9.1, Pantheon, 1959, pp. 3–41.

———. "The Psychological Aspects of the Kore." *Collected Works*, translated by R.F.C. Hull, vol. 9.1, Pantheon, 1959, pp. 182–203.

———. *The Red Book = Liber Novus*. Reader's, Norton, 2012.

———. "The Structure and Dynamics of the Psyche." *Collected Works*, translated by R.F.C. Hull, vol. 8, Princeton University Press, 1969.

———. "The Syzygy: Anima and Animus." *Collected Works*, translated by R.F.C. Hull, vol. 9.2, Princeton University Press, 1959, pp. 11–22.

Kastenbaum, Robert. *The Psychology of Death*. 3rd ed., Springer, 2000.

Kerényi, C. *Dionysos: Archetypal Image of Indestructible Life*. Vol. 2, Princeton University Press, 1976.

Kilgour, Maggie. "Satan and the Wrath of Juno." *ELH*, vol. 75, no. 3, 2008, pp. 653–71.

Laertius, Diogenes. *Lives of the Eminent Philosophers*. Translated by Robert Drew Hicks, Vol. 2, Harvard University Press, 1950.

Lake, Kirsopp, translator. *The Apostolic Fathers*. Vol. 1, Harvard University Press, 1952.

Lakoff, Robin Tolmach. "Stylistic Strategies within a Grammar of Style." *Language, Sex, and Gender: Does La Différence Make a Difference?*, edited by Judith Orasanu, New York Academy of Sciences, 1979, pp. 53–78.

Leeming, David Adams. *Mythology: The Voyage of the Hero*. Oxford University Press, 1998.

Leitzmann, Hans. *The Beginnings of the Christian Church*. Translated by Bertram Lee Woolf, Vol. 1, Meridian, 1953.

Lerro, Bruce. *From Earth Spirits to Sky Gods: The Socioecological Origins of Monotheism, Individualism, and Hyperabstract Reasoning from the Stone Age to the Axial Iron Age*. Lexington Books, 2000.

Livy. *Livy: With an English Translation in Fourteen Volumes*. Translated by Evan Sage Taylor, Vol. 11, Harvard University Press, 1965.

Mackenzie, John, translator. *Anchor Bible: Second Isaiah*. Doubleday, 1968.

Martin, Thomas. *Ancient Greece: From Prehistoric to Hellenistic Times*. Yale University Press, 1996.

Mikalson, Jon. *Ancient Greek Religion*. Blackwell, 2005.

Moore, Clifford. *Ancient Beliefs in the Immortality of the Soul*. Cooper Square Publishers, 1963.

Morris, Ian. "Attitudes Toward Death in Archaic Greece." *Classical Antiquity*, vol. 8, no. 2, 1989, pp. 296–320.

Myres, John. "Persephone and the Pomegranate (H. Dem. 372–4)." *The Classical Review*, vol. 52, no. 2, 1938, p. 51.

Neumann, Erich. *The Fear of the Feminine and Other Essays on Feminine Psychology*. Princeton University Press, 1994.

———. *The Great Mother: An Analysis of the Archetype*. Translated by Ralph Manheim, Pantheon, 1955.

Neumann, Erich, and Apuleius. *Amor and Psyche; the Psychic Development of the Feminine; a Commentary on the Tale by Apuleius*. Pantheon, 1956.

Nietzsche, Friedrich. *The Birth of Tragedy and the Genealogy of Morals*. Translated by Francis Golffing, Doubleday, 1956.

Nilsson, Martin. *The Dionysiac Mysteries of the Hellenistic and Roman Age*. Arno Press, 1975.

Nocent, Adrian. *The Liturgical Year*. Vol. 1, Liturgical Press, 1977.

Oates, Whitney, editor. *The Stoic and Epicurean Philosophers; the Complete Extant Writings of Epicurus, Epictetus, Lucretius Marcus Aurelius*. Random House, 1940.

Ogden, Daniel. *Greek and Roman Necromancy*, Princeton University Press, 2004.

Ovid. *Selected Works*. Edited by J.C. Thornton and M.J. Thornton, J.M. Dent & Sons, 1948.

Pagels, Elaine. *Revelations: Visions, Prophecy and Politics in the Book of Revelation*. Viking, 2012.

———. *The Origin of Satan*. Random House, 1995.

Plato. *Cratylus, Parmenides, Greater Hippias, Lesser Hippias*. Translated by Harold North Fowler, Harvard University Press, 1939.

———. *Laws*. Translated by R.G. Bury, William Heinemann, 1952.

———. *Phaedo*. Translated by R. Hackforth, Cambridge University Press, 1955.

———. *The Dialogues of Plato: Translated into English with Analyses and Introductions*. Translated by Benjamin Jowett, Vol. 1, Clarendon, 1953.

———. *The Republic*. Translated by Paul Shorey, William Heinemann, 1956. *Ancient World*, edited by Kimberley Stratton and Dayna Kalleres, Oxford University Press, 2014, pp. 41-70.

Plutarch. "Of Isis and Osiris, or of the Ancient Religion and Philosophy of Egypt." *Plutarch's Essays and Miscellanies, Comprising All His Works Collected under the Title of "Morals,"* edited by William Goodwin, translated by William Baxter, Little Brown and Company, 1911.

Purkiss, Diane. *At the Bottom of the Garden: A Dark History of Fairies, Hobgoblins, and Other Troublesome Things.* New York University Press, 2000.

Radin, Max. *The Jews Among the Greeks and Romans.* Jewish Publication Society of America, 1915.

Raphael, Simcha Paull. *Jewish Views of the Afterlife.* 2nd ed., Rowman & Littlefield, 2009.

Redford, Donald, editor. *Oxford Encyclopedia of Ancient Egypt.* Oxford University Press, 2001.

Relke, Joan. "The Archetypal Female in Mythology and Religion: The Anima and the Mother." *Europe's Journal of Psychology,* vol. 3, no. 1, 2007, ejop. psychopen.eu/article/view/389/html.

———. "The Archetypal Female in Mythology and Religion: The Anima and the Mother of the Earth and Sky." *EJOP: Europe's Journal of Psychology,* vol. 3, no. 2, 2007, ejop.psychopen.eu/index.php/ejop/article/view/401/html.

Rhodius, Apollonius. *Jason and the Argonauts.* Translated by Aaron Poochigian, Penguin, 2014.

Rohde, Erwin. *Psyche; the Cult of Souls and Belief in Immortality among the Greeks.* Kegan Paul, Trench, Trubner, 1925.

Russell, Jeffrey Burton. *The Devil: Perceptions of Evil from Antiquity to Primitive Christianity.* Cornell University Press, 1977.

Saraswati, Satyananda. *Chandi Path.* Devi Mandir, 2002.

Scharf Kluger, Rivkha. *The Archetypal Significance of Gilgamesh: A Modern Ancient Hero.* Daimon Verlag, 1991.

Siculus, Diodorus. *Diodorus of Sicily: In 12 Volumes.* Translated by Charles Oldfather, Vol. 2, William Heinemann, 1968.

Sophocles. "Ajax." *Sophocles II,* translated by David Grene and Richmond Lattimore, University of Chicago Press, 1957, pp. 2–62.

———. *Sophocles.* Translated by F. Storr, Vol. 2, William Heinemann, 1913.

Spence, Lewis. *Myths and Legends of Ancient Egypt.* George Harrap & Company, 1949.

Stanley Spaeth, Barbette. "From Goddess to Hag: The Greek and the Roman Witch in Classical Literature." *Daughters of Hecate: Women and Magic in the*

Ancient World, edited by Kimberley Stratton and Dayna Kalleres, Oxford University Press, 2014, pp. 41-70.

Starr, Chester. *The Origins of Greek Civilization: 1100-65 B.C.* Alfred A. Knopf, 1961.

Storey, Ian, and Arlene Allan. *A Guide to Ancient Greek Drama*. Blackwell, 2007.

Stratton-Kent, Jake. *Geosophia: The Argo of Magic: From the Greeks to the Grimoires*. Vol. 1, Scarlet Imprint, 2010.

Taylor-Perry, Rosemary. *God Who Comes: Dionysian Mysteries Reclaimed*. Algora Publishing, 2003.

Thucydides. *Thucydides*. Translated by Charles Foster Smith, Vol. 1, William Heinemann, 1930.

Ulanov, Ann Belford. *The Feminine in Jungian Psychology and in Christian Theology*. Northwestern University Press, 1971.

Varro, Marcus Terentius. *Varro on the Latin Language: In Two Volumes*. Translated by Roland Kent, Vol. 2, William Heinemann, 1958.

Ventris, Michael, and John Chadwick. "Document 172 from Pylos." *Documents in Mycenaean Greek*, Cambridge University Press, 1973.

Virgil. *The Aeneid*. Translated by Robert Fitzgerald, Vintage, 1983.

Vürtheim, J. "The Miracle of the Wine at Dionysos' Advent: On the Lenaea Festival." *Classical Quarterly*, vol. 14, no. 2, Apr. 1920, pp. 92–96.

West, Martin. *Early Greek Philosophy and the Orient*. Oxford University Press, 1971.

Wilhelm, Richard, and Carl G. Jung. *The Secret of the Golden Flower: A Chinese Book of Life*. Harcourt, Brace, Jovanovich, 1962.

Xenophanes. *Xenophanes: Fragments and Commentary*. Translated by Arthur Fairbanks, The Eleatic School, Hanover Historical Texts Project, 2013, history.hanover.edu/texts/presoc/xenophan.html.

Xenophon. *Cyropaedia*. Translated by Walter Miller, Vol. 1, Harvard University Press, 1914.

Zaidman, Louise Bruit. "Pandora's Daughters and Rituals in Grecian Cities." *A History of Women in the West*, edited by Pauline Schmitt Pantel, Belknap of Harvard University Press, 1992, pp. 338–77.

Zandee, Jan. *Death as an Enemy According to Ancient Egyptian Conceptions*. Brill, 1960.

Zeller, Eduard. *Outlines of the History of Greek Philosophy*. Humanities Press, 1951.

INDEX

Neith, 19

Nekyia, 47, 95, 106

Neoplatonism, 128, 145

Nephthys, 18, 19, 24, 28

New Kingdom, 14, 15, 22, 24

Nietzsche, Friedrich, 69, 104, 105, 110, 184

Numen, 108, 117, 118

Nut, 14, 26, 63

O

Odyssey, 33, 34, 36-39, 41, 42, 45, 46, 57, 58, 61, 65, 72, 95, 113

Oikos, 43, 44, 95, 102, 117, 119, 158, 185

Oresteia, 61, 120

Origen, 169

Orpheus, 68, 71, 75, 77-79, 81-86, 88, 104, 109, 117, 118, 171, 185

Orphism, 10, 76, 77, 81-83, 85, 106, 108, 122, 131, 139

Osiris, 14-23, 25-29, 37, 82, 131, 137, 141, 147, 148

Other, The, 2, 59, 181

P

Pandareids, 61

Papyrus of Ani, 18, 27

Parentalia, 120, 121

Paul of Tarsus (St. Paul), 1, 166, 168, 185

Pentheus, 67, 157

Persephone, 17, 39, 53, 59, 64-66, 72, 77, 80, 116, 131, 144, 146, 147

Persians, 34, 76, 93, 108, 119

Phanes, 79, 80, 109

Physis, 60, 144, 151

Plato, 33, 37, 72, 75, 83, 86, 88, 89, 91, 92, 95, 96, 101, 103, 104, 110, 123, 125, 126, 134, 144-147, 150, 157, 169, 170

Plutarch, 14, 16, 18, 19, 24, 110, 131, 137, 145, 146, 151

Polis, 38, 43, 44, 95, 102, 104, 117, 158, 182, 185

Poseidon, 32, 57, 61

Psalm 82, 98, 110

Psyche (or Psykhe), 4, 11, 21, 38, 41-43, 50, 53, 56-58, 72, 73, 78, 89, 91, 105-107, 117, 124, 130, 143, 151, 172, 174

Pyramid Texts, 15, 19, 20, 22, 39

Pythagoras, 75, 76, 82, 85-88, 90, 91, 101, 104, 109, 127

Pythagoreanism, 127

R

Ra, 16-18, 22, 24-27

Reincarnation, 84, 86, 124, 170

Rephaim, 40

S

Sahu, 21

Salvation, 2, 20, 60, 82-84, 92, 99, 101, 106, 151, 157, 168, 170, 171, 182, 185

Satan, 50, 55, 72, 99, 141, 148, 153-157, 161, 164, 166, 168, 171, 174, 178

Second Punic War, 122, 136, 141

Sekhmet, 26

Selket, 19, 24

Semnai Theai, 120, 181

Serapis, 131, 141

Seth (see also Typhon), 15-18, 24, 27, 28, 37, 108, 147, 148, 177

Shadow, 2, 5, 18, 21, 39, 41, 43, 50, 52, 58, 65, 67, 70, 71, 89, 105, 107, 131, 155, 161, 185

Shamash, 48

Shekinah, 158, 162, 164

Sheol, 40, 156

Sibyl of Cumae, 46, 125

Socrates, 37, 83, 91, 92, 96, 140, 150, 182

Socrates, 37, 83, 91, 92, 96, 140, 150, 182

Sol Invictus, 142, 184

Sophia, 19, 25, 157, 158, 162-164, 173, 174

Stoics, 123, 124, 126

Printed in the United States
By Bookmasters